When should I travel to get the best airfare?
Where do I go for answers to my travel questions?
What's the best and easiest way to plan and book my trip?

frommers.travelocity.com

Frommer's, the travel guide leader, has teamed up with **Travelocity.com**, the leader in online travel, to bring you an in-depth, easy-to-use resource designed to help you plan and book your trip online.

At **frommers.travelocity.com**, you'll find free online updates about your destination from the experts at Frommer's plus the outstanding travel planning and purchasing features of Travelocity.com. Travelocity.com provides reservations capabilities for 95 percent of all airline seats sold, more than 47,000 hotels, and over 50 car rental companies. In addition, Travelocity.com offers more than 2,000 exciting vacation and cruise packages. Travelocity.com puts you in complete control of your travel planning with these and other great features:

> **Expert travel guidance from Frommer's** - over 150 writers reporting from around the world!

> **Best Fare Finder** - an interactive calendar tells you when to travel to get the best airfare

> **Fare Watcher** - we'll track airfare changes to your favorite destinations

> **Dream Maps** - a mapping feature that suggests travel opportunities based on your budget

> **Shop Safe Guarantee** - 24 hours a day / 7 days a week live customer service, and more!

Whether traveling on a tight budget, looking for a quick weekend getaway, o planning the trip of a lifetime, Frommer's guides and Travelocity.com will make your travel dreams a reality. You've bought the book, now book the trip!

Travelocity.com
A Sabre Company

Frommer's

Also available from Hungry Minds, Inc.

Beyond Disney: The Unofficial Guide to Universal, Sea World, and the Best of Central Florida

Inside Disney: The Incredible Story of Walt Disney World and the Man Behind the Mouse

Mini Las Vegas: The Pocket-Sized Unofficial Guide to Las Vegas

Mini Mickey: The Pocket-Sized Unofficial Guide to Walt Disney World

The Unofficial Guide to Bed & Breakfasts in California

The Unofficial Guide to Bed & Breakfasts in New England

The Unofficial Guide to Bed & Breakfasts in the Northwest

The Unofficial Guide to Bed & Breakfasts in the Southeast

The Unofficial Guide to Branson, Missouri

The Unofficial Guide to California with Kids

The Unofficial Guide to Chicago

The Unofficial Guide to Cruises

The Unofficial Guide to Disneyland

The Unofficial Guide to Florida with Kids

The Unofficial Guide to the Great Smoky and Blue Ridge Region

The Unofficial Guide to Golf Vacations in the Eastern U.S.

The Unofficial Guide to Hawaii

The Unofficial Guide to Las Vegas

The Unofficial Guide to London

The Unofficial Guide to Miami and the Keys

The Unofficial Guide to the Mid-Atlantic with Kids

The Unofficial Guide to New Orleans

The Unofficial Guide to New York City

The Unofficial Guide to Paris

The Unofficial Guide to San Francisco

The Unofficial Guide to Skiing in the West

The Unofficial Guide to the Southeast with Kids

The Unofficial Guide to Walt Disney World

The Unofficial Guide to Walt Disney World for Grown-Ups

The Unofficial Guide to Walt Disney World with Kids

The Unofficial Guide to Washington, D.C.

the
Unofficial
Guide® to
Disneyland Paris®
2nd Edition

Bob Sehlinger

For Joan

Every effort has been made to ensure the accuracy of information throughout this book. Bear in mind, however, that prices, schedules, etc., are constantly changing. Readers should always verify information before making final plans.

Hungry Minds, Inc.
909 Third Avenue
New York, New York 10022

Produced by Menasha Ridge Press

UNOFFICIAL GUIDE is a registered trademark of Hungry Minds, Inc.

ISBN 0-7645-6414-5

ISSN 1532-9909

Manufactured in the United States of America

10 9 8 7 6 5 4 3 2 1

Contents

List of Maps

Acknowledgments

Special thanks to our field research team who rendered a Herculean effort in what must have seemed like a fantasy version of Sartre's *No Exit* to the tune of "It's a Small World." We hope you all recover to tour another day.

Three dedicated, professional, hard-working, and extremely talented people made this guide a reality. Neil and Carol Offen assisted in organizing and conducting the research, and wrote and developed material for a number of the topics discussed. In addition, they nursed the author's hangovers, made apologies for his terrible French, and helped him add three inches to his waist eating in French restaurants. The third person, Holly Cross, organized the writing, kept the schedule intact, and compensated miraculously for the author's deficits in spelling and punctuation.

Thanks also to Peter Inserra and Anne Balcou, who introduced us to the charming people and villages of the Seine-et-Marne region.

Dr. Karen Turnbow, Dr. Gayle Janzen, and Dr. Joan Burns, psychologists, provided much insight into the experiences of small children at Disneyland Paris.

Introduction

How Come "Unofficial"?

DECLARATION OF INDEPENDENCE

The authors and researchers of this guide specifically and cate-gorically declare that they are and always have been totally inde-pendent of the Walt Disney Company, Inc., of Disneyland Paris, S.C.A., of Walt Disney World, Inc., and of any and all other members of the Disney corporate family not listed.

The material in this guide originated with the authors and researchers and has not been reviewed, edited, or in any way approved by the Walt Disney Company, Inc., Disneyland Paris, S.C.A., or Walt Disney World, Inc.

This guidebook represents the first comprehensive critical appraisal of Disneyland Paris. Its purpose is to provide the reader with the information necessary to tour the theme park with the greatest efficiency and economy and with the least amount of has-sle and standing in line. The researchers of this guide believe in the wondrous variety, joy, and excitement of the Disney attrac-tions. At the same time we recognize realistically that Disneyland Paris is a business, with the same profit motivations as businesses the world over.

In this, the "unofficial" guide, we have elected to represent and serve you, the consumer. The contents were researched and com-piled by a team of evaluators who were, and are, completely inde-pendent of Disneyland Paris and the Walt Disney Company, Inc. If a restaurant serves bad food, or if a gift item is overpriced, or if a certain ride isn't worth the wait, we can say so; in the process we hope we can make your visit more fun, efficient, and economical.

THE IMPORTANCE OF BEING GOOFY

"Sir, we have a problem."

Disney's vice president peered over his eyeglasses to see his assistant standing there, nervously fingering a stuffed file of paperwork.

The VP sighed. "What is it now? Did the tabloids find out about Minnie and Yosemite Sam?"

The assistant shook his head. "No, we think she dumped him over hygiene issues," he said. "This is another problem. A really serious problem."

"All right, let me have it," said the VP, hoping it wasn't more trouble with Donald Duck not wearing pants.

"We," said the assistant, "are out of ideas."

After a moment, the VP laughed. "You can't be serious. We have a thousand people working overtime in the Creative Department."

"They're out," said the assistant, spreading his arms helplessly. "And it's not just them. We're all out. The entire human race is out of ideas. We have nothing left to use for next year's animated summer blockbuster, which would then lead to merchandise, theme park rides, fast-food tie-ins, and the direct-to-video sequel."

Recognizing the severity of the situation, the VP began to concentrate. He wasn't head of the department for nothing. "No problem. We'll just use an old book whose copyright has expired, like *The Hunchback of Notre Dame* or *Tarzan.*"

"They've all been done," said the assistant dolefully, opening his file folder and reading aloud. "All literature and history has been entirely optioned, produced, and/or tied up in royalties litigation by Disney or our competitors."

"Everything?" said the VP, aghast.

"Everything," answered the assistant. "Well, except *Chicken Soup for the Vegetarian's Soul,* which Marketing has some kind of problem with."

"I don't believe this," said the VP angrily. "What about, um, *The Old Man and the Sea?* I read that in high school."

The assistant looked through his papers. "In production at Universal. Voices by Brad Pitt as the old man and Julia Roberts as the fish he loves."

"Okay, we'll go back further . . . what about . . . *A Tale of Two Cities?*"

"Script is in at Miramax, with Oliver Stone attached to direct.

We could steal it for animation, but that's our big Oscar con-
tender."

"How about *Moby Dick?*"

"TV movie, with low ratings."

"Romeo and Juliet?"

"Leonardo di Caprio a few years ago. Pre-*Titanic,* yesterday's
news."

"The Old Testament?"

"Dreamworks already did *Prince of Egypt.*"

"All right!" shouted the VP angrily, slamming his fist to the
desk. "There's only one thing left to do."

"What?" asked the assistant, mystified.

The VP swiveled around in his chair, looking out over the Hollywood hills. He'd always known this day would come, but he'd
hoped not during his watch.

"It's time to start cross-pollinating our existing products," he
said calmly. "Tell everyone in Creative to start work on *Pocahontas: The Little Hunchback Mermaid of Notre Dame.*"

And so it goes. . .

What really makes writing about Walt Disney World fun is that
the Disney people take everything so seriously. Day to day, they
debate momentous decisions with far-ranging consequences: Will
Goofy look swishy in a silver cape? Have we gone too far with the
Little Mermaid's cleavage? At a time when the nation is concerned
about the drug problem, can we afford to have a dwarf named
"Dopey"? As it happens, the French, or at least some obstreperous
number of them, also take themselves very seriously. This contin-
gent, led by former French Minister of Culture Jack Lang (who is
said to receive signals through his fillings from Charles de Gaulle
in the Great Beyond), managed to elevate the opening of the Disney park to the status of Attila the Hun knocking at the gates of
Paris. Rallying around the curious notion of preserving the purity
of Gallic culture, Lang and the French press accomplished the con-
siderable feat of taking Disney more seriously than it takes itself.

Thus arose the ludicrous scenario of French xenophobes collid-
ing head-on with the Disney juggernaut, the ultimate substitution
(as the cultural purists see it) of money and technology for heritage
and cultural values. But if the French were determined to resist Disney's cultural adulteration, Disney was equally determined to
expose every soul on earth to the self-presumed superiority of the

American way of doing things. In the final analysis, there was much smoke but little fire, and showers of words on deaf ears. The result is the same silliness that always attends the posturing of the self-important when debating such matters as Disney's impact on French cultural values or how many angels can dance on the head of a pin.

Unofficially, we think having a sense of humor is pretty important. This guidebook has a sense of humor, and it is probably necessary that you do, too—not to use this book, but more significantly, to have fun at Disneyland Paris. Disneyland Paris is an exceptionally complex tourist destination. A certain amount of levity is required simply to survive. Think of the Unofficial Guide as a private trainer to help get your sense of humor in shape. It will help you understand the importance of being Goofy.

The Death of Spontaneity

One of our all-time favorite letters is from a man who places great value on spontaneity; he writes:

> *Your book reads like the operations plan for an amphibious landing . . . Go here, do this, proceed to Step 15 . . . You must think that everyone [who visits Disneyland Paris] is a hyperactive, Type-A, theme-park-commando. Whatever happened to the satisfaction of self-discovery or the joy of spontaneity? Next you will be telling us when to empty our bladders.*

As it happens, we at the *Unofficial Guide* are a pretty existential crew. We are big on self-discovery when walking in the woods or watching birds. Some of us are able to improvise jazz without reading music, while others can whip up a mean pot of stew without a recipe. When it comes to Disneyland Paris, however, we all agree that you either need a good plan or a frontal lobotomy. The operational definition of self-discovery and spontaneity at Disneyland Paris is the "pleasure" of exhaustion and the "joy" of standing in line.

It's easy to spot the free spirits at Disneyland Paris, particularly at opening time. While everybody else is stampeding to Big Thunder Mountain or Star Tours, they are the ones standing in a cloud of dust puzzling over the park map. Later they are the people running around like chickens in a thunderstorm trying to find an attraction with less than a 40-minute wait. Face it, Disneyland

Paris is not a very existential place. In many ways it's the quintessential system, the ultimate in mass-produced entertainment, the most planned and programmed environment imaginable. Spontaneity and self-discovery work about as well at Disneyland Paris as they do on your tax return.

We're not saying you can't have a great time at Disneyland Paris. What we are saying is that you need a plan. You don't have to be compulsive or inflexible about it, just think about what you want to do before you go. Don't delude yourself by rationalizing that the information in this modest tome is only for the pathological and super-organized. Ask not for whom the tome tells, mon ami, it tells for thee.

Dance to the Music

When you dance, you hear the music and move in harmony with the rhythm. Like each day at Disneyland Paris, a dance has a beginning and an end. However, your objective is not to get to the end, but rather to enjoy the dance while the music plays. You are totally in the moment and care nothing about where on the floor you stop when the dance is done.

As you begin to contemplate your Disneyland Paris vacation, you may not have much patience for a philosophical discussion about dancing, but it's relevant. If you are like most travel guide readers, you are apt to plan and organize, to anticipate and control, and you like things to go smoothly. And, truth to tell, this leads us to suspect that you are a person who looks ahead and is outcome oriented. You may even feel a bit of pressure concerning your vacation. Vacations, after all, are special events, and expensive ones to boot. So you work hard to make the most of your vacation.

As discussed in the previous section, we believe that work, planning, and organization are important, and even essential at Disneyland Paris. But if they become your focus, you won't be able to hear the music and enjoy the dance. Though much dancing these days resembles highly individualized grand mal seizures, there was a time when each dance involved specific steps that you committed to memory. At first you were tentative and awkward, but eventually the steps became second nature and you didn't have to think about them anymore.

Metaphorically, this is what we want for you and your companions as you embark on your Disneyland Paris vacation. We want you to learn the steps in advance so that when you're on vacation and the music plays, you will be able to hear it. And you will dance with effortless grace and ease.

LETTERS AND COMMENTS FROM READERS

Many readers of *The Unofficial Guide to Disneyland Paris* write to us to make comments or share their own strategies for visiting Disneyland Paris. We appreciate all such input, both positive and critical, and encourage our readers to continue writing. Readers' comments and observations are frequently incorporated into revised editions of the *Unofficial Guide* and have contributed immeasurably to its improvement. Please write to:

> Bob Sehlinger
> *The Unofficial Guide to Disneyland Paris*
> P.O. Box 43673
> Birmingham, AL 35243
> U.S.A.

Be sure to put a return address on your letter as well as on the envelope. Sometimes envelopes and letters get separated. It's also a good idea to include your phone number. And remember, our work often requires that we be out of the office for long periods of time, so forgive us if our response is a little slow.

Reader Survey

At the end of this guide, you will find a short questionnaire that can be used to express your opinions about your Disneyland Paris visit. The questionnaire is designed so each member of your party, regardless of age, can tell us what he or she thinks. Clip out the questionnaire along the dotted line, and mail to:

> Reader Survey
> *The Unofficial Guide to Disneyland Paris*
> P.O. Box 43673
> Birmingham, AL 35243
> U.S.A.

Mickey, Donald, et Moi

Twenty years ago, no matter where in France you traveled, you heard the song on the radio. It was called "Mickey, Donald, et Moi." Though the identity of *moi* was open to discussion, there was no doubt who Mickey and Donald were. Without fanfare or debate, a nation (if not a continent) had taken two diminutive animated characters lovingly to its heart. The passing of time, however, demonstrated how fickle love can be.

When Euro Disneyland (the park's former name) debuted outside Paris in April 1992, many were singing a very different song. A diverse assortment of politicians, sabre-rattling intellectuals, and sanctimonious news commentators characterized the opening as an American cultural invasion (and that was when they were being polite).

In all manner of media, Euro Disneyland was impugned as a violation of cultural space. It was, pundits pronounced, "cowboy colonialism" and "American cultural imperialism," or, as a trendy French magazine put it, "squeaky clean totalitarianism." French political writers brought out the heavy artillery: "Euro Disney," one proclaimed, "is a horror of idiotic folklore taken straight from comic books written for obese Americans."

The president of Euro Disney reminded them, however, that France has a culture with several thousand years of history and one that has successfully resisted many previous and far more malicious invasions. If France actually feels threatened by the arrival of a mouse, then the culture is in worse shape than even the most caustic of the Disney critics realize.

Disbelieving observers from other European nations were astounded by the uproar over Euro Disney. An Austrian journalist in Paris wrote, "the French press must be desperate for subject matter," while a British reporter suggested that "the behavior of the French media and intellectuals would have provided Molière material enough for ten comedies." A Danish wire service correspondent summed it up best: "My god," he exclaimed, "it's just an amusement park! Do they think Disney is going to come in and administer electro-shock treatment to the whole population of Paris?"

Undaunted by logic or reality, the nouveau Flauberts persisted in denouncing Euro Disneyland as "a cultural Chernobyl," a phrase so wickedly evocative that it was quoted in almost every feature and news report on the opening of the park. (Incidentally, the person who coined the phrase is a French theatrical producer who, while on tour in California, made a beeline straight for Disneyland.)

It is undeniable, of course, that Europe in general and France in particular has been absorbing various elements of American culture for decades. More potent than U.S. high-tech weaponry is the unremitting onslaught of American TV sitcoms, Hollywood movies, fast-food restaurants, and rock music. America *has* always been a cultural invader of Europe, but arguably at Europe's express invitation.

For the most part the invasion has been a happy one. Thirty years after the Beatles took off for Germany to practice playing the music of American songwriters, cafes and clubs across Europe still shake to the sound of Stateside rock 'n' roll. Hip Italian teens wear American baseball caps in Parma. McDonald's sells hamburgers from Moscow to London's Piccadilly, from Frankfurt to Rome's Via Veneto. Parisians wolf down Big Macs in the Latin Quarter, by the Luxembourg Gardens, and on the Champs-Elysées. Worshipers in Reims drop by for a burger and a Coke after attending mass at their world-famous cathedral. Even Disney has been around for a long time. In 1933 French publishers launched the first Mickey Mouse book published outside of the United States.

It is also clear that the importation of American products and values has had an impact on traditional customs. Many of the French have substituted fast food for the more civilized three-hour lunch. There is more rock music now, both live and on video, and fewer of the beloved music hall balladeers. Blue jeans are worn routinely by all classes of society, even to nice restaurants, and take-out food (once considered an option exclusively for the sick) is now available in almost all French cities for people who are perfectly healthy.

American influence, it should be noted, took root more gradually in France than elsewhere in Europe, so it came as somewhat of a surprise when Disney chose the Ile de France for its European beachhead. To many, France is not just another country; it is another world. The French are proud of their insularity and are fierce defenders of their uniqueness. Of course, this defense was somewhat easier to maintain in the days before satellite television, the Internet, the Concorde airplane, and the other technological developments that have brought us all so much closer together. Additional cultural blurring has occurred as a result of European Economic Community (EEC) initiatives directed toward making Europe a more unified continent.

But even as the British tuned in American TV cops and the Germans devoured American mass-market fiction, the French remained aloof. They would quit NATO military operations if the Americans were going to be there drinking Coca-Cola. They would pass laws forbidding *"franglais"* (those embarrassing anglicisms in their language) if their countrymen persisted in saying such things as *le weekend.*

In short, the French developed an "attitude," a sort of cultural arrogance behaviorally manifested in cynicism and condescension. The celebrated French writer Jean Cocteau described his countrymen as "Italians in a bad mood." A magazine reporting on the opening of Euro Disneyland ran its feature under the head, "Disney Comes to Paris, Where All the Dwarfs Are Grumpy."

In reality, the case is decidedly overstated. Not all—or even a majority of—the French were disturbed by the coming of Euro Disney. In fact, the critics were and continue to be a small (albeit very noisy) minority: a collection of intellectuals, politicians, and media commentators who regard Euro Disneyland as the cultural version of the Trojan horse. While the intellectuals issued dim predictions about the cultural contamination certain to arise from this foreign enterprise on French soil, the French people, like most Europeans, sang "Mickey, Donald, et Moi" and looked forward with great anticipation to visiting Europe's grandest theme park. They *wanted* Euro Disneyland.

So did the French government. Which is why, after all, Disney chose Paris over Barcelona, Spain, with its warmer weather and more receptive press. When Disney announced its intention to build a European theme park, a number of governments, including the French, Spanish, and Danish, began salivating. They understood that Euro Disneyland would create more than 12,000 new permanent jobs as well as 18,000 subcontracting positions during the construction phase. The Mitterrand government also knew that Euro Disneyland could bring in $700 million in foreign currency each year. No matter how the French government felt about cultural imperialism, it knew that Euro Disneyland could provide the French economy with a much-needed shot in the arm. Looking ahead and evaluating Euro Disneyland in the context of the EEC, French politicians saw the opportunity to make Paris and the Ile de France the economic capital of a rapidly unifying Europe.

Disney, however, did not choose the Paris region simply because of its central location: Euro Disneyland came to Marne-la-Vallée because it got a great deal. The French offered Disney more in the way of infrastructure than did any competing government, nearly three billion francs' worth of new highways and rail connections. To facilitate the acquisition of land, the French government provided Euro Disneyland with a declaration of public utility, which allowed the Walt Disney Company to expropriate private property and essentially to function like an arm of the government. Disney was able to buy at bargain prices 5,000 acres of flat farmland (much of which had belonged to the same families for generations), an area approximately one fifth the size of Paris. To further sweeten the deal, a loan of four billion francs at highly preferential rates was arranged, as was a reduction of the dreaded Value Added Tax on theme parks from 18.6% to 7%. When all of the i's were dotted and the t's crossed, the government's contract with Disney was 400 pages long and included the go-ahead for additional development well into the future, including a second theme park, 18,000 hotel rooms, golf courses, and even housing projects. By any standards, Disney got a sweetheart of a deal.

In addition to wanting Euro Disneyland in France, the Mitterrand government also wanted the venture to succeed. Large, American-style theme parks were generally foreign to Europe and have had a particularly disastrous track record in France. Who, after all, needs fairy-tale castles and whimsical, artificial villages when you can see the real thing five miles down the road? Predecessors to the Euro Disney project, such as the Mirapolis theme park (also near Paris), were unable to lure enough customers to keep the gates open. Operational only during the warmer months, they could not cope with the difficult weather of northern Europe (where the dampness can freeze your mouse ears off) and eventually foundered in a sea of debt.

If France was going to get into the theme park business, it wanted a partner with staying power and a history of successful operations. Disney had demonstrated spectacular success with its American parks and had even been able to operate profitably in a cold weather climate with its Tokyo park. Best of all, however, Disney's asset base and cash position, coupled with the company's long-term orientation, provided the French government with sufficient stability and security to take the risk.

Thus, with all the governmental support any enterprise could desire (and with a lot of crossed fingers), Euro Disneyland became a reality. Five years in the making and costing more than $4 billion, it is by far the largest and most ambitious development of its type in European history. With the single exception of the tunnel under the English Channel connecting England and France,

Euro Disneyland was the most expensive single construction project in the history of Europe.

DISNEY'S GALLIC WARS

As Disney discovered, seducing the French government was only
the first of many challenges. The day that stock in Euro Disney
was first offered on the Paris Stock Exchange, an unruly mob of
protesters pelted Disney chief executive Michael Eisner with farm
products from Brie, the region where the park was going to be
built. Young French Communists shouted and jeered, and even
more moderate citizens expressed anger about the forced dis-
placement of Marne-la-Vallée beet farmers.

In the wake of the political maelstrom, Disney began to
encounter unanticipated personnel problems. Even in a country
with an unusually high rate of unemployment for Western Europe,
Disney was having trouble recruiting the workers it needed.
Among those French it did manage to lure, Disney struggled
mightily to instill Orlando charm and smiliness into their difficult Gallic temperaments. Hundreds of Euro Disney management
trainees had to be dispatched to Florida to learn Disney-style cour-
tesy and friendliness. French workers, incredulous that an American company would presume to dictate how they should dress and
groom themselves, had to be cajoled and ultimately coerced to
accept *le look Disney.*

This tempest actually escalated to a national conflagration with
the media, politicians, trade unions, and even professional ath-
letes and university professors getting into the act. *Le look Disney*
transcended wearing les blue jeans down Paris's Boulevard St.
Michel. At Euro Disney, Americans were telling Frenchmen that
they must shave their mustaches, beards, and long sideburns and
that they must have their hair cut to exact specifications. French
women were admonished to keep their hair in "one natural color"
with no frosting or streaking, and to keep mascara use to a minimum. No false eyelashes, eyeliner, eyebrow pencil, or long fin-
gernails were allowed.

Disney also prohibited their employees from wearing sunglasses,
on the grounds that they "inhibit interpersonal contact," and limited women to wearing only transparent panty hose (nothing black
or with fancy designs). Only what Disney discreetly refers to as
"appropriate undergarments" were allowed. Management also

insisted that Euro Disney "cast members" (staff) show up for work each day "fresh and clean," that is, properly scrubbed with the "required" application of deodorant or antiperspirant.

In the United States and Japan, where Disney has mandated these same regulations for years, it has encountered a little grumbling but certainly nothing on the order of the outright rebellion it encountered in France. Americans and Japanese generally acknowledge the right of the employer to impose certain restrictions concerning decorum and personal appearance, but Disney's French workers showed signs of storming Sleeping Beauty's Castle. Even Sleeping Beauty, however, could be more easily awakened than Disney management, which seemed totally confused by its French workers' impassioned demands for individual liberties.

The French were not only outraged but insulted. "Of all people telling us what to wear and how to look, the *Americans?* People who have been known to wear Bermuda shorts in the streets of Paris in the spring?" Critics in the press and on university campuses upbraided the Americans for being insensitive to French culture, to French individualism, to French liberty and privacy. A Communist-led labor union distributed leaflets outside Disney's suburban Paris headquarters warning of even greater infringements of individual liberty yet to come. Another union dramatically declared Disney's dress and appearance code to be "a violation of human dignity." Lawsuits were filed, and government officials responsible for protecting workers' rights registered strongly worded complaints. Almost everyone pointed out that French law prohibits employers from restricting individual and collective liberties unless the restrictions can be justified by the nature of the job.

Disney defended the restrictions by explaining that a certain standard of personal appearance is intrinsic to its corporate image and to the image of its theme parks. "How would you like going to see *Hamlet,*" responded one Disneyland Paris official, "and finding the actors dressed differently from what you had expected?" Singularly unimpressed by this logic, an unhappy Disney cast member asked, "Why do I have to shave my mustache when I run around all day in a damned pig suit?"

THE FIRST DECADE: A TRIAL BY FIRE

Almost a decade has passed since Disneyland Paris opened its doors in April 1992. During its first several years, Disneyland Paris learned any number of valuable lessons, usually the hard way in the inimitable Disney style. European visitors, for example, forced Disney to back down on its prohibition of alcoholic beverages in the park. Disney also discovered, contrary to expectations, that European visitors didn't give a hoot for leisurely meals in the park's fancy full-service restaurants. They might linger over a three-hour lunch at home, but at Disneyland Paris they inconveniently lost their appetite. To compound matters, park visitors weren't consuming much fast food either. In fact, Europeans considered the admission cost so expensive (more expensive than any of the American Disney parks) that they were forgoing purchases of any ilk. Unlike their American cousins who bolted down Disney burgers and fries, enjoyed periodic ice cream or popcorn breaks, and bought Mickey T-shirts and Goofy hats by the gross, Europeans, once past the turnstile, kept their wallets safely in their pockets.

And then there were the Disney hotels. At Walt Disney World and Disneyland in California, Disney hotels are immensely popular and stay full in spite of (some would say exorbitantly) high rates. At the French park, practically no one was interested in expensive exile at the Disney hotels with Paris a 30-minute train ride away.

Interestingly, although not widely known, the number of guests who visited the park in its first year was almost exactly what Disney had projected (about 11 million). But between the low occupancy rates of the hotels and the anemic numbers for on-site purchases, overall revenue for Disneyland Paris fell catastrophically short of expectations. This bad news, of course, was chum to the sharks of the French press, who escalated their virulent caterwauling to yet unheard levels. Anything bad that happened in France, it seemed, was the fault of Disneyland Paris. If a bus ran off a bridge in Lyon, the French press managed somehow to connect the accident to Disney. The bottom line, however, no matter how strident the French press, was that European banks, the French government, and Disney itself had so much invested in Disneyland Paris that it could not be allowed to fail.

Thus, over time Disneyland Paris has fought its way to profitability, though you couldn't exactly characterize it as phoenix rising (clawing its way out of the abyss is closer to the truth). In the process, its debt was restructured, alcoholic beverages became more readily available, admission prices were lowered, Europeans replaced Americans in top management, thrill rides were added to the attraction mix to lure teens and young adults, and food service was tailored to European preferences. For a while, some hotels were mothballed or opened only seasonally. Gradually, over eight or so years, the resort grew its group, tour, and convention business to a level that allowed the hotels to operate year-round. Also helping significantly turn the tide was the completion of the tunnel under the English Channel, allowing Brits to commute directly to Disneyland Paris in less than three hours. Additionally, the resort enjoys direct TGV (fast train) service connecting the rest of France and all of Europe beyond. Today, most Europeans, indeed most French, regard Disneyland Paris as a fixture, its Gallic wars a thing of the past. True, the French press waits like a virus for an opportunity to erupt; otherwise, Disney's continental fledgling is enjoying tolerably good health.

THE NEWEST KINGDOM IN EUROPE

Despite all the difficulties, Disneyland Paris has proved to be a survivor. More than that, Disneyland Paris is obviously not just another amusement park. It's the arrival on European soil of a new standard in popular entertainment—a quantum leap in variety, creativity, scope, scale, spectacle, attention to detail, safety, and cleanliness. The interminable, vitriolic response of the press notwithstanding, the vast majority of the French people are apparently thrilled that Disney has come to them. Most interestingly, the French are delighted that they have gotten "le vrai Disney"; in other words, the original American version, as opposed to some ersatz Europeanized facsimile. They wanted a park equal to or better than Disney parks in Orlando, Anaheim, and Tokyo. Instead of having to travel to the Magic Kingdom, they wanted the Magic Kingdom to come to them.

Basically, that's what they got. It's all there: Pirates of the Caribbean, Big Thunder Mountain, Space Mountain, Peter Pan's Flight, the Indian Canoes, Star Tours, and more. The attractions may be running on 220 current rather than 110, and many of the signs may be in French, but otherwise it's just like in the United States.

When the first visitors passed through the gates, an international children's chorus sang the Disney canon, "It's a Small World," in French, English, and what seemed like every other language, welcoming all peoples and nations to this world within a world. "If you were dropped into Disneyland Paris in the middle of the night," a Disney cast member reflected, "there's no way you would know you were in France. When you leave the park, it's a shock to discover that Paris is right out there." But she said it proudly. Profit motivation and all manner of controversy aside, Disneyland Paris is indeed a special and happy place, a domain that transcends the natural divisiveness of humanity. For Mickey, Donald, and her, it did not matter where they were geographically. At heart, they were all at home, and it felt very, very good.

Disneyland Paris: An Overview

If you are selecting among the tourist attractions of Europe, and elect to visit Disneyland Paris, the challenge becomes how to see the best of the various Disney offerings with some economy of time, effort, and finances.

Make no mistake: There is nothing quite like Disneyland Paris. Incredible in its scope, genius, beauty, and imagination, it is a joy and wonderment for people of all ages. A fantasy, a dream, and a vision all rolled into one, it transcends simple entertainment, making us children and adventurers, freeing us for an hour or a day to live the dreams of our past, present, and future.

Disneyland Paris, even more than its Florida counterpart, embodies that quiet, charming spirit of nostalgia that so characterized Walt Disney himself. Disneyland Paris is vast yet intimate, etched in the tradition of its founder, yet continually changing. A visit to Disneyland Paris is fun, but it is also a powerful and moving experience, a living testimony to the achievements and immense potential of the loving and life-embracing side of man's creativity.

Certainly we are critics, but it is the responsibility of critics to credit that which is done well as surely as to reflect negatively on that which is done poorly. The Disney attractions are special above and beyond any man-made entertainment offering we know of.

WHAT DOES DISNEYLAND PARIS CONSIST OF?

Disneyland Paris was opened in 1992 on a 5,000-acre tract surrounded almost exclusively by farms just 30 kilometers east of Paris. Located strategically in this vast expanse are the Disneyland Paris theme park, six resort hotels, a convention center, an elaborate campground, a nighttime entertainment complex, shopping arcades, almost 30 full-service restaurants, golf courses, several large interconnected lakes, and a transportation system consisting of four-lane highways, a train station, and a system of canals.

The theme park is a collection of adventures, rides, and shows drawn from Disney cartoons and films, and symbolized by Le Château de la Belle au Bois Dormant (Sleeping Beauty's Castle). Disneyland Paris park is divided into five subareas or "lands" arranged around a central hub. The first one you encounter is Main Street, U.S.A., which connects the Disneyland Paris entrance with the central hub. Moving clockwise around the hub, the other lands are Adventureland, Frontierland, Fantasyland, and Discoveryland. All five lands will be described in detail later.

Sitting above the entranceway to the Disneyland Paris theme park is the Disneyland Hotel, the most luxurious of the development's six resort hotels. Just outside the entrance area beyond the Disneyland Hotel is a train station, which serves as the terminus of a suburban rail line connecting Disneyland Paris and Paris, as well as a stop for Eurostar international and SNCF (French National Railroad) long-distance trains. Adjacent to the train station, but on the opposite side of the tracks from the theme park, is the Disneyland Paris guest parking facility and Disney Village, a nongated (no admission charge) entertainment complex featuring restaurants, shops, production shows, and nightclubs. Beyond Disney Village is a large manmade lake fronted respectively on three sides by the Hotel New York, the Newport Bay Club, and the Sequoia Lodge Resorts. Connected to the lake complex by walkway, road, and canal are the Hotel Cheyenne and the Hotel Santa Fe. Some distance away, and accessible only by car, are the Davy Crockett tent and trailer (caravan) campground and the golf courses.

What's in a Name?

Because the Disney people have a penchant for naming everything, there is always more than enough nomenclature to keep the average person confused. Technically, the entire Marne-la-Vallée Disney complex is the "Disneyland Paris Resort." Within the resort is the theme park, "Disneyland Paris," as well as Disney Village (shopping and dining arcade), the resort hotels, the campground, and the golf courses. In daily usage, however, guests, the press, and even Disney tend to refer to the whole operation as Disneyland Paris.

SHOULD I GO TO DISNEYLAND PARIS IF I'VE SEEN WALT DISNEY WORLD OR DISNEYLAND?

Disneyland Paris is roughly comparable to the Magic Kingdom theme park at Walt Disney World near Orlando, Florida; to Tokyo Disneyland in Japan; and to the original Disneyland in southern California. All are arranged by "lands" accessible from a central hub and connected to the entrance by a Main Street. The parks feature many rides and attractions with the same name, including Pirates of the Caribbean, It's a Small World, and Dumbo the Flying Elephant. Interestingly, however, the same name does not necessarily connote the same experience. Pirates of the Caribbean at Disneyland Paris is much more sophisticated and elaborate than its Walt Disney World counterpart. Big Thunder Mountain is a little wilder in Florida, and Dumbo is about the same in all of the parks.

Disneyland Paris, created in the image of the original Disneyland, is more intimate than Florida's Magic Kingdom; though, as in Florida, pedestrian thoroughfares are spacious, and everything from Big Thunder Mountain to the castle is built on a grand scale. Large crowds, likewise, are less taxing at Disneyland Paris and at Walt Disney World's Magic Kingdom, since there is more room for them to disperse. At Disneyland Paris, however, as at the original California Disneyland, dozens of little surprises—small unheralded attractions—are tucked away in crooks and corners of the park, giving Disneyland Paris a special charm and variety that Florida's Magic Kingdom lacks.

To allow for a meaningful comparison, we have provided a summary of those features found only at Disneyland Paris.

DisneySpeak Pocket Translator

Disney has its own somewhat peculiar language. Here are some terms you are likely to bump into:

DisneySpeak	English Definition
Adventure	Ride
Attraction	Ride or theater show
Attraction Host	Ride operator
Audience	Crowd
Backstage	Behind the scenes
Bull Pen	Queuing area
Cast Member	Employee
Character	Disney cartoon character impersonated by an employee
Costume	Work attire or uniform
Dark Ride	Indoor ride
Day-Guest	Any customer not staying at a Disney resort
Face Character	A character that does not wear a head-covering costume (Snow White, Cinderella, Jasmine)
General Public	Same as day-guest
Greeter	Employee at entrance of an attraction
Guest	Customer
Hidden Mickeys	Frontal silhouette of Mickey's head worked subtly into the design of buildings, vehicles, attractions, etc.
In Rehearsal	Operating though not officially open
Lead	Person in charge of an attraction
On Stage	In full view of customers
Preshow	Entertainment at an attraction prior to the feature presentation
Resort Guest	A customer staying at a Disney resort
Role	An employee's job
Security Host	Security guard
Soft Opening	Opening a park or attraction before its stated opening time
Transitional Experience	An element of the queuing area and/or preshow that provides a story line or information essential to understanding the attraction

Attractions Found Only at Disneyland Paris

Main Street	Liberty Arcade Discovery Arcade Main Street Vehicles
Adventureland	Adventure Isle Indiana Jones and the Temple of Peril
Fantasyland	La Tanière du Dragon Les Pirouettes du Vieux Moulin Alice's Curious Labyrinth
Discoveryland	Les Mystères du Nautilus

Part One

Planning before You Leave Home

Gathering Information

In addition to this guide, information concerning Disneyland Paris can be obtained at the public library, through travel agencies, or by writing or calling (do not use 33-1 when calling locally):

Disneyland Paris Guest Relations
Boîte Postale l00
77777 Marne-la-Vallée, Cedex 4, France
telephone (33-1) 60-30-60-53

In addition to the above, Disneyland Paris information is available on the Internet at www.disneylandparis.com (U.S.) and www.disney.co.uk (U.K.). On either site you can request Disney to mail you their Disneyland Paris brochure. Reservations and additional information on special events and packages are available from Walt Disney Travel Company at (407) 828-3232 (U.S.) or Disneyland Paris U.K. Reservations at 08705 03 03 03 (billed as a National Rate Call). From Ireland call 00 44 8705 03 03 03 (billed as an International Rate call).

If your travel plans include touring Paris or elsewhere in France, additional information can be obtained by writing or calling:

Ile de France and Seine et Marne Tourist Information
Disney Village
77777 Marne-la-Vallée, Cedex 4, France
telephone (33-1) 60-43-33-33

Maison Départementale du Tourisme de Seine-et-Marne
11 rue Royale
77300 Fontainbleau, France

telephone (33-1) 60-39-60-39
mdt@tourisme77.com

Office du Tourisme et des Congrès de Paris
127, Avenue des Champs-Elysées
75008 Paris, France
telephone (33-0) 8-36-68-31-12
www.paris-touristoffice.com

BEING PREPARED

Money

When you purchase traveler's checks, get about half of them in French francs or Euros. They are your insurance against finding yourself without cash after banking hours. Euros are accepted throughout Disneyland Paris Resort. In Paris, however, the French franc is still the currency of choice. Sometimes you can obtain a better exchange rate for Euros than for francs. Check with the foreign currency department of your local bank before leaving home.

Most restaurants and hotels in France accept foreign traveler's checks, of course, but the exchange rate you get can be far below a bank's rate. Get some of the French checks in small denominations, so you can use them as cash if necessary in most establishments. Also, be sure to have some actual French cash on you when you arrive in the country in case them is a long line at the airport or railway station foreign currency exchange booth. If you already have French coins for bus and train fare machines, you could save yourself a lot of time and headaches.

Clothing

Because of Paris's temperate but cool, damp weather even in summer, dressing in lightweight layers is the most comfortable and practical approach for both men and women. This is particularly true if you will be leaving your hotel early and will not be getting back to change clothes. If you find the extra layers cumbersome at the height of the afternoon heat, you can just peel them off and put them in a Disneyland Paris Main Street locker.

It rains frequently, so pack a fold-up umbrella; always bring it along even on what looks like a clear day. The weather can change several times in the course of a few hours. An anorak that folds up small also comes in handy.

Informal attire is acceptable, but extremely casual dress, such as torn cut-offs or short shorts, should be left at home.

ADMISSION OPTIONS

One-day, two-day, and three-day admission passes are available for purchase for both adults (12 years and up) and children (3 to 11 years inclusive). All rides, shows, and attractions (except the Frontierland shooting gallery) are included in the price of admission. Multiday passes do not have to be used on consecutive days.

Admission prices, not unexpectedly, are increased from time to time. For planning your budget, however, the following provides a fair estimate:

One-Day Passport Adult	About FF 225 ($30)
One-Day Passport Child (3–11)	About FF 175 ($23)
Two-Day Passport Adult	About FF 435 ($58)
Two-Day Passport Child (3–11)	About FF 340 ($45)
Three-Day Passport Adult	About FF 610 ($82)
Three-Day Passport Child (3–11)	About FF 474 ($64)

There is no denying that admission to Disneyland Paris is very expensive. People who have never visited a Disney theme park, however, are usually not prepared for the scope, variety, and quality of the attractions and entertainment. It literally takes 10 to 12 hours just to sample the many offerings of the Disneyland Paris theme park and twice that long for a truly comprehensive tour. First-run movies in Europe cost about FF 52 ($7) and average two hours in duration. If we compare the cost of a first-run movie to a day at Disneyland Paris on an hourly basis (for adult admission), the movie costs FF 26 ($4) per hour while a ten-hour visit to Disneyland Paris costs FF 22.50 ($3) per hour. During holidays and warm weather months, Disneyland Paris is open 14 to 16 hours a day. If, by some miracle, you possessed the stamina to stay all day, your visit would cost less than FF 16 ($2) per hour! Don't you feel better? Admission passes can be ordered through the mail by writing:

Disneyland Paris Ticket Service
Boîte Postale 103
77777 Marne-la-Vallée, Cedex 4, France
telephone (33-1) 64-74-43-03

The Disneyland Paris Ticket Service accepts credit cards, Eurochèques, bank drafts, and personal checks written in French francs. Allow two weeks for processing for orders placed from Europe, three to four weeks for orders placed from other continents.

How Much Does One Day at Disneyland Paris Cost?

Let's say we have a family of four—Mom and Dad, Paul (age 12), and Marie (age 8)—driving their own car. Since they plan to be in the area for a few days, they intend to buy the Two-Day Passports. Here is how much a typical day would cost, excluding lodging and transportation:

Breakfast for four at a hotel with tax and tip	FF 140.00 ($19)
Disneyland Paris parking fee	FF 45.00 ($6)
One day's admission on a Two-Day Passport:	
Dad: Adult, Two-Day Passport = FF 425 ($57) divided by 2 (days)	FF 212.50 ($28)
Mom: Adult, Two-Day Passport = FF 425 ($57) divided by 2 (days)	FF 212.50 ($28)
Paul: Adult, Two-Day Passport = FF 425 ($57) divided by 2 (days)	FF 212.50 ($28)
Marie: Child, Two-Day Passport with tax FF 330 ($44) divided by 2 (days)	FF 165.00 ($22)
Morning break (soda or coffee)	FF 47.00 ($6)
Fast-food lunch (burger, fries, soda), no tip	FF 190.00 ($25)
Afternoon break (soda and popcorn)	FF 74.00 ($10)
Dinner in park at full-service restaurant with tax and tip	FF 775.00 ($103)
Souvenirs (Mickey T-shirts for Paul and Marie) with tax*	FF 240.00 ($32)
One-day Total (not including lodging and transportation)	FF 2,313.50 ($312)

* Incidentally, prices for everything at Disneyland Paris are 12 to 45% higher than at the Disney theme parks in the United States. But cheer up, the food is much better at Disneyland Paris, and you will not have to buy souvenirs every day.

Rides and Shows Closed for Repairs or Maintenance

Rides and shows at Disneyland Paris are sometimes closed for maintenance or repairs. If there is a certain attraction that is important

to you, call (33-1) 60-30-60-53 before your visit to make sure it
will be operating. A mother wrote us, lamenting:

> We were disappointed to find La Cabane des Robinson
> [Swiss Family Treehouse] and the Riverboat closed for
> repairs. We felt that a large chunk of the [park] was not
> working, yet the tickets were still full price and expensive!

Timing Your Visit

SELECTING THE TIME OF YEAR FOR YOUR VISIT

Crowds are largest at Disneyland Paris during the summer and
during specific holiday periods during the rest of the year. The
busiest time of all is Christmas Day through New Year's Day. The
two weeks around Easter are also extremely busy. To give you some
idea of what busy means at Disneyland Paris, more than 65,000
people have toured the park on a single day! Although this level
of attendance is far from typical, the possibility of its occurrence
should prevent all but the ignorant and the foolish from challenging this mega-attraction at its busiest periods.

The least busy time of all, of course, is during the cold-weather
months. With waiting areas for most attractions protected from the
weather, and with covered walkways allowing guests to move around
much of the park without being exposed to the elements, cold
weather touring is tolerable, if not exactly comfortable. While lines
for the attractions are short to nonexistent from late fall to early
spring, the park's hours of operation are likewise short, usually 9
a.m. to 6 p.m. These hours are sufficient to enjoy the attractions
but do not leave enough time for parades, live entertainment, full-
service dining, or shopping. Also, during the colder months (except
holiday periods), all evening parades and fireworks and some stage
shows are discontinued. Even so, and at the risk of being blas-
phemous, our research team was so impressed with the relative
ease of touring in the fall, spring, and other "off" periods that we
would rather take our children out of school for a few days than
to do battle with the summer crowds.

Disneyland Paris and Paris

Most people visiting Disneyland Paris are likely to be combining
the trip with a stay in Paris. First, let's consider the best time of year
to visit the entire area (taking into consideration that the best time

to go to Disneyland Paris is not always the best time to visit Paris).

Paris's weather, while temperate, is only slightly more appealing than London's. It's not as cold, and there is no fog, but it's damp and overcast much of the time. From November to March you can almost count on rain at some point in the day. Even in summer, damp, dreary days are not uncommon.

Luckily, most precipitation is not in the form of heavy downpours that interfere with activity. Usually they are light rains that start and stop throughout the day, just enough to be annoying. Get used to carrying around a fold-up umbrella or using that anorak.

The good news is you do not have to worry about the scorching hot days that can wilt enthusiasm at Walt Disney World and Disneyland in the United States. Eighty degrees Fahrenheit (27°C) is a hot summer day in Paris.

Paris's best weather—when you can almost count on delightfully clear blue skies and temperatures around 70° (21°C)—is in September. The air is dry, it's still light late, and the Parisians are in a noticeably better mood.

Naturally, any day the weather is good the park will be more crowded. Touring the park on a clear day is, of course, vastly preferable to getting poked with someone's umbrella as you stand in line for Dumbo. But unless you have a lot of time and flexibility, you should not let rain keep you away from Disneyland Paris. (For one thing, even if it's raining when you leave your hotel, it might have stopped by the time you get to the theme park.) Even when the rain is coming down in torrents, Disneyland Paris is a spectacle. Imagine swarms of guests in yellow Disney ponchos racing frenetically from one covered area to another. If you could see Disneyland Paris from the air on such a day, you might think the park was being attacked by giant killer bees.

Getting Down to Specifics

Although vacation patterns of neighboring countries are apt to affect the park's attendance throughout the year, the Paris school calendar has the biggest potential impact.

Paris's School Vacations

Fall Break	Last week in October through November 1
Christmas Break	The week before Christmas through New Year's weekend
Winter Break	Mid-February through March 1

Easter/Spring Break   Two and a half weeks beginning at Easter
Summer Vacation   Early July to second week in September

Additionally, the periods during which neighboring countries have school breaks should be taken into consideration.

Major European School Vacation Periods

Christmas/New Year's   Mid-December to early January
Winter Break   Mid-February to mid-March
Easter/Spring Break   Mid-April to early May
Summer Vacation   Late June to early September
Fall Break   Mid-October to early November

Best Periods to Visit Disneyland Paris

A careful reading of the above lists will point to a few periods throughout the year when crowds should be the lightest:

- January (after New Year's weekend) through the first half of February
- Second half of March through the first half of April (or a week before Easter)
- Second half of May through first three weeks in June
- Mid-September through the first half of October
- Mid-November through the first half of December

Mid-September through the first half of October is the time of year that combines the fewest crowds with the best weather. The next best time is the second half of May through the first three weeks in June.

SELECTING THE DAY OF THE WEEK FOR YOUR VISIT

The crowds at Disneyland Paris are made up mostly of out-of-France visitors during the off-season and shoulder seasons, with the French accounting for 50% or more of the gate during warm weather months. Though the French think Disneyland Paris terribly expensive, the quality of the entertainment is slowly winning them over. In time, the people of Paris will probably come to think of Disneyland Paris as their own private theme park. Yearly passes are available at less cost than a year's membership to a health club, and the Disney management has intensified its efforts to appeal to the local market.

What all this means is that weekends are usually packed. Sundays, followed closely by Saturdays, are the busiest days of the week, combining local patronage with weekend and holiday travelers. Because some French schoolchildren still attend school on Saturday mornings when school is in session, the park usually does not get extremely crowded until late morning or early afternoon. Additionally, many visitors coming from afar use part of Saturday morning to get settled into their hotels. All of this is relative, of course. Saturday mornings are always much busier than weekday mornings.

After weekends and holidays, Wednesday is likely to be the next busiest day of the week. This is because during the school year, French schools are closed on Wednesday. Monday and Tuesday are generally the quietest days of the week. Since most museums are closed on Tuesdays, others on Mondays, the beginning of the week is an ideal time to schedule your visit to the park in all months except July and August. Thursdays, likewise, are usually not too crowded, and Fridays will vary.

All things considered, we recommend the following on any week without holidays, except during the months of July and August:

Best Days	Worst Days
1 Monday	1 Sunday
2 Tuesday	2 Saturday
3 Thursday	3 Wednesday
4 Friday	

In July and August, Saturday and Sunday will continue to be the busiest days, followed by Monday and Tuesday. Wednesday and Friday will usually be days of lighter attendance, and Thursdays will vary.

OPERATING HOURS

It cannot be said that the Disney folks are not flexible when it comes to hours of operation for the park. They run a dozen or more different operating schedules during the year, making it advisable to call 60-30-60-53, locally, the day before you arrive at the theme park.

Official Opening Time vs. Real Opening Time

The hours of operation that the Disney folks will give you when you call are "official hours." In reality, the park will open earlier. If the official hours of operation are 9 a.m. to 9 p.m., for example, the Main Street section of Disneyland Paris will open at 8 or 8:30 a.m., and the remainder of the park will open at 8:30 or 9 a.m.

The Disney folks publish their hours of operation well in advance but allow themselves the flexibility to react to gate conditions on a day-by-day basis. To avoid bottlenecks at the parking facilities or theme park ticket lines, the theme park is frequently opened early, absorbing the crowds as they arrive. Many visitors, relying on the accuracy of the information disseminated by the Disney Guest Relations service, arrive at the stated opening time to find the park fairly thronged with people.

We recommend arriving an hour before the official opening time regardless of the time of year you visit. If you happen to go on a major holiday, arrive an hour and 20 minutes in advance of the official opening time.

Closing time is another matter. The Disney people usually close all rides and attractions at approximately the official stated closing time. If you are in line for an attraction at closing time, however, you will usually be allowed to ride or see the show. Main Street remains open a half hour to an hour after the rest of the park has closed.

Star Nights

From early July to early September, the park is open 9 a.m.–11 p.m. Launched in 2000, the Star Nights program offers a special passport that is good from 5 p.m. until closing. The Star Nights passport costs FF 110 ($15) for both adults and children. We like the program because it allows you to enjoy the attractions during a comparatively less crowded time of day. Plus, the park is quite beautiful at night. For the hungry, most restaurants remain open.

Getting There

GETTING THERE BY AIR

Which Airport Should I Use?

Paris has two international airports: Charles de Gaulle (CDG), also known as Roissy because it's located in the northern suburb of Roissy, is the larger and busier of the two airports and is about 25 kilometers northeast of Paris and 56 kilometers from Disneyland. The older and smaller airport, Orly (OLY), is located about 15 kilometers south of Paris and around 50 kilometers west of the park. Both are easily accessible to and from Paris by a commuter subway line called the RER, public buses, Air France buses, and taxis. Airport signs are mostly in both French and English and are sufficiently clear.

You probably won't have a choice of which Paris airport you'll be using, but most, although not all, flights from North America arrive at Charles de Gaulle. If you do have a choice and are staying in Paris, note that Charles de Gaulle is slightly more convenient to Paris's Right Bank and Orly is closer to Paris's Left Bank. Even more important, those of you who travel lightly and are receptive to using Paris's excellent and inexpensive public transportation system should note that hotels located within walking distance of an RER stop in Paris are easily accessible from either airport.

We advise the following:

- If you don't have a lot of luggage, take the RER train. It's fast and reliable, and there are no traffic snarls.

- If you do have a lot of luggage and would rather not incur the cost of a taxi, take the Air France bus into Paris or arrange for a pick-up service. If your hotel is near one of the Air France bus stops in Paris you may prefer this option whether you have a lot of luggage or not.

- If you're in a hurry and don't mind spending some cash, take a taxi.

For some of the bus and train options described in the sections below, you will need to buy a ticket from a fare machine before boarding. If you have French francs but do not have coins, locate the *Caisse Monnaie* (cash booth). At Orly Sud, for example, there is one right next to the Airport Information desk. If the booth is closed for some reason, you may have to stand in line at the *Change* (currency exchange) booth or obtain change by buying something in a shop, though this shouldn't be necessary. If you need assistance, go to Airport Information in the terminal. There are also fare machines that take Visa and MasterCard, known in France as CB *(carte bleue)*. Remember to ask your bank for your international pin code number before leaving home; you'll need this here, as well as to withdraw francs from ATMs in France.

Flying into Charles de Gaulle (Roissy) Airport

You will experience your first Disneyesque "attraction" when you arrive at one of the satellites of Charles de Gaulle Airport. There are two major terminals: Terminal 1, for most foreign carriers, and Terminal 2, predominantly for Air France flights. (Note that many Air France flights to and from North America are jointly operated with an American carrier, so an Air France flight may also be a Delta Airlines flight, taking two flight numbers.) There is also Terminal T9, which is primarily for charters. Shuttle buses operate between the terminals. A moving sidewalk (conveyer belt for pedestrians) will transport you to passport control, from which you may proceed to the arrivals level and Baggage Claim. Here you will find everything you might need: foreign currency exchange, tourist office, airport information desk, car rental firms, and transportation to Paris.

RER   If you take the RER, count on about 40 minutes of travel time to central Paris. There is direct access by foot to the RER station at Charles de Gaulle Airport from Terminal 2. Follow the signs for RER. From Terminal 1, take the free airport shuttle *(navette)* to the RER station, which is only five minutes away.

Trains run every 15–20 minutes from 5 a.m. until 11:45 p.m. and cost 45 FF per person each way. It's always best to ask your hotel in advance which RER stop you should get off at, but when in doubt get off at Gare du Nord and either transfer to the Métro or take a taxi to your hotel. The RER stops in Paris at Gare du Nord, Châtelet-Les Halles, Cluny-La Sorbonne, Luxembourg, Port Royal, Denfert-Rochereau, and Cité Universitaire. One way to select a hotel is by its convenience to one of these stops.

Above the platform you'll see a lit-up sign indicating which train is the next to depart for Paris. The airport is the end of the line, so you can't possibly take the train the wrong way.

Air France Airport Bus   This is a very convenient and comfortable way to get in and out of town. It is accessible to everyone; do not be confused—you do not need an Air France plane ticket or need to be an Air France passenger to use the Air France airport bus service. From your terminal, follow the well-marked signs for Buses to Paris. From Charles de Gaulle, take either line 2 or line 4, depending where in Paris you'd like to be dropped off, Etoile/Porte Maillot or Gare de Lyon. All Air France buses offer disabled access, and there is a baggage handler at each stop. You do not need to pre-purchase tickets; you pay onboard. Children pay half-price.

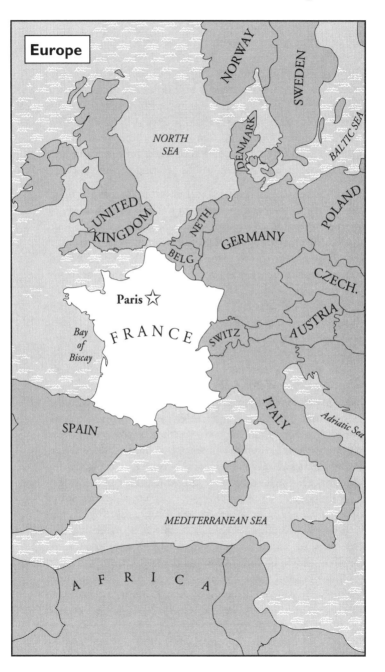

If a Paris destination is served by both train and bus, the train will usually get you there in less time, especially during the morning rush hour. Having arrived from the airport at a given Paris train station or bus terminus, you probably will need to transfer (to another train or bus), catch a taxi, or both, to actually reach your hotel. The idea is to use cheap and convenient public transportation (train or bus) to get within easy striking distance of your Paris hotel. Once you have arrived by train or bus in the neighborhood, so to speak, taking a taxi the remaining distance to your final Paris destination will be practical and affordable.

Taxis   Paris taxis, incidentally, are not as expensive as you might think. One driver was quick to point out that Paris taxis are the cheapest in France and among the least expensive in Europe. Rates outside the city are about 50% higher than in town. If there are three people in your party, taking a taxi directly to your hotel might be cheaper than each of you paying full fare on the bus or train.

At the airports, there are always plenty of taxis lining up for fares. Follow the signs for *Taxis* and get in line on the sidewalk as the next available taxi pulls up to the curb. Parisians do not share taxis, and drivers do not appreciate your attempts to make a deal with the people in front or in back of you in line. Paris taxi drivers are not known for their loquaciousness or general friendliness. Few speak English. Some smoke. Others drive around with a dog in the front seat. In terms of honesty, it's not common that a driver tries to rip you off; nonetheless, make sure the meter only starts when you get in the taxi. You should have a rough idea where your hotel is situated and not appear hopelessly dependent. From Charles de Gaulle Airport to central Paris, count on 250–300 FF. You'll be charged 7 FF extra for each piece of luggage and a small surcharge for bikes, skis, etc. Rates are posted on the window of all Paris taxis and are in English. *Note:* Nighttime taxi rates (8 p.m.–8 a.m.) are roughly 50% higher than daytime rates. Count on an hour from the airport to or from central Paris, depending on time of day and traffic.

If you take the train to town, then want to catch a taxi from the station to your hotel, it is much easier to get one at a taxi stand than to hail one in the street. In fact, taxi drivers are not allowed to pick up passengers in traffic.

Only take taxis that are marked Taxi on the roof and are equipped with meters. For safe keeping you may ask the driver for the approximate fare to your hotel: *"Combien ça va couter, s'il vous plâit, monsieur?"* (You may wish to hand the driver a piece of paper and pencil to write it down if you do not speak French.) Limos, which are often difficult to differentiate from taxis, can charge FF 300 ($40) for a short ride within the city that would run under FF 50 (less than $10) in a taxi, tip and surcharges included!

A small tip of FF 10 to FF 20 for a fare to or from the airport is customary—no more. Inside the city, a few francs is all that's ever expected. For comfort's sake, just round off your fare to the next increment of five francs.

If You Are Going Directly to Paris   Your choice of ground transportation will depend on where in Paris you are staying, how mobile you are, and your budget requirements. Bear in mind that Charles de Gaulle is northeast of the city and that most of the coach transportation service from the airport goes to the Right Bank (the part of the city north of the Seine). If you need to go to the Left Bank, you can transfer or catch a taxi from your Right Bank terminus. The RER serves both sides of the city.

The following transportation options are listed in order from the least expensive to the most expensive.

Transportation Options	To: Terminus	Sites Nearby	Transit Time	Cost
RER/RoissyRail	Gare du Nord	Châtelet—Les Halles	35 mins.	FF 49
Air France Coach	Place Charles de Gaulle–Etoile	Champs-Elysées	40 mins.	FF 65
Air France Coach	Porte Maillot	Neuilly/Palais de Congrés	40 mins.	FF 65
Air France Coach	Montparnasse	Montparnasse TGV station	1 hr.	FF 75

If You Are Going Directly to the Disneyland Paris Resort
After you come through baggage claim, follow signs for VEA Navettes Disneyland Paris. Shuttle bus coach service to Disneyland Paris operates from Charles de Gaulle every 45 minutes, and schedules are posted at all shuttle bus stops. Service runs every day, 8:30 a.m.–7:45 p.m., with extra departures from Charles de Gaulle to the park on Friday night at 8:30 p.m., 9:15 p.m., and 10 p.m.

Additionally, VEA runs a 7:30 a.m. departure from Disneyland Paris to the airport seven days a week. Tickets cost FF 85 ($12) for adults and FF 65 ($9) for children ages 3–11 each way; those under age 3 ride free. Tickets can be purchased on the bus or even in advance from a travel agent. Information is available at www.vea.fr or in France at 01-60-31-72-00.

You can board the shuttle bus at Terminal 1, Departures level (Porte 30); Terminal 2A and 2C (Porte A-11, C1); Terminal 2F, Level O-Arrivals (Porte 0.05); and Terminal 2B and 2D (Porte D-12). The ride is usually about 45 minutes, longer during rush hours. The shuttle stops at all six Disneyland Paris Resort hotels and at the Disneyland Paris Resort bus station, the starting point for the internal shuttle.

Flying into Orly Airport

Orly is more compact than CDG but is also less organized. Orly Sud (South) is used for international flights, Orly Ouest (West) for domestic and inter-European ones. You will arrive on the first floor (one floor up). Follow the large yellow signs down to the street level for the Exit and Baggage Claim. After you retrieve your luggage, look for a large sign listing ground transportation options. The sign will tell you what level and gate each option leaves from. All gates are nearby.

RER/Orlyval   When using the commuter train, follow the signs for the RER/Orlyval. Trains are accessed from both terminals. The Orlyval is a fast, fully automated train offering a connection service between Orly Airport and the RER (Line B) intersection at a station called Antony. The trip takes 32 minutes to Châtelet in the center of Paris. *Tip:* show up with francs and, if possible, enough coins to be able to buy your ticket from a machine and not have to stand in line. Follow the well-marked signs for the RER/Orlyval train toward Paris. The train stops in Paris at Cité Universitaire, Denfert-Rochereau, Port-Royal, Luxembourg, Cluny-La Sorbonne, St. Michel/Notre-Dame, Châtelet-Les Halles, and Gare du Nord.

You can count on the shortest wait with Orlyval, which leaves every 4–8 minutes between 6 a.m. and 10 p.m., with Sunday service beginning at 7 a.m. and ending at 11 p.m. The price, including continued use of the Métro (subway), is 57 FF per person each way and half-price for children ages 4–10. The round-trip price is exactly double, so there is no advantage to buying your return portion in advance.

To catch the Orlyval from Orly Sud take Exit K near the baggage claim area. From Orly Ouest use Exit W on the departure level.

The RER C line departs every 15 minutes from 5:45 a.m. to 9 p.m. and every 30 minutes after that until 10:50 p.m. This is a useful option if you are heading toward Gare d'Austerlitz.

Air France Airport Bus   From your terminal, follow the well-marked signs for Buses to Paris. From Orly Sud or Ouest, line 1 takes you to Montparnasse (in front of the Hotel Meridien, 1 rue du Commandant-Mouchotte, Métro: Montparnasse) and The Air France Terminal at Invalides. The bus will also stop, if you request it, at Porte d'Orléans and Duroc, but only for passengers who do *not* have luggage stowed underneath.

All Air France buses offer disabled access, and there is a baggage handler at each stop. You do not need to prepurchase tickets; you pay onboard. Children pay half-price.

Air France buses leave every 12 minutes between 6 a.m. and 11:30 p.m. from Exit K (platform 6) in Orly Sud and Exit D in Orly Ouest. The cost is 50 FF per person each way. Round-trip costs 85 FF, so if you'll be using the service to get back to the airport, consider buying the round-trip ticket for the savings. Children ages 2–12 pay 25 FF. A 24-hour information service can be called at 01-41-56-89-00.

Orlybus   The Paris transport authority (RATP) offers a regular Orly Airport bus service to the RER station at Denfert-Rochereau. Travel time is 30 minutes. Catch this bus at Porte H at Quai 4 in Orly Sud or Porte J on Niveau 0 in Orly Ouest. Service runs Monday–Friday 6 a.m.–11:30 p.m. every 13 minutes and Saturday and Sunday 6 a.m.–11:30 p.m. every 15–20 minutes. Cost is 35 FF per person each way. Tickets are purchased on the bus or at the ADP window in the airport. Many travelers take this service to Denfert-Rochereau, then take a taxi or jump on the Métro to their hotel.

Taxis   Follow the signs for taxi and wait in line on the sidewalk as taxis pull up curbside. The ride into town from Orly takes roughly half an hour, considerably more during peak traffic. The cost is about FF 160 ($22) at daytime rates to or from the center of Paris, plus 7 FF per piece of luggage.

If You Are Going Directly to Paris   Orly is south of the city, and most of the coach transportation serves the Left Bank (the part of the city south of the Seine). If you need to go to the Right Bank, you can transfer or catch a taxi once you arrive at a Left Bank terminus.

Transportation Options	To: Terminus	Sites Nearby	Transit Time	Cost
Orlybus	Denfert-Rochereau	Montparnasse	25 min.	FF 48
Orly Rail (RER C)	Gare d'Austerlitz	Latin Quarter	35 min.	FF 33
Air France Coach	Montparnasse & Invalides	St. Germain-des-Près	30 min.	FF 50
Orlyval & RER B	Antony Denfert-Rochereau	Montparnasse	21 min.	FF 57
Orlyval	Châtelet-Les Halles	Les Halles	29 min.	FF 57
Orlyval	St. Michel	Latin Quarter	27 min.	FF 57

If You Are Going Directly to the Disneyland Paris Resort
After you come through baggage claim, follow the signs for VEA Navettes Disneyland Paris. Shuttle bus coach service to Disneyland Paris operates from Orly every 45 minutes, and schedules are posted at all shuttle bus stops. Service runs every day, 8:30 a.m.–7:45 p.m., with extra departures from Orly to the park on Friday night at 8:30 p.m., 9:15 p.m., and 9:45 p.m. Additionally, VEA runs a 7:30 a.m. departure from Disneyland Paris to the airport seven days a week. Tickets cost FF 85 ($12) for adults and FF 65 ($9) for children ages 3–11 each way; those under age 3 ride free. Tickets can be purchased on the bus or even in advance from a travel agent. Information is available at www.vea.fr or in France at 01-60-31-72-00.

You can board the shuttle bus at Orly South (Sud) at the Coach Station (Gare routière) Platform 2 (Quai 2) or at Orly West (Ouest) on Level 0 (Niveau 0) Gate C (Porte C). The ride is usually about 45 minutes, longer during rush hours. The shuttle stops at all six Disneyland Paris Resort hotels and at the Disneyland Paris Resort bus station, the starting point for the internal shuttle.

Taxis to the park from Orly are available but will run at least FF 400 ($53).

GETTING TO DISNEYLAND PARIS BY THE FRENCH TRAIN SYSTEM (SNCF AND EUROSTAR)

You can actually take the famous TGV (Train à Grande Vitesse) line serving Paris, Lille, Brussels, and London via the Eurotunnel directly to Disneyland Paris. The train stops at the Marne-la-Vallée–Chessy station, a few minutes' walk from the entrance to the park—and the Disney characters will be there to greet you! Along the same line, Paris is just a few minutes away. The London–Disneyland Paris journey takes a total of three hours, or two hours when leaving from Ashford International station in Kent. The train stops in Lille. This means that you can easily combine a London and/or Paris trip with an easy stop at Disneyland Paris.

Disneyland Paris is also served by the RER A (Rèseau Express Regional) at the Marne-la-Vallée–Chessy station, the last stop on the line. The trip between the park and the city is about 35 minutes. And the Paris Métro, one of the world's great subway systems, links up with the RER at the following stations: Nation, Gare de Lyon, Châtelet, Auber, and Etoile.

If you are arriving in Paris by train from another French or European destination, note that the Gare de Lyon train station, in eastern Paris, is the station most convenient to Disneyland Paris since the RER A line stops there.

Les Gares (Train Stations)

Paris has six main train stations, so the first point is to make sure you know which station you're coming into and from which station you're departing. There is nothing more stressful than showing up on time for a train that leaves from another station. All Paris train stations are accessible by at least two Métro lines. For information and ticket sales at all stations, call 08-36-35-35-35; for recorded train times (in French), call 08-36-67-68-69.

Here are the main stations:

Gare du Nord   75010 Paris, Métro: Gare du Nord on Lines 4 and 5, RER B and D. Served by Bus Lines 42, 43, 46, 47, 48, and 49. This enormous Neoclassical train station was designed by Jacques-Ignace Hittorf in 1863 and crowned with statues representing the larger cities of France. As its name suggests, it serves destinations in the north of France. It is also the departure point for the Eurostar (Brussels, London) and Thalys (Brussels, Amsterdam, Cologne, Düsseldorf) train lines.

Gare du l'Est   75010 Paris, Métro: Gare de l'Est on Lines 4, 5, and 7. Served by Bus Lines 30, 31, 32, 38, and 39. One of the more modest stations in Paris, it serves destinations in the east of France such as Nancy, Reims, and Strasbourg, as well as Switzerland and Luxembourg. An enormous fresco by A. Herter illustrating French soldiers departing for the "Grande War," as WWI is called in French, is worth a look.

Gare Montparnasse   75014/75015 Paris, Métro: Gare du Montparnasse on Lines 4, 6, 12, and 13. Served by Bus Lines 91, 92, 94, 95, and 96. This station lies beneath the 209-meter Tour de Montparnasse and serves destinations southwest of Paris such as Poitiers, La Rochelle, Bordeaux, Toulouse, Biarritz, and Lourdes. Organized in two areas, Montparnasse 2 is where the TGV departs from.

Gare d'Austerlitz   75005 Paris, Métro: Gare d'Austerlitz on Lines 5 and 10, RER C. Served by Bus Lines 61 and 65. Trains leaving from this station link Spain and Portugal with France.

Gare Saint Lazare   75008 Paris, Métro: Gare St. Lazare on Lines 3, 12, and 13. Served by Bus Lines 20, 21, 24, 26, 27, 28, and 29. This station has been called a "factory of dreams" because of its steel-and-glass architecture. It was built by J. Litsch in 1885 and acts as the commuter hub for most of the suburbs to the west of Paris. Note the bronze sculpture of piled-up battered suitcases in front of the station. It was here that thousands of homeless and uprooted eastern Europeans arrived at the end of World War II.

Gare de Lyon   75012 Paris, Métro: Gare de Lyon on Line 1 and RER A. Served by Bus Lines 20 and 63. This station has been remodeled several times since its construction (1847–52). It has had its present-day modern style since the arrival of the TGV. It serves destinations in the Midi (middle of France) and the Côte d'Azur, including Dijon, Lyon, Montpellier, Marseilles, and Nice. It is also the departure point for the Artesia train line that links France and Italy (you can reach Torino in 5 1/2 hours and Milan in 3½ hours).

Train Reservations and Tickets

Any SNCF office, train station, or travel agent can sell you train tickets and reservations. Travel agents usually charge 30–50 FF above the ticket price as their service fee. This is often worth it since you won't have to go to the train station or wait in lines prior to your departure. The SNCF maintains an information phone line, but you may spend a long time on hold and then the staff may not speak adequate English or may become impatient if you ask too many questions. Ask your hotel concierge if he can help you make reservations. For information, call 01-53-90-20-20 (Ile de France) or 08-36-35-35-35 (Grandes Lignes)

GETTING TO DISNEYLAND PARIS BY CAR

In France just about all major roads lead to Paris. And if you can find Paris, then you can find Disneyland Paris. The theme park is just 32 kilometers (19 miles) east of Paris, right off the A4 autoroute, sometimes known as the *autoroute de l'est.* Disneyland Paris is connected to the A4 autoroute by a direct access loop. Once on the loop, follow the signs to the park. The upcoming Parc Disneyland Paris exit is well marked along the autoroute, in both directions, way before you reach the exit.

The other major French autoroutes—to the north, south, northwest, and southwest—all emanate from Paris, like spokes from the hub of a wheel. Easy link-ups to the A4 are by N104 (called the Francilienne) from the south connecting the A6 near Orly Airport, the A86 from the southwest, and A104 from the north, which links with the A1 near Charles de Gaulle Airport.

If you are traveling to Disneyland Paris from the north, or from the United Kingdom, Ireland, Belgium, Holland, or northern Germany, take the A2 or A26 autoroutes into the A1 (also known as the *autoroute du nord*). Take the A1 into the A4. Head east (direction: Reims) to the Disneyland Paris exit.

If you are traveling to Disneyland Paris from the south, or from Switzerland, Italy, or parts of Spain, take the A6 autoroute (also known as the *autoroute du soleil* or *autoroute du sud*) to the N104. Take the N104 to the A4, head east (direction: Reims) to Disneyland Paris.

If you are coming from the southwest, or from Spain and Portugal, take the A10 (also known as *L'Aquitaine*) a short distance to the A6. Take the A6 to the A86, and then take the A86 to the A4 and head east (direction: Reims).

If you are coming from the east, or from central or southern Germany or Austria, take the A4 west from Strasbourg. Head west (direction: Paris).

Disneyland Paris is located at Exit 14 on the A4 marked "Val d'Europe, Parc Disneyland." You can't miss it!

Getting around Paris and the Ile de France

RENTING A CAR

If you are staying in Paris, skip ahead to the section on using the Métro and RER. You do not want to have a car in Paris, unless your idea of a vacation is driving through Alice's Curious Labyrinth in a Renault that seems to get bigger as the streets get smaller. Negotiating Paris's narrow, congested streets can be challenging even for honor graduates of the macho school of driving. Traffic can be nerve-wracking, and parking is often a major problem. This is definitely not our idea of a vacation. If, however, you are staying at Disneyland Paris or elsewhere outside the city, read on.

Frankly, if you are staying at Disneyland Paris, you really do not need a car either. Free and efficient Disney bus transportation will get you around the resort. If you wish to see some of the nearby countryside (in addition to Disneyland Paris and Paris) and are contemplating renting a car, consider the following:

1. Do you really *need* a car? The French rail system is extremely efficient, takes you just about everywhere, and is reasonably priced. Car rentals are generally high priced, and gasoline is a lot more expensive than wine, currently about FF 8 per liter, or over $4 a gallon.

2. Will your own car insurance policy cover a rental car—a rental car in France? Will the policy make it unnecessary to buy collision damage and other insurance from the rental agency? These are important questions, because the per-day cost of collision and other insurance can boost the overall rental cost by as much as 45%.

3. What about your credit card company? Does it provide total or supplemental insurance on a rental car in France? Rental car insurance provided by credit card companies almost always serves as secondary or back-up coverage. In other words, it will pay certain costs not covered by your primary policy. Before you leave home, find out: (a) if your credit card coverage is operative in France and (b) if it will cover you even if your primary auto insurance policy will not. Finally, (c) determine the extent of coverage.

4. Be aware that smaller, local rental car companies may offer lower daily rates but demand (as a condition of rental) that you buy insurance from them. This is nothing but a scam, pure and simple, and is one of the best reasons we know for dealing with the larger multinational companies.

5. If you plan to drive in other countries besides France, make sure you are authorized by your rental contract to drive the car in those countries. Many rental companies will not allow their cars to be taken into Eastern European countries, for example.

6. Sometimes, when your primary auto insurance policy does not cover rental vehicles (abroad and/or at home), your agent will be able to sell you a policy on a trip-by-trip basis. Insurance purchased from your own agent will almost always be less expensive than that purchased from the car rental company.

7. Be aware that many tour operators and airlines offer packages that include rental cars. Also be aware that a multinational rental car company may offer different deals in different countries at the same time. We got a much better deal on an Avis car, for example, by booking through the U.S. reservation system as opposed to the French. If you reserve from home, you may be able to get a flat rate—and thus avoid France's exorbitant Value Added Tax (TVA), which is 19.2%. In any case, when you book, ask if the rate you've been quoted is TVA inclusive. Often it is not, and you will find yourself with a bill 20% higher than you expected.

8. Where do you want to leave your rental car? Not all rental companies allow you to pick-it-up-here and drop-it-off-there. Even when allowed, there are usually extra charges associated with turning in your car at a location different from where you rented it. If you rent your car at Disneyland Paris and drop it off at one of the Paris airports, there should be no extra charges. Ask.

If you do decide to go ahead and rent, here is what you should know:

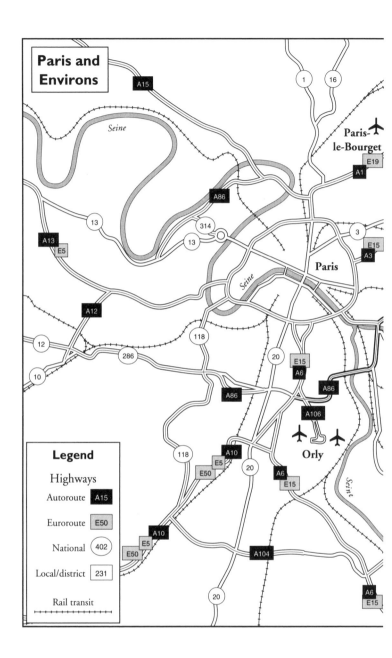

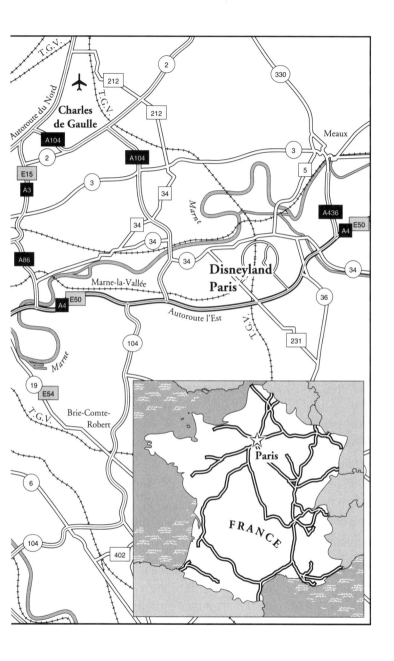

43

You must be at least 21 years old to rent a car, and there is a sup-plementary fee for drivers ages 21–25. You need a valid driver's license (if you are coming from abroad, an international driver's license—although sometimes useful—is not obligatory). If you are a foreigner and have not arranged payment before leaving home, you will need to show a valid passport and a valid credit card.

All major car rental companies are represented in the Paris region, but Hertz is an official sponsor of Disneyland Paris and, consequently, is the only rental company on the Disneyland Paris premises. The Eurostar/RER station outside the park now hosts several major car rental companies, including Avis and Hertz. You can rent Hertz vehicles at the same time you book your Disney-land Paris reservations. Avis's central reservation number in France is 0-802-05-05-05. The branch office number at the Chessy sta-tion is 01-60-43-70-93.

Both airports, Orly and Charles de Gaulle, have all the major rental car agencies. When returning a rental car at the airports, pay attention to the signs; particularly at Orly, the directions to the rental car return point are confusing.

USING THE PARIS MÉTRO AND THE RER

Here's an overview of Paris's public transportation system (RATP), which is one of the most extensive in the world. Don't be afraid to use the Paris Métro!

Hours   5:30 a.m. to 12:30 a.m. (These times are from the depar-ture points, so if you board at a station several stops away, you could conceivably get a train as late as 1 a.m.)

Frequency of Departure   Métro trains run very frequently throughout the day, even during off hours. RER trains have a posted schedule, about every 10 minutes during the day and every 15 minutes to a half hour at night, depending on the line.

Prices   A single Métro/RER ticket, good throughout Paris, costs FF 8 ($1), but you almost need never pay full price (see Unlim-ited Travel Passes; also Carnets, below). Children under age four ride for free; ages four to nine pay half-price (tarif réduit). Chil-dren ten years of age and up pay full fare. *Note:* Outside Paris city limits, RER fares are based on zones. A single ticket on the RER (including the Paris Métro) between Paris and Disneyland Paris costs FF 39 each way.

The Paris mass-transit system is comparatively clean, safe, comfortable, inexpensive, and extremely well marked. In short, it's easy to use even if you do not speak French and do not know your way around the city.

The Paris region is divided into mass-transit zones forming concentric circles around the city. Zone 1 covers Paris proper and the immediate suburbs. As you move farther out of the city, you pass through Zone 2, Zone 3, and so on. Both airports fall within Zone 4, and Disneyland Paris is in Zone 5. You will be charged according to the number of zones you cross.

Unlimited Travel Passes

Before making your trek out to Disneyland Paris from Paris (round-trip: FF 78 or $10.50), consider buying a pass that will entitle you to unlimited use of trains and buses. A weekly Carte Orange is the optimum choice if you are staying for several days (even if it's not a full week), but the RATP offers other options for one, two, three, and five days that are worth checking out. Here are some of your choices:

Carte Orange The weekly Carte Orange, a personal favorite, is an unbelievable bargain. It covers unlimited Métro, bus, and RER from a Monday through the following Sunday. It can be bought as early as Friday of the preceding week and as late as Wednesday of the use week. The card that covers Disneyland Paris (five zones) costs FF 173 ($23). If you go out to Disneyland Paris from Paris more than twice during your stay, you will have paid for your pass even before using it for sight-seeing.

The Carte Orange requires an identity photo. If you can bring a small ID photo from home, you will save yourself some time and trouble. If you forgot to bring a photo, most major Métro and RER stations have photo booths (Photomatons) where you can get four head shots for FF 25 ($3.50). The station clerk will usually let you pass through the turnstile to use a photo booth inside the station.

Paris Visite Paris Visite is the much-touted tourist card that can be bought in many countries (and major French cities) before you leave home. It's available as a one-, two-, three-, or five-day pass (the days must be consecutive) and covers Métro, bus, and RER, as well as savings on numerous tourist attractions. The pass that includes the airports and Disneyland Paris (five zones total) is considerably more costly than a Carte Orange: one-day passes cost FF 110 ($15) for adults, FF 55 ($5.50) for children under age 12; two-day passes cost FF 175 ($23.50) for adults, FF 85 ($11.50) for children under age 12; three-day passes cost FF 245 ($33) for adults, FF 120 ($16) for children under age 12; and five-day passes cost FF 300 ($40) for adults, FF 150 ($20) for children under age 12.

Mobilis (formerly Formule 1)   Mobilis is a one-day pass the same as Paris Visite except it does not include access to the airports. Less advantageous than the Paris Visite pass, Mobilis costs FF 74 ($10) for one day.

Carnets

If you do not buy one of the above-described passes, try to avoid buying Métro tickets one at a time as you go along. A single ticket is FF 8 ($ 1), but if you buy tickets in packets of ten, called a *carnet* (pronounced car-nay), the price is FF 58 ($7.75) or FF 5,80 ($0.75) each. A family or any group traveling together can divide the tickets among themselves.

Using Métro Tickets on Buses

Individual Métro tickets, as well as passes, can be used on regular buses. The number of tickets needed depends on the length of your ride, which is based on sections. Put the ticket in the machine next to the driver. The machine reads and punches the ticket and then returns it to you. Signs posted inside the bus, as well as at bus stops, show the route and where each new section begins. If you have a Carte Orange, you need only hold up the pass to show your photo; you do not punch *(composter)* the ticket.

Riding the Métro

Métro stations are everywhere, and you cannot miss them: A giant "M" looms above the art deco entrances. Large Métro maps are posted inside the station before you reach the turnstiles and also on the platform. Small fold-out maps are readily available in the stations, at tourist offices, and hotels. Larger stations additionally have electronic Métro maps with lights to guide your route. If you press the button corresponding to your destination, the map will illuminate your path, including where, if necessary, you should switch to another line.

CORRESPONDANCE

 ← (M) (1) CHATEAU DE VINCENNES
LA DEFENSE

SORTIE →

 (RER) (A) SAINT-GERMAIN-EN-LAYE →
CERGY • POISSY
BOISSY-SAINT-LEGER
MARNE-LA-VALLEE

⠿ Gares desservies	⠿ VAL DE FONTENAY
⠿ NATION	⠿ NEUILLY-PLAISANCE
⠿ VINCENNES	⠿ BRY-SUR-MARNE
⠿ FONTENAY-SOUS-BOIS	⠿ NOISY-LE-GRAND - MONT-D'EST
⠿ NOGENT-SUR-MARNE	⠿ NOISY - CHAMPS
⠿ JOINVILLE-LE-PONT	⠿ NOISIEL
⠿ SAINT-MAUR - CRETEIL	⠿ LOGNES
⠿ LE PARC DE SAINT-MAUR	⠿ TORCY
⠿ CHAMPIGNY	
⠿ LA VARENNE - CHENNEVIERES	⠿ MARNE-LA-VALLEE - CHESSY
⠿ SUCY - BONNEUIL	
⠿ BOISSY-SAINT-LEGER	
	⠿ TRAIN COURT

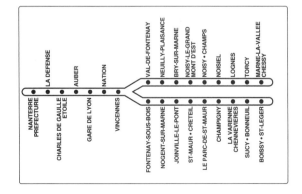

Métro lines have numbers, but they are identified in practice by the name of the terminus at each end. For example, the major east-west Right Bank line is Grande Arche de La Défense–Château de Vincennes (often seen on signs in its shortened version: La Défense–Château de Vincennes). If you are headed in the direction of La Défense, follow signs for *direction* La Défense. Conversely, if you are headed in the direction of Vincennes, follow signs for *direction* Château de Vincennes.

Using a route map or consulting the front desk of your hotel, identify the Métro line you need and the station most convenient for it (there could be more than one station in walking distance of your hotel). All the passes described above, as well as carnets, can be purchased at any Métro ticket window, inside the station. No matter which pass or fare you purchase (even the Carte Orange with the photo ID card), you will receive a ticket, which you must use for passing through the turnstiles. Insert your ticket into the slot in front of the turnstile. Upon insertion, your ticket will disappear briefly into the turnstile to be read and validated and then pop up in another slot on top of the turnstile. This is your indication that you have been cleared to proceed through the turnstile. Always remember to retrieve your ticket from the second slot when it pops up and to put it away someplace safe where it will not be bent or torn, because you may need it again.

Once past the turnstiles, follow the signs to your line or your direction. If there is more than one Métro line serving the station, direction signs will first show the name by giving both termini; for example: Porte de Clignancourt–Porte d'Orléans.

As you proceed through the station, continue to follow the signs for your line and then for your direction (Porte de Clignancourt or Porte d'Orléans). You will ultimately be guided to the correct platform. In the corridor en route to your platform, you will see a sign listing all the stops for trains headed in your direction.

On most Métro lines within Paris, there are no forks, so you should almost never find yourself on a platform wondering which train to take. Generally speaking, if you make it to the correct platform, you will catch the right train. The few lines that do fork will have an illuminated sign on the platforms. Check out the sign before the next train arrives; that particular train will be going only to those stops that are illuminated.

When the train pulls up, the doors do not open automatically. The first passenger getting on or off opens the door. On some trains, there's a large button to press. If there is a handle, lift the lever in a counterclockwise movement, and the door will readily open.

As you enter the train car and get settled in, you will notice that there are signs above and beside the doors. The one above the door is a very straightforward route map that lists all the stops the train makes. When the train reaches the next stop, use the route map to verify that you are going in the right direction. Of course, you can also use the route map to figure how many stops the train will make before it reaches your destination.

If you do not speak French and are concerned about the signs next to the door, the following should help:

"Il est interdit de monter ou descendre dès que le signal sonore fonctionne; gêner la fermeture des portes,"

means:

"It is forbidden to get on or off once the tone sounds, or to block the closing of the doors."

"Conservez votre billet jusqu'à la sortie,"

means:

"Keep your ticket until the exit." The sign also reminds riders that tickets can be checked in the car or in the station, pointing out that offenders have to pay a penalty on the spot.

Transferring

When you get off the train, you may need to transfer to another line to reach your final destination. If so, look for a sign indicating *"Correspondance"* (transfer), instead of *"Sortie"* (exit). In stations with several lines, a number of different transfers might be possible. Exit your arrival platform by following the *Correspondance* signs, and then look for signs directing you to the next line you need. Once again, the line will be identified on signs by the abbreviated names of the last stop in each direction (La Défense–Château de Vincennes, for example). Your walk to the appropriate platform could take 30 seconds or up to 5 minutes (most are a minute or two). Transfers at stations with several Métro lines, or from Métro to RER, involve the most walking. If you ride the Métro enough, you will learn which transfers are the quickest.

Unless the weather is awful, it's usually not worth transferring to another line to go just one Métro stop, since the stations are so close to one another. Learn which stops for which lines are within walking distance of your hotel. Most hotels provide the name of the nearest station, but one or even two others could be within a ten-minute walk. Choosing the right station can often eliminate the need to transfer.

When you finally arrive at your destination station, follow the signs to the *sortie* (exit). Watch for a *Plan du Quartier,* a large, easy-to-read wall map of the immediate neighborhood. It shows nearby streets and major landmarks (not just tourist sites but also useful things like post offices, churches, and pharmacies). A *Plan du Quartier* is particularly useful at a large square like Etoile, République, or Nation, where a dozen or more streets feed into the traffic circle. You might want to know which side of the square you are getting out on, particularly if it's raining. In cases of large boulevards, signs over the exits indicate whether it's the side with odd *(côté numéros impairs)* or even numbered *(côté numéros pairs)* addresses.

The Métro does not go to Disneyland Paris (Marne-la-Vallée). To travel to Disneyland Paris by train, you must take the RER. Of course, you can use the Métro to reach a station from which you can transfer to the RER. As mentioned above, the various fares for both the RER and the Métro are sold at all stations.

The RER

RER lines are indicated by letters on Paris Métro maps. Within Paris you can use the Métro or RER suburban trains interchangeably; outside town, however, with distance determining cost, you will need more than one ticket unless you have a pass that covers the extra number of zones.

If you are transferring from a Métro to an RER line, you will pass through a set of turnstiles and follow signs for the RER, then for the appropriate RER line. Before entering the RER section, you will have to go through another turnstile; remember to retrieve your ticket whether you have a pass or not. Once on the RER platform, pay close attention to the display showing the names of stops served (les gares désservies). A small square or circle will be illuminated next to the names of the stops the next train will make.

You need to pay attention because, unlike (most) Métro lines, RER lines fork. You could be on the right RER platform for Disneyland Paris, for example, but still take the wrong train. The A line forks just outside Paris at Vincennes, with one line, the A4, going to Marne-la-Vallée–Chessy (and Disneyland Paris), and the other going toward Boissy–St. Uger. If you take the wrong one, you will need to go all the way back to Vincennes to catch the correct train. On the return trip, from Marne-la-Vallée to Paris, there is no possibility of catching the wrong train.

Sometimes a train will take the correct fork but not go all the way to Marne-la-Vallée at the end of the RER line. It's not uncommon for a train to go even as far as Torcy, the next-to-last stop, but not to the terminus. Of course, if you get on a train that is not going as far as you need to go, it's just a matter of waiting right there for the next train.

Posted on the walls of RER stations is a complicated, hard-to-read schedule for the lines stopping there. Always check the top of the column to see if there is a symbol: a circled A indicates workdays only; a circled C, Saturday and Sunday only. If there is no circled letter at the top of the column, you can assume the train runs every day. Still, check at the information booth or call 08-36-68-77-14 for a 24-hour information line. Also consult www.ratp.fr for additional information and routing suggestions.

When you arrive at your RER line destination, you run your ticket through another turnstile on exiting the station. If your ticket is good for additional travel, it will be returned to you in the usual manner via the slot on the top of the turnstile. If, on the other hand, you have used up all of your fare, the turnstile will keep your ticket.

GETTING TO DISNEYLAND PARIS FROM YOUR PARIS HOTEL

On Your Own: Timing Your Ride

Throughout this guide we emphasize the importance of arriving at Disneyland Paris before the theme park opens. You can experience more attractions (with less waiting in line) in the first two hours the park is open than in the following five hours. There is nothing, repeat, nothing more contributory to fun, stress-free touring than arriving at the theme park early. This is true regardless of whether your hotel is at Disneyland Paris, in Paris, or someplace in between. For visitors lodging in Paris, the following information should allow you to calculate how long it will take to commute to Disneyland Paris.

Your door-to-door trip from most places in central Paris will take about an hour with walking and waiting. From Châtelet–Les Halles, in the dead center of Paris, the ride on the RER to Disneyland Paris is 37 minutes; if you board at another station on the RER

A line within Paris, add or subtract 3 minutes for each stop (for example, it takes 34 minutes from the Gare de Lyon RER stop, one stop down the line toward Marne-la-Vallée).

If you must transfer from a Métro line to the RER, or from one Métro line to another, remember that the walk inside the station can often add as much as five minutes, in addition to waiting time. Changing from one RER line to the other, however, is quick.

On most Métro lines the stops are only about one and a half minutes apart, so you can estimate the full time for your trip before you check the RER schedule. You will rarely wait more than a few minutes for a Métro train during the day.

The following guidelines will assist you in determining your route and estimating the duration of your travel. The times given are only for the ride and for the walk within the transfer station in those cases when a transfer is required. Waiting time at the original departure station (and at the transfer station when applicable) is not included. Also, if you are leaving from a large station like Charles de Gaulle–Etoile or Châtelet–Les Halles, allow five minutes just to walk to the platform from the entrance of the station.

Note: Châtelet and Châtelet-Les Halles are not the same station, though they are within walking distance of one another. Châtelet is a Métro station, while Châtelet-Les Halles is an RER station.

If your hotel is on the Right Bank and near:

Arc de Triomphe

Start at This Station:	Charles de Gaulle-Etoile
Type of Station:	Métro and RER
Train to Take:	RER A4
Direction:	Marne-la-Vallée–Chessy
Final Stop:	Marne-la-Vallée–Chessy
Commuting Time:	43 minutes plus waiting time

Place de la Concorde/Tuileries Gardens

Start at This Station:	Concorde or Tuileries
Type of Station:	Métro
Train to Take:	La Défense–Château de Vincennes
Direction:	Château de Vincennes
Transfer at:	Châtelet
Transfer to:	RER A4
Direction:	Marne-la-Vallée–Chessy
Final Stop:	Marne-la-Vallée–Chessy
Commuting Time:	45–50 minutes plus waiting time

Paris Opéra

Start at This Station:	Auber
Type of Station:	RER
Train to Take:	RER A4
Direction:	Marne-la-Vallée–Chessy
Final Stop:	Marne-la-Vallée–Chessy
Commuting Time:	42 minutes plus waiting time

Centre Georges Pompidou/Les Halles

Start at This Station:	Châtelet-Les Halles
Type of Station:	RER
Train to Take:	RER A4
Direction:	Marne-la-Vallée–Chessy
Final Stop:	Marne-la-Vallée–Chessy
Commuting Time:	37 minutes plus waiting time

Bastille/Opéra Bastille

Start at This Station:	Bastille
Type of Station:	Métro
Train to Take:	La Défense–Château de Vincennes
Direction:	Château de Vincennes
Transfer at:	Nation
Transfer to:	RER A4
Direction:	Marne-la-Vallée–Chessy
Final Stop:	Marne-la-Vallée–Chessy
Commuting Time:	40 minutes plus waiting time

Place de la Nation

Start at This Station:	Nation
Type of Station:	Métro and RER
Train to Take:	RER A4
Direction:	Marne-la-Vallée–Chessy
Final Stop:	Marne-la-Vallée–Chessy
Commuting Time:	31 minutes plus waiting time

If your hotel is on the Left Bank and near:
Place St. Michel/Latin Quarter

Start at This Station:	St. Michel–Notre Dame
Type of Station:	RER
Train to Take:	Any northbound RER B line
Direction:	Roissy–Aéroport Charles de Gaulle or Mitry-Claye

Transfer at: Châtelet-Les Halles
Transfer to: RER A4
Direction: Marne-la-Vallée–Chessy
Final Stop: Marne-la-Vallée–Chessy
Commuting Time: 40 minutes plus waiting time

Montparnasse
Start at This Station: Vavin (or Montparnasse-Bienvenue)
Type of Station: Métro
Train to Take: Pte. de Clignancourt–Pte. d'Orléans
Direction: Pte. de Clignancourt
Transfer at: Châtelet
Transfer to: RER A4
Direction: Marne-la-Vallée–Chessy
Final Stop: Marne-la-Vallée–Chessy
Commuting Time: 50 minutes plus waiting time

Luxembourg Gardens
Start at This Station: Luxembourg
Type of Station: RER
Train to Take: Any northbound RER B line
Direction: Roissy–Aéroport Charles de Gaulle
                            or Mitry-Claye
Transfer at: Châtelet
Trawfer to: RER A4
Direction: Marne-la-Vallée–Chessy
Final Stop: Marne-la-Vallée–Chessy
Commuting Time: 40 minutes plus waiting time

Musée d'Orsay/St. Germain-des-Prés
Start at This Station: St. Germain-des-Prés
Type of Station: Métro
Train to Take: Pte. de Clignancourt–Pte. d'Orléans
Direction: Pte. de Clignancourt
Transfer at: Châtelet
Transfer to: RER A4
Direction: Marne-la-Vallée–Chessy
Final Stop: Marne-la-Vallée–Chessy
Commuting Time: 45–50 minutes plus waiting time

Place Denfert-Rochereau
Start at This Station: Denfert-Rochereau
Type of Station: RER

Train to Take:	Any northbound RER B line
Direction:	Roissy–Aéroport Charles de Gaulle or Mitry-Claye
Transfer at:	Châtelet-Les Halles
Transfer to:	RER A4
Direction:	Marne-la-Vallée–Chessy
Final Stop:	Marne-la-Vallée–Chessy
Commuting Time:	45 minutes plus waiting time

Eiffel Tower

Start at This Station:	Champs de Mars–Tour Eiffel
Type of Station:	RER
Train to Take:	The RER C line
Direction:	Montigny-Beauchamp or Argentueil
Transfer at:	Pte. Maillot–Neuilly
Transfer to:	RER A4
Direction:	Marne-la-Vallée–Chessy
Final Stop:	Marne-la-Vallée–Chessy
Commuting Time:	55 minutes plus waiting time

Before you head into the park, check the return train schedule (generally every 15 minutes at night; every 10 minutes during peak hours, sometimes more frequently). The time of the last train is usually displayed in an illuminated sign above the information booth in the center of the street-level area. The usual 12:30 a.m. departure gives you plenty of time to linger.

A Word about Lodging

We have found lodging to be a primary concern for Disneyland Paris visitors. The most convenient, as well as the most expensive, accommodations are generally to be found at the Disneyland Paris Resort hotels. Though there are very few hotels in the small villages surrounding Disneyland Paris, a limited number of affordable modern hotels can be found within an 8–15-minute ride on the RER commuter train or via car along the A4 highway. Hundreds of hotels of all sizes, of course, are available in Paris. Commuting time on the RER from Paris to Disneyland Paris is about an hour one-way. Specifics concerning use of the RER as well as some information on air and auto travel are detailed in the section titled "Getting There."

In addition to proximity and a certain number of guest privileges, there is a certain peace of mind associated with staying inside

Disneyland Paris. "I feel more a part of everything and less like a visitor," is the way one guest described it.

There is no real hardship, however, in staying outside Disneyland Paris and driving or taking the RER to the theme park for your visit. Meals can be had much less expensively, too, and there is this indirect benefit: Rooming outside Disneyland Paris puts you in a more receptive mood for enjoying Paris and other area attractions.

Some of our research team lodged in a comfortable (though not plush) hotel within easy walking distance of the train station in Torcy for less than half the cost of staying in the least expensive Disneyland Paris Resort hotel. Our commuting time was 8 minutes one-way by RER to the Disneyland Paris station or 15 minutes by car to the Disneyland Paris parking complex.

STAYING IN DISNEYLAND PARIS

Here are the specific privileges and amenities of staying in a Disneyland Paris lodging property:

1. Vastly decreased commuting time made possible by easy access to the Disneyland Paris Resort internal transportation system. This is especially advantageous if you stay in the Disneyland Hotel, which literally sits astride the entrance to the theme park. All of the other Disneyland Paris Resort hotels are connected to the theme park by bus, though the walking time from the most distant hotel is less than 20 minutes for most people. The single exception is Davy Crockett Ranch, which is ten minutes away by car.

2. Preferential treatment in making advance reservations to Disneyland Paris evening entertainment.

3. The privilege of making lunch and dinner reservations over the phone, one or two days in advance, at the Disneyland Paris full-service restaurants.

4. Various kinds of preferential treatment at the theme park. Sometimes Disneyland Paris lodging guests are allowed into the theme park ahead of other guests, and sometimes they are given special admission discounts. These benefits and extras are subject to change without notice.

5. A number of alternatives for baby-sitting, child care, and special children's programs.

6. Only Disneyland Paris Resort guests may leave pets overnight in the kennels.

7. On days of particularly heavy attendance, Disneyland Paris Resort guests are guaranteed admission to the theme parks.

8. Disneyland Paris Resort guests with cars do not have to pay for parking in the theme park guest lot. Disneyland Paris Resort guests are accorded preferential treatment for tee times at the golf course.

All Things Considered

1. Ease of Access   If you stay at Disneyland Paris (except at the campground), you are within walking distance of everything at the theme park and at the resort, and you are within a half-hour to 45-minute train commute of Paris, depending where you want to go. If you stay either in Paris or at Disneyland Paris, you will not need a car.

2. Small Children   Although the actual hassle of commuting to most hotels outside Disneyland Paris is not great, a definite peace of mind results from staying at the Disneyland Paris Resort. If you are traveling with small children and can afford it, go for the Disneyland Hotel at the entrance to the theme park. If the Disneyland Hotel is too expensive, try to book the Hotel Cheyenne.

3. Splitting Up   If you are in a party that will probably be splitting up (as frequently happens in families with children of widely varying ages), staying in Disneyland Paris offers more transportation options and therefore more independence.

4. All's Hungry on the Western Front   If you have a large crew that can eat more than a platoon of French paratroopers, you might be better off staying outside Disneyland Paris, where food is far less expensive.

5. Visiting Paris and Other Area Destinations   If you plan to visit Paris or tour the Ile de France, it may be more convenient to stay outside the Disneyland Paris Resort.

The Goofy World of Disneyland Paris
Hotel Reservations

There are three ways to do just about anything: the right way, the wrong way, and the Disney way. Regarding the latter, whether it's right, wrong, or a little of both, you can count on it being complex and confusing. Predictably, trying to get a hotel room at Disneyland Paris is only slightly less effortful than building your own hotel. For starters, you cannot simply reserve a hotel room. Unless you are attending a convention at Disneyland Paris, you must buy a package. That's right—a package. One that includes lodging in one of the seven hotels, park admission, and various other goodies like buffets, continental breakfasts, and even transportation.

Package prices are per person per night with different rates for adults (age 12 and over) and children (ages 3–11). The maximum number of persons allowed to share a Disney hotel room is four, including children. At Davy Crockett Ranch, the maximum number allowed to share a cabin is six, including children. Disney also offers packages that include lodging in ten independent (i.e., non-Disney) hotels. Five are located in Paris, four in neighboring Bussy-Saint-Georges (on the RER train line), and two just off the A-4 Motorway. All but one are three- or four-star hotels, and all are as expensive as or more expensive than the Disney hotels. Unlike the Disney hotels, the independents can be booked directly if you simply want a room as opposed to a package (which must be booked through Disney).

The cost of your package is determined (among other things) by the number of nights and your choice of hotel. Among the Disney hotels, the Disneyland Hotel is most expensive, followed by Hotel New York, Newport Bay Club, Sequoia Lodge, Hotel Cheyenne, and Hotel Santa Fe, in that order. To get a feel for the difference, the most costly hotel, the Disneyland Hotel, is more than twice as expensive as the Hotel Santa Fe, the least costly. The seventh Disney property is Davy Crockett Ranch, which offers free-standing cabins for up to six people. The cabins are only a good buy if you have four or more in your party.

Then there are the seasons. Package prices vary according to season. At Disneyland Paris, of course, these are not seasons of the year but seasons that Disney makes up, like "Value Season, Regular Season, Low Season, High Season, and Holiday Season," to name a few. Logic would suggest that the seasons flow in sequential order through the year so that you could say, for example, that Value Season is January 9–March 15. But no, with Goofy creating the calendar, all seasons can be scrambled up in a single month—sometimes in a single week. Seasons (and therefore hotel prices) vary according to time of year, time of month, and even day of week. In December 2000, for example, it was Value Season on December 1, 3–8, 10–15, and 17–21; Intermediate Season on December 2, 9, 16, and 22; and Holiday Season December 23–31.

The season flip-flop is so confounding that you'll need either a Disney reservationist or a Disneyland Paris brochure (which you can order on the Internet or obtain from a travel agent) to figure it out. But figure it out you must because package prices for the respective seasons vary by as much as 56%! Here's how it works: the cost per night of your package is determined by what season it is on your arrival day.

Let's say you wanted a four-day package at Christmas time. If you arrive on the 21st of December, you'll pay FF 675 ($91) per person per night for you and your spouse at the Hotel Santa Fe. If you arrive on the 22nd, you'll pay FF 930 ($125) per night, and if you arrive on the 23rd your package will cost FF 1056 ($143) per person per night. What a difference a day makes!

To get the best deal, be flexible in your travel plans. Be willing to move your visit up or back a few days to cash in on lower rates. Because seasons (and rates) change an average of ten times a month, you should be able to get pretty close to the dates you prefer. Also, before making reservations, ask if there are any special deals available (Disney reservationists usually won't volunteer this information). Sometimes you can get a three-night package for the price of a two-night package or a four-night package for the price of a three-night package; at other times there's a reduced rate for specific hotels. Another frequently run special is one child (ages 3–11) stays free for each paying adult sharing the same room.

If you own or purchase stock in Euro Disney S.C.A. you are eligible to join the Shareholders' Club. It offers 5–16% discounts on passports, packages, and purchases and permits the cardholder to enter the park 30–60 minutes ahead of the general public.

Many Disneyland Paris visitors, especially those coming from the Low Countries and the UK, need only one night's lodging. The good news is that such a package exists. It's called "Bella Notte" package. It also includes two days' admission to the park (whether you want two days or not) and a buffet breakfast. The bad news is the package is not available some nights, including Saturday, the night most folks would prefer.

Magic Kingdom Club Member Discounts   The Magic Kingdom Club is offered as a benefit by employers, credit unions, and organizations. Membership entitles you to a 10–20% discount on Disney lodging and a 5% discount on theme park tickets, among other things. Some government employees are Magic Kingdom Club members (though many of them don't know it). If you work for a large company or organization (anywhere in the world), ask your personnel department if the Magic Kingdom Club benefit is provided.

Individuals who do not own stock, and whose employer does not provide Magic Kingdom Club benefits, can join under the Magic Kingdom Gold Card program. Membership is about $50 if you join in the United States, or FF 300 ($40) if you join in France. For information call or write either of the following:

Magic Kingdom Club
Gold Card
P.O. Box 3850 Anaheim, CA 92803-9832
U.S.A.
telephone (800) 49-DISNEY

Magic Kingdom Club
Gold Card
Boîte Postale 122
77777 Marne-la-Vallée, Cedex 4, France
telephone (33-1) 49-32-44-00

DISNEYLAND PARIS RESORT HOTELS AND THE DAVY CROCKETT RANCH

There are six resort hotels at Disneyland Paris, all designed to reflect a particular American region and historical period. The flagship property, rated luxury class, is the Disneyland Hotel, at the entrance to the theme park. Also rated luxury class is the Hotel New York, fronting manmade Lake Buena Vista and about a 12-minute walk from the entrance of the park. The Newport Bay Club and the Sequoia Lodge are also on the lake and are rated first class. Walking time from the Newport Bay Club or the Sequoia Lodge to the Disneyland Paris park is about 15–18 minutes. Rated moderate class, and located farthest from the theme park, are the Hotel Santa Fe and the Hotel Cheyenne, each about 20–24 minutes by foot. Finally, a couple of kilometers away, is the Davy Crockett Ranch, which offers cabins as well as camping emplacements for tents and recreational vehicles (caravans).

Reservations for all of the hotels and for the campground can be made through a central reservations center. Disney reservationists are multilingual, but separate phone numbers are assigned for information and assistance in each of 16 languages and dialects. Write or call:

Réservation Centrale
Disneyland Paris S.C.A.
Boîte Postale 100
77777 Marne-la-Vallée, Cedex 4
France
Fax for all languages: (33-1) 49-30-71-00 and
(33-1) 49-30-71-70

DISNEYLAND PARIS RESORT HOTELS RANKED AND DESCRIBED

All of the Disneyland Paris Resort hotels offer exceptionally comfortable guest rooms that sleep four persons. American in design, decor, and appointments, each guest room has a private bath with one or two sinks plus tub and shower. The Disneyland Hotel, the Hotel New York, the Newport Bay Club, and the Sequoia Lodge feature large, spacious guest rooms, and the rooms at the Hotel Santa Fe and the Hotel Cheyenne are smaller. All guest rooms are equipped with a telephone, a television, and a small refrigerator. All of the resort hotels have a bar, at least one restaurant, and one shop where necessities as well as international newspapers and magazines can be purchased.

Each resort hotel has its own parking facility. Bus transportation is provided from all hotels (except the Disneyland Hotel, located at the park entrance) to the transportation/train station located between Disney Village and the theme park. Walking time from the bus unloading area to the entrance of the Disneyland Paris park is about 4–5 minutes.

While all of the hotels are expensive, price does not always correlate directly with quality. In our opinion, for instance, both the first-class Newport Bay Club and Sequoia Lodge are superior to the luxury-class Hotel New York in terms of guest-room quality, ambience, and livability.

Nicest Guest Rooms

1. Disneyland Hotel
2. Newport Bay Club
3. Sequoia Lodge
4. Hotel New York
5. Hotel Santa Fe
6. Hotel Cheyenne

Best Value

1. Newport Bay Club
2. Disneyland Hotel
3. Sequoia Lodge
4. Hotel Cheyenne
5. Hotel Santa Fe
6. Hotel New York

Most Convenient to Theme Park

1. Disneyland Hotel
2. Hotel New York
3. Newport Bay Club
4. Sequoia Lodge
5. Hotel Cheyenne
6. Hotel Santa Fe

Best Atmosphere and Theme Presentation

1. Sequoia Lodge
2. Hotel Cheyenne
3. Newport Bay Club
4. Disneyland Hotel
5. Hotel New York
6. Hotel Santa Fe

Best for Activities and Recreation

1. Hotel New York
2. Newport Bay Club
3. Sequoia Lodge
4. Disneyland Hotel
5. Hotel Cheyenne
6. Hotel Santa Fe

Best Hotel Restaurants

1. Disneyland Hotel
2. Newport Bay Club
3. Hotel New York
4. Sequoia Lodge
5. Hotel Cheyenne
6. Hotel Santa Fe

Best for Families with Children

1. Disneyland Hotel
2. Hotel Cheyenne
3. Newport Bay Club
4. Sequoia Lodge
5. Hotel Santa Fe
6. Hotel New York

Most Romantic

1. Newport Bay Club
2. Sequoia Lodge
3. Disneyland Hotel
4. Hotel New York
5. Hotel Cheyenne
6. Hotel Santa Fe

Disneyland Hotel   479 Rooms   Bus Service

The Disneyland Hotel is modeled after an American, turn-of-the-century Florida resort hotel. Easily distinguished by its many spires and cupolas, flamingo-colored facade, and white-trimmed balconies, it is the most luxurious of the Disneyland Paris Resort hotels. It is also the most convenient to the theme park, lying directly over the Disneyland Paris entranceway. This proximity makes it easy to return to the hotel for meals and rest, an important consideration if there are small children or seniors in your party.

The spacious guest rooms feature restful pastels and light woods. Baths, with two sinks, are the nicest of any Disneyland Paris hotel. Additionally, many guest rooms afford an excellent view of the theme park. The hotel offers the best food available anywhere in the Disneyland Paris Resort, plus an array of services and amenities appropriate to the Disneyland Hotel's luxury classification, including an indoor pool and health club.

On the negative side, the Disneyland Hotel is extremely expensive. Our only other complaint relates to how incredibly spread out the property is. Guests in the west wing must hike a couple of hundred yards to reach the lobby. Conversely, guests in the east wing must walk a comparable distance to reach the pool.

Hotel New York   539 Rooms   Bus Service

The Hotel New York is supposed to capture the sophistication and grandeur of Manhattan. Consisting of a center high rise flanked by smaller wings, the building is intended to create the illusion of a skyscraper positioned among elegant brownstone row houses from New York's East Side. In our opinion, the hotel's cluster of buildings more closely resembles a factory in Detroit. On inspection, it is not only the architecture that falls short of the mark at Hotel New York. Indeed, with extremely high package rates per night and with a luxury-class rating, there is very little about this property that lives up to expectations.

The lobby and public areas of both the hotel and the adjoining convention center are cold and impersonal, probably the closest approximation of New York the hotel has managed to achieve. The large and comfortable guest rooms are unique if not exactly restful in decor, with rust-colored furniture and lamps in the shape of the Empire State Building. The baths are luxurious, however, and tastefully appointed.

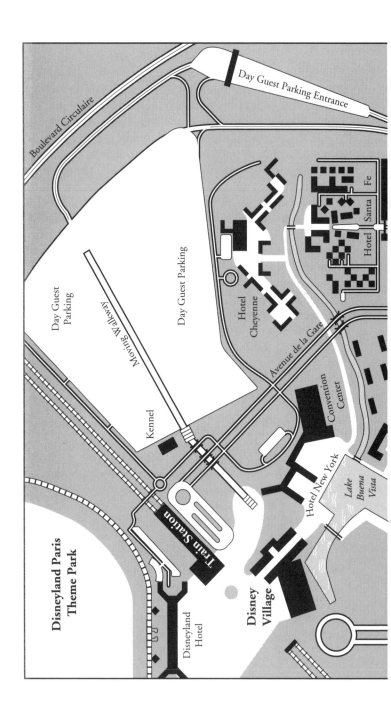

Disneyland Paris
Theme Park

Day Guest Parking Entrance

Boulevard Circulaire

Day Guest Parking

Moving Walkway

Day Guest Parking

Kennel

Hotel Cheyenne

Hotel Santa Fe

Avenue de la Gare

Convention Center

Train Station

Hotel New York

Lake Buena Vista

Disney Village

Disneyland Hotel

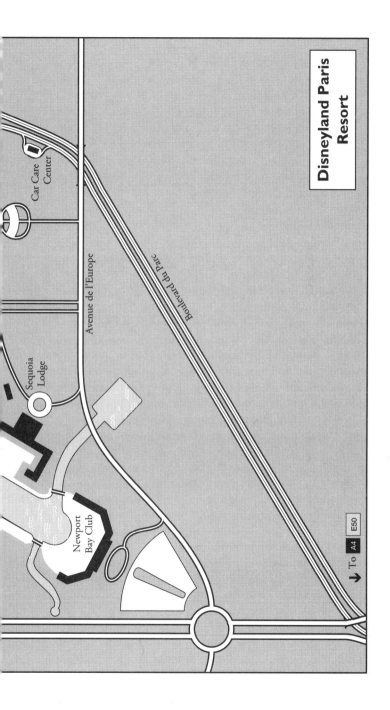

Car Care Center

Avenue de l'Europe

Sequoia Lodge

Boulevard du Parc

Newport Bay Club

→ To A4 E50

Disneyland Paris Resort

65

The restaurants in the Hotel New York serve palatable but vastly overpriced food. Amenities and recreational offerings include indoor and outdoor pools, winter ice skating, a health club, lighted tennis courts, and even ballroom dancing. The Hotel New York is located at the end of Lake Buena Vista. Disney Village, a shopping, dining, and entertainment complex, is an easy four-minute walk from the hotel. Bus shuttles to the theme park are available, though the walk is only about 10–12 minutes. Bus service is also available to the golf course.

Sequoia Lodge   997 Rooms   Bus Service

The Sequoia Lodge is reminiscent of the massive, rugged log and stone hotels that grace American national parks and many western U.S. ski resorts. Located along Lake Buena Vista, the Sequoia consists of a U-shaped main lodge flanked on one side by six smaller lodges. The public areas of the main lodge, including the fireside Redwood Bar & Lounge, are warm, cozy, and exceedingly beautiful with high-beamed ceilings, natural wood trim, and a huge hearth. Though rated first class, the Sequoia is in many ways more beautiful and luxurious than the luxury-class Disneyland Hotel or Hotel New York. Amenities are comparable to the more expensive hotels and include indoor and outdoor pools and a health club. The Hunter's Grill Restaurant, though not cheap, is one of the better hotel eating establishments at Disneyland Paris. Like most other Disneyland Paris Resort hotels, however, the Sequoia Lodge is large and rambling, which means that some guests must trek a long way to reach the restaurants, lobby, shops, or pool from their rooms.

Guest rooms at the Sequoia Lodge are characterized by their elegant simplicity, much in the style of a Canadian hunting club. Dark wood furniture contrasts with clean white walls. Beds are high and covered with colorful patterned quilts. Wall lamps are carved to resemble deer antlers. Baths are attractive and especially well designed, with a dressing bench next to the shower and tub.

The Sequoia Lodge provides bus service to the transportation/train station located between Disney Village and the theme park entrance. If the weather is good, you can walk to the Disney Village in about 8–10 minutes and to the park entrance in about 15 minutes. Along with the Newport Bay Club, the Sequoia Lodge is our preferred hotel for couples on a romantic holiday.

Newport Bay Club   1,083 Rooms   Bus Service

Located at the far end of Lake Buena Vista and facing the Hotel New York at the opposite end of the waterfront promenade, the Newport Bay Club is a careful re-creation of the grand, New England seaside resorts of the late nineteenth century. An imposing structure of seven stories, the cream-colored facade is punctuated with striped awnings over small balconies. A lakeside lighthouse and immaculately manicured lawns complete the picture.

Rated first class, the Newport Bay Club rivals the Disneyland Hotel in terms of luxury and surpasses it in style and ambience. There are indoor and outdoor pools, a health club, two decent restaurants, a lovely lobby, and a lounge that overlooks the waterfront. The Newport Bay Club is an 8–10-minute walk from the Disney Village and about 15–18 minutes on foot from the theme park entrance. If you do not want to walk shuttle buses run about every 15–20 minutes.

Guest rooms at the Newport Bay Club reflect a clean, nautical theme with gleaming white enameled furnishings offset with navy patterns on the bedspreads and drapes. The baths are elegant and well designed with plenty of counter space. The Newport Bay Club ranks with the Sequoia Lodge as one of the better values in Disneyland Paris lodging. It also ranks with the Sequoia Lodge as a great place for a romantic getaway.

Hotel Cheyenne   1,000 Rooms   Bus Service

The Hotel Cheyenne is a huge, sprawling complex of two-story lodges designed to resemble an 1880s Old Western trail town. By far the most exotic of the Disneyland Paris hotels, the Cheyenne is Disney carrying a theme to its limits. If there is any place in the entire Disneyland Paris Resort where you will forget you are in France, it is here. Gaily colored wood buildings with covered boardwalks flank two intersecting gravel thoroughfares. There are water towers, bunkhouses, a saloon with swinging doors, Indian tepees, a Western-theme children's play area, and even covered wagons to complete the illusion.

Rated moderate class, the hotel guest rooms are small and contain a double bed and (even) a set of bunk beds. Rooms are appointed in Western decor with cowboy boot lamps and drapes patterned after the traditional Western red and blue bandanna.

The decor is so juvenile it makes you feel as if you have taken over the bedroom of someone's ten-year-old son. While there is no air-conditioning at the Hotel Cheyenne, each room does contain a ceiling fan. The baths are not large but are well designed. As in the more expensive hotels, there is a phone and a television.

We found the rooms at the Hotel Cheyenne very comfortable. During warm weather, however, when it is necessary to sleep with the window open, noise from the street and American country music (broadcast from speakers seemingly 24 hours a day) conspire to make rest a difficult proposition. Getting to an ice machine is also a hassle at the Hotel Cheyenne. If you want ice, you must troop up the street to a separate building to obtain it.

You could argue that amenities at the Hotel Cheyenne are limited: no swimming pool, no health club, and only one (cafeteria-style) restaurant. To most guests, and particularly to children, however, the whole place is an amenity—and a great adventure to boot. Shuttle buses connect the hotel with the Disney Village and the theme park. If you prefer to walk, you should be able to reach Disney Village within 12–15 minutes and the theme park entrance in about 20 minutes.

Hotel Santa Fe   1,000 Rooms   Bus Service

Intended to look like a Southwestern adobe pueblo, the Hotel Santa Fe more closely resembles a Los Angeles housing project (there are even junk autos!) or a large 1950s American chain motel. The Hotel Santa Fe also has the unfortunate distinction of being the only Disneyland Paris Resort hotel to have its parking lot insinuated around and alongside its guest-room buildings. Why import the boxy ugliness of an Oklahoma, Route 62, Travelodge motel all the way to France? That's Disney for you!

The best feature of the Hotel Santa Fe is its entrance, which cleverly resurrects the look of a typical American drive-in movie. Sitting under the huge movie screen (bearing the permanent image of Clint Eastwood in one of his spaghetti Western roles) is the reception area, a bar and lounge, a food court–style restaurant specializing in Mexican food, a gift shop, and a game arcade. All are located a pretty fair distance from the great majority of the guest rooms. At one end of this complex—and on the roof, no less—is a children's playground. During our stay, few children were able, apparently, to locate the playground. Whenever we stopped by, it was full of Disney employees on break, napping in the sun. There is no pool at the Hotel Santa Fe.

Guest rooms at the hotel are small but tastefully decorated in American Southwestern earth tones. Bedspreads and wall friezes bear colorful Navajo Indian designs. Baths are small but very pleasant.

As at the Hotel Cheyenne, there is no air-conditioning, though ceiling fans are provided. Finding an ice machine can be a challenge here, too. The Hotel Santa Fe is quieter at night, however, and you do not have to fall asleep to the crooning of Johnny Cash.

The Hotel Santa Fe is a good 16–18-minute walk from the Disney Village and a 21–24-minute walk from most guest buildings to the main entrance of the Disneyland Paris Park. Buses run every 15–20 minutes to and from the transportation/train station.

Davy Crockett Ranch 181 campsites   Bus Service
414 cabins (sleep up to 6)   Bus Service

Set in a 56-hectare wooded area about 2 kilometers from the Disneyland Paris theme park, Davy Crockett Ranch is a large resort campground for both tent and recreational vehicle (caravan) camping. Each camping emplacement is equipped with a grill, picnic table, electrical outlet, and a garbage can cleverly disguised as a plastic log. Endowed with little grass or foliage, and placed close together, the campsites do not allow much privacy. A very good bathhouse containing toilets and showers is provided for tent campers.

In addition to the campsites, 414 fully equipped air-conditioned cabins are also available for rent. Each cabin is designed to accommodate four persons (pleasant) to six persons (claustrophobic), and contains a kitchenette, bath, television, and phone. Cookware, dishes, cutlery, bedclothes, and towels are provided, as is maid service.

Aside from camping and cabin accommodations, Davy Crockett Ranch features include a petting farm, a stunning indoor swimming pool, tennis courts, basketball courts, sports fields, evening campfire entertainment, bike and golf-cart rentals (for traveling around the campground), a general store that sells groceries and other necessities, hiking and jogging trails, and pony rides.

The only place to park a car at the campground is at your campsite. There is no parking at the restaurant, pool, or recreation area.

If you want to travel around the campground, you must walk, use the in-ranch bus service, or rent a bike or golf cart. Guests at the ranch must provide their own transportation to Disneyland, a 15-minute drive away (i.e., no bus service). On the bright side, ranch guests are not charged to park in the Disneyland Paris lot.

SEEING THE PARIS SIGHTS

If you are staying at the Disneyland Paris Resort and want to visit Paris, transportation is fast, easy, and economical by train. Since you will be traveling to Paris on the RER, whenever possible we have routed these trips to the nearest RER stop (rather than the Métro), assuming you would rather do your walking in Paris above ground than below.

If you get tired of walking, bear in mind that the La Défense–Château de Vincennes Métro line (I) runs parallel to much of the RER A line within Paris. This line includes stops at the Louvre (Palais Royal–Musée du Louvre and Louvre-Rivoli), the Tuileries, Concorde, and Champs-Elysées–Clemenceau (the beginning of the Champs-Elysées).

If you want to go from Disneyland Paris (Marne-la-Vallée–Chessy), to:

Arc de Triomphe/Champs-Elysées   Take the RER all the way to Charles de Gaulle–Etoile.

The Paris Opéra (Opéra Garnier)   Take the RER line to Auber (this is in the center of the Paris department store area Boulevard Haussmann). Auber is a short walk from the Opéra Garnier.

Centre Georges Pompidou (known to locals as Beaubourg)/Forum des Halles   Take the RER to Châtelet–Les Halles, which leaves you right in the center of Les Halles. Beaubourg is a ten-minute walk away—by way of a colorful, boisterous pedestrian zone that is worth experiencing.

The Louvre/Tuileries Gardens   Take the RER to Châtelet–Les Halles, walk to the rue de Rivoli, and then head west (toward the Arc de Triomphe in the distance). It will take you less than 15 minutes to get to the Louvre or the Tuileries. Or, transfer to the La Défense–Château de Vincennes Métro line, *direction* La Défense, and get off at Palais Royal–Musée du Louvre or at Tuileries.

The Eiffel Tower   Take the RER A line to Porte Maillot, and change to the RER C line (C2, C4, or C6 only; be careful, you do not want the southbound western fork, which goes to Versailles); take it to Champs de Mars–Tour Eiffel.

Musée d'Orsay Take the RER to Châtelet–Les Halles; transfer to the Métro, *direction* La Défense, to Tuileries. Walk through the gardens and across the Seine. The museum is on the opposite bank of the Seine—you can't miss it.

Latin Quarter (Quartier Latin) Take the RER to Châtelet–Les Halles and switch to the southbound RER B line (*direction* Robinson or St. Rémy-lès-Chevreuse) to St. Michel–Notre Dame; or if the weather is nice, walk straight south, and cross the Seine.

Montmartre Take the RER to Nation; transfer to the Métro Nation–Porte Dauphine line (2), (*direction* Porte Dauphine), and get off at Anvers; look for signs for Sacré-Coeur, and be prepared for a long walk uphill.

LODGING OUTSIDE DISNEYLAND PARIS

Staying in Paris

Because many visitors will be combining a visit to the park with a stay in Paris, we will not try to present a guide to Paris hotels here. We recommend *The Unofficial Guide to Paris* (Hungry Minds) and the red *Michelin France* (Michelin Travel Publications) to guide your selection.

The Paris Convention and Visitors Bureau publishes a booklet (not comprehensive) that lists hotels for Paris and the surrounding Ile de France region. It gives details on number of rooms and services, in addition to prices. The main office, near the Arc de Triomphe, as well as those at most SNCF stations, can also provide same-day hotel reservations for a fee that varies with the type of accommodations. Office hours are 9 a.m. to 8 p.m.; during off-season, Sunday 11 a.m.–6 p.m. If you take the Métro, use the George V Métro stop instead of the stop at Charles de Gaulle–Etoile; there's much less walking inside the station. Their address is:

Office du Tourisme et des Congrés de Paris
127, avenue des Champs-Elysées, 75008 Paris
phone 33 (0) 8-36-68-31-12
fax 33 (0) 1-49-52-53-00
www.paris-touristoffice.com

A toll-free number anywhere in France for English information on hotels, as well as transportation and general tourist information, operates from May through October; call 05-201-202 (Monday through Saturday, 8:30 a.m. to 8 p.m.).

In the United States, the French Government Tourist Office provides a list of "Hotels in France with U.S. Representatives." Many of these reservation services have toll-free numbers and are not necessarily limited to chain hotels or even to large establishments.

French Government Tourist Offices in the United States:
New York: 444 Madison Avenue, 16th Floor, New York, NY 10022-6903; (212) 838-7029
Chicago: 676 N. Michigan Avenue, Chicago, IL 60611-2819; (312) 751-7800
Los Angeles: 9454 Wilshire Boulevard, Beverly Hills, CA 90212-2967; (213) 272-2665
Miami: 1 Biscayne Tower Suite 1750 or 2 South Biscayne Boulevard, Miami, FL 33131; (305) 373-8177

Busy Times for Hotels in Paris   Paris hotels book up farther in advance for trade shows than they do for tourist periods. It's actually easier to find a hotel room in Paris during July and August than it is in June and October.

The Paris Convention and Visitors Bureau listed the following periods as the most heavily booked dates for all classifications of visitors (tourists, businesspeople, trade show and convention attendees):

Second week in January	All of June
Last weekend in January and first week of February	First two weeks of September
First two weeks of March	All of October
First week of April	Third week of November
Last three weeks of May	Last week of December

Most Convenient Lodging outside the Park

"Outside" Disneyland Paris does not have to mean an hour's trek away to Paris. There are a number of lodging alternatives along the A4 autoroute and on the Marne-la-Vallée–Chessy RER line. In addition, there are several small villages near Disneyland Paris, but they do not offer much in the way of lodging options. These tiny, charming villages do, however, offer some wonderful dining alternatives to the restaurants of Disneyland Paris.

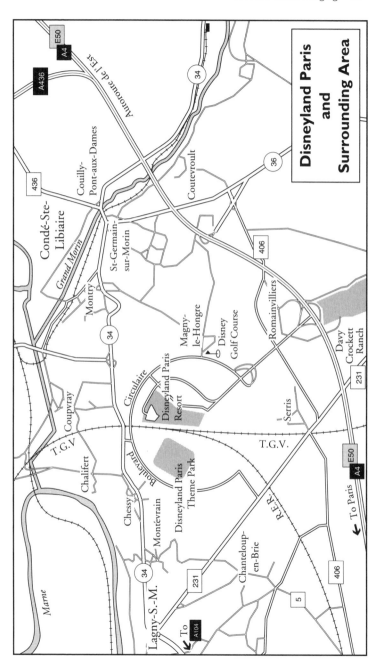

Disneyland Paris
and
Surrounding Area

Staying in a Town along the RER Line   If you want to be near, but not in, Disneyland Paris, we recommend staying in one of the nearby towns accessible by RER. Even if you have come to the area by car, you can park at your hotel and walk to the train station. Small and mid-sized hotel chains offer a sizable reservoir (some have up to 200 rooms) of comfortable accommodations, which can usually be booked through a central number from abroad, often without a deposit. The rooms tend to be small, but they are fairly inexpensive, clean, and pleasant, albeit largely devoid of any charm.

All the hotels listed here are within easy walking distance from the RER station in their respective towns and ten minutes or less from Disneyland Paris by rail.

Torcy   Torcy is the stop right before Marne-la-Vallée on the RER, a seven-minute ride. It is a fairly nondescript—bordering on dreary—industrial town, whose sole attraction is its proximity to Disneyland Paris coupled with low-priced lodging options. It also has a *centre-commercial* (shopping mall) right behind the train station that provides an interesting glimpse of life in modern, suburban France.

Les Relais Bleus   FF 360–440 ($48–60)   Tel. 64-80-02-32
Les Relais Bleus is an attractive hotel with a nicely appointed restaurant, located within a two-minute walk from the Torcy RER station. The continental breakfast is expensive at FF 42 ($6). Pass it up and stop at a cafe or the *centre-commercial.* You can get fresh croissants at the *boulangerie* or in the *hypermarché* (a mega supermarket where you can find anything from baguettes to a television set).

Campanile   FF 370 ($50)   Tel. 60-17-84-85
The Campanile is warm and surprisingly homey for a chain hotel. A hearty breakfast buffet is offered daily for only FF 29 ($4). Unfortunately, the Campanile is a boring ten-minute walk from the RER.

Première Classe   FF 179 ($24)   Tel. 60-17-30-19
This budget hotel is comfortable but offers very little in the way of services or amenities and is essentially without reception staff. Check-in is fully automated, using your credit card as if you were making a transaction at an automatic banking machine. A self-service breakfast is offered for FF 20 ($3). The hotel, located right behind the Campanile, is a ten-minute walk from the RER station.

Lognes   Lognes is two stops and nine minutes down the line toward Paris on the RER. Predominantly a modern town with boxlike buildings, it does have an older section with some provincial charm. There is a good country-style restaurant, Auberge de la Fontaine (26, rue de la Mairie), where two can eat well for about the price of a one-day Disneyland Paris pass. There is also a pretty pond with a grassy area right behind the station, where you can relax and watch people fish or walk their dogs while you wait for your train. Unfortunately, Lognes has only one hotel, but it's a very attractive option:

Frantour   **FF 405–490 ($54–66)**   **Tel. 64-80-02-50**
The Frantour is a three-star hotel with full restaurant and bar located within a seven-minute walk of the RER station. Regular duplexes offer privacy and the best value for families; duplex suites are available with a second shower or bath for FF 750–950 ($101–128).

Noisiel   Noisiel is a new and fairly bland town, 11 minutes from Disneyland Paris by RER. It offers another inexpensive chain hotel:

Climat   **FF 325–340 ($43–45)**   **Tel. 60-06-15-40**
The Climat offers spartan but comfortable rooms and a restaurant. The hotel is an easy three- to five-minute walk from the RER station.

Staying Near the Autoroute   If you are arriving by car and looking for reliable accommodations with an easy route to the park, we recommend one of the following chain hotels convenient to the A4. These hotels, except for those in Noisy-le-Grand, are not accessible by the RER.

Champs-sur-Marne   Take the A199 to the N104 and then the A4 (*direction:* Reims).

Arcade   **FF 310–340 ($41–46)**   **Tel. 64-68-00-83**
A property with a restaurant and bar.

Collégien   Near the autoroute A4 interchange for Lagny.

Novotel   **FF 470–550 ($63–74)**   **Tel. 64-80-53-53**
Marne-la-Vallée
A three-star hotel with restaurant and bar.

Noisy-le-Grand   Near the A4 but closer to Paris (also served by the RER).

| Climat | FF 310–345 ($41–46) | Tel. 43-05-22-99 |
| Novotel | FF 590–650 ($79–87) | Tel. 48-15-60-60 |

Making the Most of Your Time

ALLOCATING TIME

The Disney people recommend a day and a half to three full days at Disneyland Paris. Although this may seem a little self-serving, it is not without basis. Disneyland Paris is *huge,* with something to see or do crammed into every conceivable space. In addition, touring requires a lot of walking and often a lot of waiting in lines. Moving in and among large crowds all day is exhausting, and the unpredictable French weather makes tempers short. In our many visits to Disneyland Paris we observed, particularly on warm days, a dramatic transition from happy, enthusiastic touring upon arrival to an almost zombielike plodding along later in the day. Visitors who began their day enjoying the wonders of the Disney imagination ultimately lapsed into an exhausted production mentality ("We've got two more rides in Fantasyland, then we can go back to the hotel.")

OPTIMUM TOURING SITUATION

The optimum touring situation would call for having three days of touring time at your disposal. Buy the Three-Day Passport, which entities you to admission plus unlimited use of attractions; it does not have to be used on consecutive days.

Day One

Tour Disneyland Paris early in the morning when the lines are short, following Day One of the Two-Day Touring Plan A provided in this guide to help you avoid long lines. At about noon go back to your hotel for lunch and maybe a swim or a nap—whatever you feel like.

If the park closes early (6–8 p.m.) return refreshed about two hours before closing and continue your visit among the less populous crowds of the evening. Eat dinner somewhere outside of Disneyland Paris after the park closes.

If Disneyland Paris closes late (after 8 p.m.), take a relaxing dinner break outside the park and return refreshed to enjoy yourself until closing time. Evenings on a late-closing night are special at Disneyland Paris. We recommend this time for taking in special events and live performances. If you stay until near closing, you will find the lines for the more popular rides vastly diminished.

Day Two

Arrive early in the morning, and follow Day Two of Two-Day Touring Plan A provided in this guide.

If the park closes early, stick around for the afternoon parade and some of the other live performances around the park. Ride the Indian Canoes before dusk. If you enjoy shopping, this is a good time to explore the shops.

If the park remains open late, eat an early dinner outside Disneyland Paris, and return around 7:30 p.m. to enjoy the evening festivities.

Day Three

Arrive early and experience again those rides and attractions you enjoyed most from the first two mornings. Catch any of the shows or rides you missed on the previous days.

The essence of the "Optimum Touring Situation" is to see the various attractions of Disneyland Paris in a series of shorter, less exhausting visits during the more temperate, less crowded parts of the day, with plenty of rest and relaxation in between visits. Since the "Optimum Touring Situation" calls for leaving and returning to the theme park on most days, it obviously makes for easier logistics if you stay fairly close to the park (at a Disneyland Paris Resort hotel, a nearby small village inn, or a hotel within 15 minutes on the RER commuter train or the A4 highway). If you are staying too far away for much coming and going, try relaxing during the crowded middle of the day in the lounges or at the pools of the Disneyland Paris Resort complex.

SEEING DISNEYLAND PARIS ON A TIGHT SCHEDULE

Most visitors admittedly do not have three days to devote to Disneyland Paris. Some are en route to other French or European destinations, and others wish to spend time sampling other nearby attractions. For these visitors, efficient, time-effective touring is a must. They cannot afford long waits in line for rides, shows, or meals.

Even the most efficient touring plan will not allow the visitor to cover Disneyland Paris in one day without making some choices. The basic trade-off is between enjoying the attractions or catching specially scheduled live entertainment, such as parades or concerts. If the park closes late (after 8 p.m.), you can have the best of both worlds—with a little organization. Otherwise, you will probably have to accept some sacrifices.

ONE-DAY TOURING

Touring Disneyland Paris comprehensively in one day is possible but requires knowledge of the park, good planning, and no small reserve of energy and endurance. It does not leave much time for leisurely meals in sit-down restaurants, prolonged browsing in the many shops, or lengthy rest periods. Even so, one-day touring can be a fun and rewarding experience.

Successful one-day touring hinges on *Three Cardinal Rules:*

1. Decide in Advance What You Really Want to See

What are the rides and shows that appeal to you most? Which additional attractions would you like to experience if you have any time left? What are you willing to forgo? The section of this guide labeled "Disneyland Paris in Detail" will help you sort out your choices. Also refer to the section on Live Entertainment.

2. Arrive Early! Arrive Early! Arrive Early!

This is the single most important key to touring efficiently and avoiding long lines. With your admission pass in hand, be at the gate ready to go about 50 minutes before the theme park's stated opening time. First thing in the morning there are no lines and relatively few people. The same four rides that you can experience in one hour in the early morning will take more than three hours to see after 11 a.m. Have breakfast before you arrive, so you will not have to waste prime touring time sitting in a restaurant.

3. Avoid Bottlenecks

Helping you avoid bottlenecks is what this guide is all about. Bottlenecks occur as a result of crowd concentrations and/or less-than-optimal traffic engineering. Concentrations of hungry people create bottlenecks at restaurants during the lunch and dinner hours; concentrations of people moving toward the exit near closing time create jams in the gift shops en route to the gate; concentrations of visitors at new and unusually popular rides create congestion and long lines; rides slow in loading and unloading passengers create bottlenecks and long waiting lines. Avoiding bottlenecks involves being able to predict where, when, and why they occur. To this end we provide field-tested touring plans to keep you ahead of the crowd or out of its way. In addition we provide critical data on all rides and shows, which help you estimate how long you might have to wait in line, which compare rides in terms of their capacity to accommodate large crowds, and which rate the rides according to our opinions as well as the opinions of other Disneyland Paris visitors.

TRAFFIC PATTERNS INSIDE DISNEYLAND PARIS

When we began our research on Disneyland Paris, we were very interested in traffic patterns throughout the park, specifically:

What attractions and which sections of the park do visitors head for when they first arrive?   When guests are admitted to the various lands from Main Street, the flow of people to Discoveryland and Frontierland is heaviest. The next most crowded land is Fantasyland, followed by Adventureland. In our research we tested the often-heard assertions that most people turn right into Discoveryland and tour Disneyland Paris in an orderly counterclockwise fashion; or, turn left into Frontierland and tour the park in a sequential clockwise direction. Americans, Japanese, and Australians, interestingly, seem to prefer counterclockwise touring, while Europeans and North Africans almost invariably move in a clockwise direction. In that Europeans constitute the vast majority of any day's attendance, Frontierland fills up first.

Many guests, however, attracted by the castle, initiate their rotation from Fantasyland, making it the third most crowded land in the morning. Repeat visitors appear to head directly to specific favored attractions that they wish to ride before the lines get long. These more than other factors determine traffic patterns in the mornings and account for the early distribution of visitors throughout Disneyland Paris. Attractions that are heavily attended in the early morning are:

Big Thunder Mountain	Frontierland
Space Mountain	Discoveryland
Dumbo the Flying Elephant	Fantasyland

How long does it take for the park to reach peak capacity for a given day? How are the visitors dispersed throughout the park? There is a surge of early birds who arrive before or around opening time but are quickly absorbed into the empty park. After opening there is a steady stream of arriving visitors that peaks between 10 and 11:30 a.m.

Lines sampled reached their longest length between noon and 2 p.m., indicating more arrivals than park departures into the early afternoon. For general touring purposes, most attractions develop substantial lines between 10:30 and 11:30 a.m. Through the late hours of the morning and the early hours of the afternoon, attendance is equally distributed through all of the "lands." By midafternoon, however, we noted a concentration of visitors in Fantasyland and Discoveryland and a slight decrease of visitors in Frontierland.

Late afternoon and early evening normally found attendance more heavily distributed in Discoveryland and Fantasyland. Though Big Thunder Mountain remained inundated throughout the day, most of the other attractions in Frontierland had reasonable lines. In Adventureland, the clockwise touring multitudes had rotated into Fantasyland by dinnertime. Frontierland, and particularly Adventureland, therefore, became less congested as the afternoon and evening progressed.

How do most visitors go about touring the park? Is there a difference in the touring behavior of first-time visitors and repeat visitors? Many first-time visitors are accompanied by friends or relatives who are familiar with Disneyland Paris and who guide their tour. These tours sometimes, but not always, proceed in an orderly (clockwise or counterclockwise) touring sequence. First-time visitors without personal touring guidance tend to be more orderly in their touring. Many first-time visitors, however, are drawn to Le Château de la Belle au Bois Dormant (the castle) on entering the park and thus commence their rotation from Fantasyland. Repeat visitors usually proceed directly to their favorite attractions.

What effect do special events, such as parades and the evening fireworks, have on traffic patterns? Special events such as parades, evening fireworks, and live performances pull substantial numbers of visitors from the lines for attractions, but the key to the length of the lines continues to be how many people are in the park.

What are the traffic patterns near to and at closing time? On our sample days, recorded in and out of season, park departures outnumbered arrivals beginning in midafternoon, with a wave of departures following the parades and fireworks show. A substantial number of visitors departed during the late afternoon as the dinner hour approached. When the park closed early, there were steady departures during the two hours preceding closing, with a mass exodus of remaining visitors at closing time. When the park closed late, departures were distributed throughout the evening hours, with waves of departures following the evening parade(s) and fireworks, increasing as closing time approached. The balloon effect of mass departures at the end of the day primarily affects conditions on Main Street and in the parking complex. In the lands other than Main Street, just prior to closing, touring conditions are normally uncrowded.

SAVING TIME IN LINE BY UNDERSTANDING THE RIDES

There are many different types of rides in Disneyland Paris. Some, like It's a Small World, are engineered to carry several thousand people every hour. At the other extreme, rides such as Dumbo the Flying Elephant can accommodate only about 480 persons in an hour. Most rides fall somewhere in between. Lots of factors figure into how long you will have to wait to experience a particular ride: the popularity of the ride, how it loads and unloads, how many persons can ride at one time, how many units (cars, rockets, boats, flying elephants, gondolas, etc.) of those available are in service at a given time, and how many Disney staff are available to operate the ride. Let's take them one by one:

1. Popularity of the ride Thrill rides like Space Mountain, Star Tours, and Big Thunder Mountain attract a lot of people, as do children's rides such as Dumbo. If you know a ride is popular, you need to learn a little more about how it operates to determine when might be the best time to ride. But a ride need not be especially popular to form long lines: the lines can be the result of less-than-desirable traffic engineering; that is, it takes so long to load and unload that a long line builds no matter what. This is the situation at the Flying Elephant, for example. Only a small percentage of Disneyland Paris land visitors (mostly children) ride Dumbo, but because it takes so long to load and unload, this ride can form long waiting lines.

2. How the ride loads and unloads   Some rides never stop. They are like a circular conveyor belt that goes around and around. We call these "continuous loaders." The Phantom Manor is a continuous loader. The more cars or ships or whatever on the conveyor, the more people can be moved through in an hour. The Phantom Manor has lots of cars on the conveyor belt and consequently can move more than 2,400 people an hour.

Other rides are interval loaders. This means that cars are unloaded, loaded, and dispatched at certain set intervals (sometimes controlled manually and sometimes by a computer). Blanche-Neige et les Sept Nains (Snow White and the Seven Dwarfs) is an interval loader. It dispatches nine cars at set time intervals, usually one car every 15 seconds. In one kind of interval loader, such as Blanche-Neige, empty cars are returned to the starting point, where they line up, waiting to be reloaded. In a second type of interval loader, one group of riders enters the vehicle while the last group departs. We call these "in and out" interval loaders. It's a Small World is a good example of an "in and out" interval loader. As a boat pulls up to the dock, those who have just completed their ride exit to the left. At almost the same time, those waiting to ride enter the boat from the right. The boat is released to the dispatch point a few yards down the line, where it is launched according to whatever time interval is being used. Interval loaders of both types can be very efficient at moving people if (1) the release (launch) interval is relatively short, and (2) the ride can accommodate a large number of vehicles in the system at one time. Since many boats can be floating through Pirates of the Caribbean at a given time, and since the release interval is short, almost 2,800 people an hour can see this attraction. The River Rogue Keelboats is an "in and out" interval loader, but runs only three keelboats at a time. Thus the River Rogue Keelboats can handle only about 650 people per hour.

A third group of rides are "cycle rides." Another name for these is "stop and go" rides; people waiting to ride exchange places with those who have just ridden. The main difference between "in and out" interval rides and cycle rides is that with a cycle ride the whole system shuts down when loading and unloading is in progress. While one boat is loading and unloading in It's a Small World, many other boats are proceeding through the ride. But when Dumbo the Flying Elephant touches down, the whole ride is at a standstill until the next flight is launched. Likewise, with the Orbitron ride in Discoveryland, all riders dismount, and the rockets stand stationary until the next group is loaded and ready to ride. In discussing a cycle ride, the amount of time the ride is in motion is called "ride time." The amount of time that the ride is idle, while loading and unloading, is called "load time." Load time plus ride time equals "cycle time," or the time expended from the start of one run of the ride until the start of the succeeding run. Cycle rides are the least efficient of all the Disneyland Paris rides in terms of traffic engineering.

3. How many persons can ride at one time   This figure is defined in terms of "per-ride capacity" or "system capacity." Either way the figure refers to the number of people who can be riding at the same time. Our discussion above illustrates that the greater the carrying capacity of a ride (all other things being equal), the more visitors it can accommodate in an hour.

4. How many units are in service at a given time   A "unit" is simply our term for the vehicle you sit in during your ride. At the Mad Hatter's Tea Cups, the unit is a Tea Cup; at Star Tours, it's a spaceship; at Pirates of the Caribbean, it's a boat. On some rides, notably cycle rides, the number of units in operation at a given time is fixed; thus there are always 16 Flying Elephant units operating on the Dumbo ride, 86 horses on Le Carrousel de Lancelot, and so on. What this all means to you is that there is no way to increase the carrying capacity of the ride by adding more units. On a busy day, therefore, the only way to carry more people each hour on a fixed-unit cycle ride is to shorten the loading time (which, as we will see in section 5 below, is sometimes impossible) or to decrease the riding time, the actual time the ride is in motion. The bottom line on a busy day for a cycle ride is that you might wait longer and perhaps be rewarded for your wait with a shorter ride. This is why we try to steer you clear of the cycle rides, unless you are willing to ride them early in the morning or late at night. The following rides are cycle rides:

Fantasyland	Dumbo the Flying Elephant
	Le Carrousel de Lancelot
	Mad Hatter's Tea Cups
Discoveryland	Orbitron

Other rides at Disneyland Paris can increase their carrying capacity by adding units to the system as the crowds build. Big Thunder Mountain is a good example. If attendance is very light, Big Thunder can start the day by running one of its five available mine trains on one out of two available loading platforms. If lines start to build, the other loading platform can be activated and more mine trains placed into operation. At full capacity a total of five trains loading from two platforms can carry about 2,400 persons an hour. Likewise, Pirates of the Caribbean can increase its capacity by adding more boats, and Autopia by adding more sports cars. Sometimes a long line will disappear almost instantly when new units are brought on line. When an interval-loading ride places more units into operation, it usually shortens the dispatch interval, so more units are being dispatched more often.

5. How many staff personnel are available to operate the ride
Allocation of additional staff to a given ride can allow extra units to be placed in operation or additional loading areas or holding areas to be opened. Pirates of the Caribbean and It's a Small World can run two separate waiting lines and loading zones. The Phantom Manor has a short "preshow," which is staged in a "stretch room." On busy days a second "stretch room" can be activated, thus permitting a more continuous flow of visitors to the actual loading area. Additional staff make a world of difference on some cycle rides. Sometimes one attendant will operate the Mad Hatter's Tea Cups. This individual must clear the visitors from the ride just completed, admit and seat visitors for the upcoming ride, check that all Tea Cups are properly secured (which entails an inspection of each Tea Cup), return to the control panel, issue instructions to the riders, and finally, activate the ride (whew!). A second attendant allows for the division of these responsibilities and has the effect of cutting loading time by 25–50%.

SAVING TIME IN LINE BY UNDERSTANDING THE SHOWS

Many of the featured attractions at Disneyland Paris are theater presentations. They are not as complex from a traffic engineering viewpoint as rides, but a little enlightenment concerning their operation may save some touring time.

Most of the theater attractions at Disneyland Paris operate in three distinct phases:

1. There are the visitors who are in the theater viewing the presentation.
2. There are the visitors who have passed through the turnstile into a holding area or waiting lobby. These people will be admitted to the theater as soon as the current presentation is concluded. Several attractions, including *Le Visionarium* and *Honey, I Shrunk the Audience,* offer a preshow in their waiting lobby to entertain the crowd until they are admitted to the main show.

3. Finally, there is the outside line. Visitors waiting here will enter the waiting lobby when them is room and then move into the theater when the audience turns over (is exchanged) between shows.

The theater capacity and popularity of the presentation, along with the level of attendance in the park, determine how long the lines will be at a given theater attraction. Except for holidays and other days of especially heavy attendance, the longest wait for a show usually does not exceed the length of two complete performances.

Almost all Disneyland Paris theater attractions run continuously, stopping only long enough for the previous audience to leave and the waiting audience to enter, so a performance will be in progress when you arrive. If a showing of *Honey, I Shrunk the Audience* in Discoveryland lasts 17 minutes, and if you were to arrive just after the show began, the wait under optimal circumstances should be 17 minutes.

All Disneyland Paris theaters (except some amphitheater productions) are very strict when it comes to controlling access. Unlike a movie theater at home, you cannot just walk in during the middle of a performance; you will always have at least a short wait.

FASTPASS

In 1999 Disney launched a new system for moderating the waiting time for popular attractions. Called FASTPASS, it was originally tried at the Animal Kingdom at Walt Disney World and then subsequently expanded to cover attractions at the other Disney parks, including Disneyland Paris. Here's how it works.

Your handout park map, as well as signage at respective attractions, will tell you which attractions are included. Attractions operating FASTPASS will have a regular line and a FASTPASS line (marked "ENTRÉE FASTPASS AVEC TICKETS"). A sign at the entrance will tell you how long the wait is in the regular line. If the wait is acceptable, hop in line. If the wait seems too long, insert your park admission pass into a special FASTPASS machine and receive an appointment time (for sometime later in the day) to come back and ride. When you return at the appointed time, you will enter the FASTPASS line and proceed directly to the attraction's preshow or boarding area with no further wait. Interestingly, this procedure was pioneered by Universal Studios Hollywood many years ago and has been pretty much ignored by major theme parks ever since. It works well, however, and can save a lot of time standing in line. There is no extra charge to use FASTPASS.

FASTPASS is still evolving, and attractions continue to be added and deleted from the lineup. Pending changes aside, here's an example of how to use FASTPASS: Let's say you have only one day to tour the park. You arrive early and ride Space Mountain and Big Thunder Mountain with minimal waits. Then, following our touring plan, you head across the park to Indiana Jones and the Temple of Peril and find a substantial line. Because Indiana Jones is designated as a FASTPASS attraction, you can insert your admission pass into the machine and receive an appointment time to come back and ride, thus avoiding a long wait.

We found FASTPASS to work remarkably well, primarily because Disney provides amazingly preferential treatment for FASTPASS holders. In fact, the effort to accommodate FASTPASS holders makes anyone in the regular line feel like an illegal immigrant. As a telling indication of their status, guests in the regular lines are referred to as "standby guests." Indeed, we watched guests in the regular lines stand by and stand by, shifting despondently from foot to foot, while dozens, and sometimes hundreds, of FASTPASS holders were ushered into the boarding area ahead of them. Clearly Disney is sending a message here, to wit: FASTPASS is heaven; anything else is limbo at best and probably purgatory. In any event, you'll think you've been in purgatory if you get stuck in the regular line during more crowded times of the day.

FASTPASS doesn't eliminate the need to arrive at the theme park early. Because the park offers four or fewer FASTPASS attractions, you still need to get an early start if you want to see as much as possible in a single day. Plus, as we'll discuss later, there is a limited supply of FASTPASSes available for each attraction on a given day. If you don't show up until the middle of the afternoon, you might find that all the FASTPASSes have been distributed to other guests. FASTPASS does make it possible to see more with less waiting than ever before, and it's a great benefit to those who like to sleep late or who enjoy an afternoon or evening at the theme park on their arrival day at Disneyland Paris

Understanding the FASTPASS System

The basic purpose of FASTPASS is to reduce the waiting time for designated attractions by more equally distributing the arrival of guests at those attractions over the course of the day. This is accomplished by providing an incentive, a shorter wait in line, for guests who are willing to postpone experiencing the attraction until later. The system also, in effect, imposes a penalty (i.e., being relegated to standby status) on those who opt not to use it. However, distributing guest arrivals more equally also decreases the waiting time for standby guests.

When you insert your admission pass into a FASTPASS time clock, the machine spits out a small slip of paper—small enough to fit in your wallet but also small enough to lose easily. Printed on the paper is the name of the attraction and a specific one-hour time window, for example 1:15–2:15 p.m., during which you can return to enjoy the ride.

When you report back to the attraction during your one-hour window, you'll enter a line marked "FASTPASS Return" that will route you more or less directly to the boarding or preshow area. Each person in your party must have his or her own FASTPASS and be ready to show it to the Disney cast member at the entrance of the FASTPASS Return line. Before you enter the boarding area or theater, another cast member will collect your FASTPASS.

You may show up at any time during the period printed on your FASTPASS, and from our observation, no specific time within the window is better or worse. This holds true because cast members are instructed to minimize waits for FASTPASS holders. Thus, if the FASTPASS Return line is suddenly inundated (something that occurs essentially by chance), cast members rapidly intervene to reduce the FASTPASS line. This is done by admitting as many as 25 FASTPASS holders for each single standby guest until the FASTPASS line is reduced to an acceptable length. Although FASTPASS will eliminate as much as 80% of the wait you'd experience in the regular line, you can still expect a short wait, but it's usually less than 20 minutes.

You can obtain a FASTPASS anytime after a park opens, but the FASTPASS Return lines do not begin operating until about an hour after opening. Thus, if the park opens at 9 a.m., the FASTPASS time clock machines will also be available at 9 a.m., and the FASTPASS Return line will begin operating at 10 a.m.

Whenever you obtain a FASTPASS, you can be assured of a period of time between when you receive your FASTPASS and the period to report back. The interval can be as short as 30 minutes or as long as several hours, depending on park attendance, the popularity of the attraction, and the attraction's hourly capacity. As a rule of thumb, the earlier in the day you secure a FASTPASS, the shorter the interval between time of issue and your one-hour return window. If the park opens at 9 a.m. and you pick up a FASTPASS for Space Mountain at 9:25 a.m., your appointment window for returning to ride would be something like 10–11 a.m. The exact time of your return window will be determined by how many other guests have obtained FASTPASSes before you.

To more effectively distribute guests over the course of a day, the FASTPASS machines bump the one-hour return period back five minutes for a set number of passes issued (usually the number is equal to about 6% of the attraction's hourly capacity). For example, when Space Mountain opens at 9 a.m., the first 125 people to obtain a FASTPASS will get a 10–11 a.m. return window. The next 125 guests are issued FASTPASSes with a 10:05–11:05 a.m. window, and the next 125 are assigned a 10:10–11:10 a.m. time slot. And so it goes, with the time window dropping back five minutes for every 125 guests. The fewer guests who obtain FASTPASSes for an attraction, the shorter the interval between the receipt of your pass and the return window. Conversely, the more guests issued FASTPASSes, the longer the interval. If an attraction is exceptionally popular and/or its hourly capacity is relatively small, the return window might be pushed back all the way to park closing time. When this happens the FASTPASS machines simply shut down and a sign is posted saying FASTPASSes are all gone for the day. For example, it's not unusual for Indiana Jones and the Temple of Peril to distribute an entire day's allocation of FASTPASSes by 2 or 3 p.m.

When to Use FASTPASS

Except as discussed below, there's no reason to use FASTPASS during the first 30–40 minutes a park is open. Lines for most attractions are quite manageable during this period, and this is the only time of day when FASTPASS attractions exclusively serve those in the regular line. Regardless of time of day, however, if the wait in the regular line at a FASTPASS attraction is 25–30 minutes or less, we recommend joining the regular line.

Think about it. Using FASTPASS requires two trips to the same attraction: one to obtain the pass and another to use it. This means you must invest time to secure the pass (sometimes there are lines at the FASTPASS machines!) and then later interrupt your touring and backtrack to use your FASTPASS. The additional time, effort, and touring modification required are justified only if you can save more than 30 minutes. And don't forget: Even in the FASTPASS line you must endure some waiting.

If you're wondering how FASTPASS waits compare with waits in the standby line, here's what we observed at Space Mountain during a school holiday on a day when the park opened at 9 a.m. From 9 to 10 a.m. Space Mountain served standby guests. At about 10 a.m. the FASTPASS line opened and the progress of those in the regular line was significantly retarded. At 10:45 a.m. the posted standby wait time was 45 minutes, while the FASTPASS wait was only 10 minutes. At 1:45 p.m., the posted standby wait time was 60 minutes, with 10 minutes for FASTPASS. These observations, in addition to documenting the benefit of FASTPASS, also reveal shorter waits in the regular line than those observed at the same time of day prior to the advent of FASTPASS.

Tricks of the Trade

Although Disney stipulates that you can hold a FASTPASS to only one attraction at a time, it's possible to acquire a second FASTPASS before using the first. Let's say you obtain a FASTPASS to Peter Pan's Flight with a return time slot of 10:15–11:15 a.m. Any time after your FASTPASS window begins (i.e., after 10:15 a.m.), you can obtain another FASTPASS. This is possible because the FAST-PASS computer system only monitors the distribution of passes, ignoring whether or when an issued FASTPASS is used.

When obtaining FASTPASSes, it's faster and more considerate of other guests if one person obtains passes for your entire party. This means entrusting one individual with both your valuable park admission passes and your FASTPASSes, so choose wisely.

Don't try to pack too much into the time between obtaining your FASTPASS and the end of your return window. We interviewed a number of families who blew their FASTPASS time slot by trying to cram an extra attraction or two into their touring scheme before returning to use their FASTPASS.

FASTPASS Guidelines

- Don't mess with FASTPASS unless it can save you 30 minutes or more.

- If you arrive *after* the park opens obtain a FASTPASS for your preferred FASTPASS attraction first thing.

- Don't depend on FASTPASSES being available after 2 p.m. during busier times of year.

- Make sure everyone in your party has his or her own FASTPASS.

- Be mindful of your FASTPASS time slot and plan intervening activities accordingly.

Part Two

Tips and Warnings

Before You Get to the Theme Park

Exchange Offices   Exchanges are open every day at both airports and all Paris railway (SNCF) stations except the Gare Montparnasse; there are several others in major tourist areas such as near the Louvre and the Champs-Elysées. A complete list is provided on the back of the tourist office's city map. The exchange window in the main tourist office near the Arc de Triomphe is closed on Sundays.

Warning: If you notice a sign for a Change near the Centre Georges Pompidou, or any nondesignated location, look closely before changing your money. The attractive rate posted is often for the *sale* of foreign currency; such places tend to pay scandalously low rates *to buy* foreign money.

Bank Hours   Banks are open 9 a.m.–4 p.m., Monday to Friday, except on public holidays. Some banks close for an hour or so around lunch, and some are open on Saturday morning.

Telephones   Most public telephones operate with a special card called a *télécarte,* which can be purchased at *tabacs* (certain cafes where stamps are sold), post offices, and Métro stations. If you will be making only an occasional local call while you are away from your hotel, however, they are not worth buying. The cheapest one available covers 50 units for FF 40 ($5.40). They can also be used for out-of-town and overseas calls.

Coin-operated phones take half-, one-, two-, and five-franc pieces. Pick up the receiver and insert one franc; dial your number. You can talk for six minutes if it's a local call; local exchanges will be listed in the telephone booth. Charges vary from FF 1.00 to 3.50 outside the calling area.

If you cannot find a phone that takes coins, try the nearest cafe. If all phones there are card-operated, then look for the nearest post office (PTT), where coin phones are available; instructions for use translated.

<table>
<tr><td colspan="2">**Making a Call with a Télécarte**</td></tr>
<tr><td colspan="2">An electronic screen will instruct you in French:</td></tr>
<tr><td>1. *Dérocher*</td><td>Pick up the receiver.</td></tr>
<tr><td>2. *Introduire carte ou faire numero libré*</td><td>Insert card or dial toll-free number.</td></tr>
<tr><td>3. *Fermer le volet, SVP*</td><td>Please close the flap.</td></tr>
<tr><td>4. *Solde x unités*</td><td>Number of call unit, remaining on your card.</td></tr>
<tr><td>5. *Numéroter*</td><td>Dial number.</td></tr>
<tr><td>6. *Numéro appelé*</td><td>Screen shows the number you dialed. After you hang up, the flap opens automatically.</td></tr>
<tr><td>7. *Retirer carte*</td><td>Take your card.</td></tr>
</table>

Inside Disneyland Paris

Credit Cards

American Express, MasterCard, EuroCard, VISA, Diners Club, and JCB are accepted for theme park admission, dining, entertainment, and shopping.

Traveler's Checks and Personal Checks

American Express Traveler's Checks, French Francs Traveler's Checks, Eurochèques, and personal checks drawn on French banks (with proper identification) are accepted for theme park admission, full-service meals, and shopping purchases. Refunds for lost American Express Traveler's Checks and other banking services are available at the American Express office in the Disneyland Hotel.

Rain

If it rains, go anyway; the bad weather will serve to diminish the crowds. Additionally, most of the rides and attractions in Disneyland Paris are under cover. Likewise, all but a few of the waiting areas are protected from inclement weather. If you get caught by an unexpected downpour, rain gear of varying sorts can be purchased at a number of Disneyland Paris shops.

Cold Weather

Disneyland Paris's objective is to operate the entire park and all of its attractions throughout the dead of winter. Attendance at this time of year, needless to say, is normally minimal, and you can enjoy most rides and shows without waiting. Live entertainment such as parades, amphitheater productions, and fireworks, however, are either discontinued or drastically curtailed during the cold-weather months. During this period, benignly referred to as the "off season," the park operates on a shortened schedule, usually 9 a.m.–8 p.m. Finally, some attractions may be out of service for maintenance or refurbishing.

Getting around the park in nasty weather is no problem. Covered walkways and queuing areas allow guests to amble from land to land and wait comfortably for attractions without getting wet. Outdoor pedestrian paths and railings, happily, are treated with chemicals to prevent icing.

While some rides, such as the Riverboats and Keelboats, have small internal cabins, others are totally exposed to the weather. Only one of these, however, Big Thunder Mountain (mine train), is rated "not to be missed," and even the mine train is actually outdoors only 90 seconds or so during the course of the ride. Of the other totally exposed rides, Orbitron, Autopia, and Dumbo are midway-type rides and considered expendable by most. If your children insist on riding Dumbo in winter, pack them in goose down and check to make sure Dumbo's ears have been de-iced.

Le Carrousel de Lancelot merry-go-round and the Mad Hatter's Tea Cups, while not completely enclosed, are at least under a roof. Likewise, the walk-through attractions La Cabane des Robinson (Swiss Family Treehouse) and Adventure Isle are partially covered, but not protected against the wind. Les Mystères du Nautilus is completely covered. Only Alice's Curious Labyrinth (a walk-through maze) is totally at the mercy of the elements. The remainder of Disneyland Paris's continuously operating attractions are comfortably tucked away indoors.

The bottom line on winter touring is that half of Disneyland Paris's attractions are indoors (including all but one of the featured rides), and another 35% are outdoors but covered. Only about 15% of the attractions are totally exposed to the weather, and most of these are midway-type rides. The cold-weather months are not optimal if you are big on parades and live outdoor performances, but they can be a great time of year if you just want to see the park without fighting the crowds.

Same Day Re-Entry to Disneyland Paris Theme Park

If you wish to leave the theme park and return on the same day, you must have your hand stamped at the park exit on departure. The stamp is very durable and will not (usually) come off when swimming or washing your hands. When you return to the park, you must show your hand stamp (visible only under ultraviolet light) along with your valid Disneyland Paris admission passport.

Visitors with Special Needs

Disabled Visitors   Rental wheelchairs are available if needed. Most rides, shows, attractions, rest rooms, and restaurants are engineered to accommodate the disabled. For specific inquiries or problems, call 60-30-10-20. If you are in Disneyland Paris and need some special assistance, go to City Hall, just inside the park entrance on Town Square. Close-in parking is available for the disabled; inquire when you pay your parking fee.

A special information booklet for disabled guests is available at City Hall and at the wheelchair-rental location just inside the park entrance and on the far right side of the train station or by calling 60-30-10-20.

Visitors with Dietary Restrictions   Visitors on special or restricted diets, including those requiring kosher meals, can arrange for assistance at City Hall on Main Street. For Disneyland Paris hotel restaurants, call the restaurant one day in advance for assistance.

Sight- and/or Hearing-Impaired Guests   The Disneyland Paris theme park provides complimentary tape cassettes and portable tape players to assist sight-impaired guests. They are available at

City Hall at the Town Square end of Main Street. A deposit is required. Seeing eye guide dogs are permitted in the theme park, but are not allowed on certain rides (generally the ones that would make the dogs go bonkers or throw up). Also at City Hall, hearing-impaired guests can obtain a Telecommunications Device for the Deaf (TDD).

Foreign-Language Assistance   Most Disneyland Paris "cast members" are fluent in one or two foreign languages and functional in a couple of others. It is easy to find employees who speak English, German, Dutch, and, of course, French. It is somewhat more difficult to find Disney staff who are fluent in Spanish, Italian, or Danish. Speakers of Greek, Japanese, eastern European languages, Arabic, and Hebrew are in short supply.

Most restaurants throughout Disneyland Paris offer menus in French, English, German, and Spanish translations. Signs are usually in French and/or English, or use nonlinguistic internationally recognizable symbols. If you will need language assistance, call 60-30-60-53 in advance of your visit; in the theme park, request help at City Hall in the Town Square area of Main Street.

Lost Adults   Arrange a plan for regrouping with those in your party should you become separated. Failing this, you can leave a message at City Hall for your missing person.

Lost Children   Lost children should be reported to the first aid center or to the Lost Children center (in the Baby Care Center) adjacent to the Plaza Gardens Restaurant at the central-hub end of Main Street. For more on lost children, see the chapter "Disneyland Paris with Kids."

Messages   Anyone can leave messages at City Hall.

Car Trouble   If the problem is simple, one of the security patrols, which continually cruise the parking lots, might be able to put you back in business. Otherwise, ask a Disney cast member to contact the Car Care Center for you.

Lost and Found   If you lose (or find) something, go to the lost and found office, located in City Hall, at the Town Square end of Main Street. If you do not discover your loss until after you have left the park, call (33-1) 64-74-25-00.

Excuse Me, but Where Can I Find …

Someplace to Put All These Packages?   Coin-operated lockers are available on the ground-floor level of the train station on Main Street.

A Mixed Drink or Beer?   Beer and wine are available in the theme park. If you want a mixed drink, you will have to exit the park and go to one of the bars or restaurants at the Disney Village or in the hotels.

Some Rain Gear?   If you get caught in one of the frequent northern France downpours, you can buy a poncho or an umbrella in most any shop. Though readily available, rain gear is not always displayed. As the Disney people say, it is sold "under the counter." In other words, you have to ask for it. If you are caught without protection on a rainy day, do not slog around dripping. Rain gear is one of the few shopping bargains at Disneyland Paris. Ponchos can be had for FF 35 ($4.70). Umbrellas are also available but are expensive.

A Cure for This Headache?   Aspirin and various other sundries can be purchased on Main Street at the Emporium (they keep them behind the counter, so you have to ask).

Pharmacy to Fill a Prescription?   Unfortunately, there is no place in Disneyland Paris to have a prescription filled.

Suntan Lotion?   Suntan lotion and various other sundries can be purchased on Main Street at the Emporium (they keep them behind the counter, so you have to ask).

A Smoke?   Cigarettes are readily available throughout Disneyland Paris.

Feminine Hygiene Products?   Feminine hygiene products are available in most of the women's rest rooms at Disneyland Paris.

Cash?   BNP automatic teller machines are located in each of the covered arcades that parallel Main Street. Outside the park, an automatic teller machine is located in the Disney Village Post Office. ATM machines accept *cartes bancaires françaises,* MC, EuroCard, and VISA. Additionally, American Express operates an office (in Disney Village), which offers many of the same services as a bank.

Exchange of Foreign Currency?   As you would expect, cash transactions at Disneyland Paris are executed in French francs. Currency can be exchanged at the reception desks of the resort hotels, at the Disney Village Post Office, at the Foreign Currency Exchange Booths outside the main entrance to the theme park, and inside the park at Information Booths in the Main Street and Frontierland train stations, and at the Adventureland and Fantasyland Information Kiosks.

A Place to Leave My Pet?   Cooping up an animal in a stuffy car while you tour can lead to disastrous results, and pets are not allowed in Disneyland Paris (except seeing-eye dogs). Kennels and holding facilities for the temporary care of your pets are located at the end of the guest parking lot to the right of the moving sidewalk. If you are adamant, the folks at the kennels will accept custody of just about any type of animal. Owners of pets, exotic or otherwise, must themselves place their charge in the assigned cage. Small pets (mice, hamsters, birds, snakes, turtles, alligators, whatever) must arrive in their own escape-proof quarters.

In addition to the above, them are several other details you may need to know:

- Pets must have a tattoo identification mark and a certificate of vaccination and immunization.
- Advance reservations for animals are not accepted.
- Kennels open one hour before the theme park opens and close one hour after the park closes.
- Pets may not be boarded overnight.
- Guests leaving exotic pets should supply food for their pet.
- On busy days there is a one- to two-hour bottleneck at the kennel, beginning a half hour before the park opens. If you need to use the kennel on such a day, arrive at least an hour before the park's stated opening time.
- Guests who board their pets should be advised that only the most elementary and essential services are provided; the kennels are not staffed overnight, and Disney personnel will not exercise pets.

A Telephone?   Telephones are located throughout the park, usually near the rest rooms. While most require a special card (see

"Making a Call with a Télécarte," above), coin-operated phones still are easy to find.

Cameras and Film?   Photo tips, including recommendations for settings and exposures, are provided in the Disneyland Paris map brochure, available free when you enter the park. If you do not have a camera, Disney will rent you a 35 mm camera for FF 70 ($9.40) a day and a FF 705 ($95) deposit, or a video camcorder for FF 430 ($58) a day with a FF 7,000 ($945) deposit. All deposits are refundable. If you rent a camcorder, be advised that your video system at home might not be compatible with the rental camcorder. American and Japanese videos, for example, will not work on most European systems. Rental equipment is available at Town Square Photography on Main Street. You can buy film throughout the park.

Film-developing services are provided by most Disneyland Paris hotel gift shops as well as the Camera Center in the theme park. The Camera Center offers 2-hour processing for film dropped off at the center; allow 24 hours for film deposited at "film drops" in the various lands.

We encountered a couple whose film was not developed when they called for it at the Camera Center just before park closing. Scheduled to go home the next morning, they naturally did not want to pay another day's admission just to enter the park for the purpose of claiming their processed film. They had to return to the park entrance in the morning and explain their problem to a Disney supervisor. The supervisor assigned an escort to admit the couple to the park and walk them over to the Camera Center. After the couple reclaimed their film, the escort ushered them to the exit. If you have problems regarding film processing or rented equipment, the direct phone number of the Camera Center is 64-74-28-70.

Part Three

Disneyland Paris with Kids

The Agony and the Ecstasy

The international media and advertising presence of Disney is so overwhelming that any child who watches TV or shops with Mom is likely to get all revved up about going to a Disney park. Parents, if anything, are even more susceptible. Almost every parent has brightened with anticipation at the prospect of guiding their children through the wonders, of this special place. "Imagine little Marie's expression when she first sees Mickey Mouse. Think of her excitement and awe as she crosses the moat to Sleeping Beauty's Castle, or her small arm around me when Dumbo takes off." Are these not the treasured moments we long to share with our children?

While dreams of visiting Disneyland Paris are tantamount to nirvana for a three-year-old and could melt the heart of any parent, the reality of actually taking that three-year-old is usually a lot closer to the "agony" than the "ecstasy."

A mother wrote us describing her visit with her five-year-old to the Magic Kingdom in Walt Disney World, Florida, but it could just as easily have been Disneyland Paris:

I felt so happy and excited before we went. I guess it was all worth it, but when I look back I think I should have had my head examined. The first day we went [the park] was packed. By 11 in the morning, we had walked so far and stood in so many lines that we were all exhausted. Kristy cried about going on anything that looked or even sounded scary, and was frightened by all of the Disney characters (they are so big!) except Minnie and Snow White.

> *We got hungry about the same time as everyone else,*
> *but the lines for food were too long and my husband said*
> *we would have to wait. By one in the afternoon, we were*
> *just plugging along, not seeing anything we were really*
> *interested in, but picking rides because the lines were*
> *short, or because whatever it was was air-conditioned. We*
> *rode Small World three times in a row and I'll never get*
> *that song out of my head (Ha!). At around 2:30 we finally*
> *got something to eat, but by then we were so hot and tired*
> *that it felt like we had worked in the garden all day.*
> *Kristy insisted on being carried, and we had 50 fights*
> *about not going on rides where the lines were too long. At*
> *the end, we were so P.O.'d and uncomfortable that we*
> *weren't having any fun. Mostly by this time we were just*
> *trying to get our money's worth.*

Before you stiffen in denial, let me assure you that this family's experience is fairly typical. Most small children are as picky about the rides as they are about what they eat, and more than 50% of preschoolers are intimidated by the friendly Disney characters. Few humans (of any age), moreover, are mentally or physically equipped to march all day in a throng of 40,000 people under the summer sun. Finally, would you be surprised to learn that almost 52% of preschoolers said the thing they liked best about their Disneyland Paris vacation was the hotel swimming pool?

REALITY TESTING—WHOSE DREAM IS IT?

Remember when you were little, and you got that nifty electric train for Christmas—the one your Dad wouldn't let you play with, Did you ever wonder who that train was really for? Ask yourself the same question about your vacation to Disneyland Paris. Whose dream are you trying to make come true, yours or your child's?

Small children are very adept at reading their parents' emotions. When you ask, "Honey, how would you like to go to Disneyland Paris?" your child will be responding more to your smile and excitement and the idea of doing something with Mom and Dad, than to any notion of what Disneyland Paris is all about. The younger the child in question, the more this is true. For many preschoolers you could elicit the same enthusiastic response by asking, "Honey, how would you like to go to Cambodia on a dogsled?"

So, is your warm, fuzzy fantasy of introducing your child to the magic of Disney a pipe dream? Not necessarily, but you will have to be practical and open to a little reality testing. For instance, would you increase the probability of a happy, successful visit by holding off a couple of years? Is your child spunky and adventuresome enough to willingly sample the variety of Disneyland Paris? Will your child have sufficient endurance and patience to cope with long waits in line and large crowds?

RECOMMENDATIONS FOR MAKING THE DREAM COME TRUE

When contemplating a Disneyland Paris vacation with small children, anticipation is the name of the game. Here are some of the things you need to consider:

Age   Although the color and festivity of Disneyland Paris excite children of all ages, and though there are specific attractions that delight toddlers and preschoolers, the Disney entertainment mix is generally oriented to older kids and adults. We believe that children should be a fairly mature seven years old to appreciate Disneyland Paris.

Time of Year to Visit   If there is any way you can swing it, avoid the crowded summer months. Try to go in September, October, early November, late April (except Easter), or May. If your kids are preschoolers, don't think about going during the summer. Nothing, repeat nothing, will enhance your Disneyland Paris vacation as much as avoiding summer months and holiday periods.

Building Naps and Rest into Your Itinerary   Disneyland Paris is huge. If your schedule allows, try to spread your visit over at least two days. Tour in the early morning, and return to your hotel around 11:30 a.m. for lunch, a swim, and a nice nap. Even during the off-season, when the crowds are smaller, the sheer size of the park will exhaust most children under age eight by lunchtime. Go back to the park in the late afternoon or early evening, and continue your touring.

Neglecting to relax and unwind is the best way we know to get the whole family in a snit and ruin the day (or the entire vacation). Relief from the frenetic pace of the theme park is indispensable. Although it's true that you can gain some measure of peace by retreating to the Disneyland Hotel for lunch, or by finding a quiet spot or restaurant in the theme park, there is really no substitute for returning to the familiarity and security of your own hotel room.

Where to Stay   The time and hassle involved in commuting to and from Disneyland Paris will be somewhat reduced if you can afford to stay at one of the Disneyland Paris Resort hotels, or at another hotel within easy striking range on the RER line or along the A4 highway. Thousands of rooms are available in and near Disneyland Paris, some of them very affordable. With sufficient lead time you should have no difficulty finding accommodations that fulfill your requirements. But even if, for financial or other reasons, you lodge relatively far away, it remains imperative that you get small children out of the park each day for a few hours to rest and recuperate.

Being in Touch with Your Feelings   We acknowledge that a Disneyland Paris vacation seems like a major capital investment, but remember that having fun is not necessarily the same as seeing everything. When you or your children start getting tired and irritable, call time-out and regroup. Trust your instincts. What would really feel best right now? Another ride, a rest break with some ice cream, going back to the room for a nap? *The way to protect your investment is to stay happy and have a good time, whatever that takes.* You do not have to meet a quota for experiencing a certain number of attractions or watching parades or anything else. It's your holiday; you can do what you want.

Least Common Denominators   Remember the old saying about a chain being only as strong as its weakest link? The same logic applies to a family touring Disneyland Paris. Somebody is going to run out of steam first, and when they do the whole family will be affected. Sometimes a cold soda and a rest break will get the flagging member back into gear. Sometimes, however, as Napoleon said in Russia, "It's time to go home." Pushing the tired or discontented beyond their capacity is like driving on a flat tire: It may get you a few more miles down the road, but you will further damage your car in the process. Accept that energy levels vary among individuals, and be prepared to respond to small children or other members of your group who poop out. (Hint: "After we've driven 300 kilometers to take you to Disneyland Paris, you're going to ruin everything!" is not an appropriate response.)

Setting Limits and Making Plans   The best way to avoid arguments and disappointment is to develop a game plan *before* you go. Establish some general guidelines for the day and get everybody committed in advance. Be sure to include:

1. Wake-up time and breakfast plans.

2. What time you need to depart for the park.

3. What you need to take with you.

4. A policy for splitting the group up or for staying together.

5. A plan for what to do if the group gets separated or someone is lost.

6. How long you intend to tour in the morning, and what you want to see, including fall-back plans in the event an attraction is closed or too crowded.

7. A policy on what you can afford for snacks and refreshments.

8. A target time for returning to the hotel to rest.

9. What time you will return to the park and how late you will stay.

10. Plans for dinner.

11. A policy for shopping and buying souvenirs, including who pays: Mom and Dad or the kids.

Flexibility   Having a game plan does not mean giving up spontaneity or sticking rigidly to the itinerary. Once again, listen to your intuition. Alter the plan if the situation warrants. Any day at Disneyland Paris includes some surprises, so be prepared to roll with the punches.

Overheating, Sunburn, and Dehydration   Even in the temperate climate of France, overheating, sunburn, and dehydration sometimes occur. A small bottle of sunscreen carried in a pocket or fanny pack will help you take precautions against overexposure to the sun. Be sure to put some on children in strollers, even if the stroller has a canopy. Some of the worst cases of sunburn we have seen were on the exposed foreheads and feet of toddlers and infants in strollers. To avoid overheating, rest at regular intervals in the shade or in an air-conditioned restaurant or show.

Do not count on keeping small children properly hydrated with soft drinks and water fountain stops. Long lines often make buying refreshments problematic, and water fountains are not always handy. What's more, excited children may not realize or inform you that they're thirsty or overheated. We recommend renting a stroller for children up to five years old and carrying plastic water bottles with you. If you forget to bring your own water containers, plastic squeeze bottles with caps are sold at the Emporium on Main Street for about FF 23 ($3).

Cold Weather   Families visiting Disneyland Paris from warmer climates should anticipate vastly varying daily temperatures, especially during the fall and spring. Dress children warmly in layers that can be added or removed as needed. Bring along a small daypack or a bag with a shoulder strap to carry clothing not being worn. Be forewarned: If you are forced to buy a sweatshirt, hat, or some other article of apparel at the park in order to stay comfortable, it will cost a mint.

Foot Comfort   Blisters and sore feet are common for visitors of all ages, so wear comfortable, well-broken-in shoes and two pairs of thin socks (preferable to one pair of thick socks). If you or your children are unusually susceptible to blisters, carry some precut "Moleskin" bandages; they offer the best possible protection, stick great, and won't sweat off. When you feel a hot spot, stop, air out your foot, and place a Moleskin bandage over the area before a blister forms. Moleskin is available by name at all pharmacies. Sometimes small children won't tell their parents about a developing blister until it's too late. We recommend inspecting the feet of preschoolers two or more times a day.

First Aid   Registered nurses are on duty at all times in the First Aid Center, located adjacent to the Plaza Gardens Restaurant at the central hub end of Main Street. If you or your children have a medical problem, do not hesitate to use the First Aid Center. It's warmer and friendlier than most doctor's offices and is accustomed to treating everything from paper cuts to allergic reactions.

Children on Medication   For various reasons, some parents of children on medication for hyperactivity elect to discontinue or decrease the child's normal dosage at the close of the school year. Be forewarned that Disneyland Paris might stimulate such a child to the point of system overload. Consult your physician before altering your child's medication regimen.

Sunglasses   If you want your smaller children to wear sunglasses, it's a good idea to affix a strap or string to the frames so the glasses will stay on during rides and can hang from the child's neck while indoors.

Things You Forgot or Things You Ran Out of   Rain gear, diapers, diaper pins, formula, film, aspirin, topical sunburn treatments, and other sundries are available for sale at Disneyland Paris. For some reason, rain gear is a bargain, but the cost of most other items is pretty high. Ask for goods you do not see displayed; some are stored behind the counter.

Strollers   You can rent strollers (push chairs) for a modest fee just inside the main entrance and to the right. The rental covers the entire day. If you rent a stroller and later decide to go back to your hotel for a nap, turn in your stroller, but hang on to your rental receipt. When you return to the park later in the day, present your receipt. You will be issued another stroller without additional charge.

Strollers at Disneyland Paris are small, collapsible models, unfortunately, that will not accommodate most children over the age of five. In fact, the park will not rent you a stroller if your child weighs more than 20 kilograms (44 pounds). The rental procedure is fast and efficient; likewise, returning the stroller is a breeze. Even in the evening when several hundred strollers are turned in following the parade and fireworks show, there is little wait or hassle.

For infants and toddlers the strollers are a must, but we have observed many sharp parents renting strollers for somewhat older children (as long as they will fit in the stroller). The stroller prevents parents from having to carry children when they run out of steam and provides an easy, convenient way to carry water, snacks, diaper bags, and other essentials.

Stroller Wars   Sometimes rental strollers disappear while you are enjoying a ride or a show. Do not be alarmed. You won't have to buy the missing stroller, and you will be issued a new stroller for your continued use. At Disneyland Paris, replacement centers are located at the information kiosks in Adventureland and Fantasyland. Lost strollers can also be replaced at the main rental facility near the park entrance.

While replacing a missing stroller is no big deal, it is an inconvenience. One family complained that their stroller had been taken six times in one day. Even with free replacements, larceny on this scale represents a lot of wasted time. Through our own experiments and suggestions from readers, we have developed several techniques for hanging on to a rented stroller:

1. Write your name in Magic Marker on a six-by-nine-inch card, put the card in a transparent freezer bag, and secure the bag to the stroller with masking or duct tape.

2. Affix something personal (but expendable) to the handle of the stroller. Evidently most strollers are pirated by mistake (since they all look the same) or because it's easier to swipe someone else's stroller (when yours disappears) than to troop off to the replacement center. Because most stroller theft is a function of confusion, laziness, or revenge, the average pram pincher will balk at hauling off a stroller bearing another person's property. After trying several items, we concluded that a bright, inexpensive scarf or bandanna tied to the handle works well. A sock partially stuffed with rags or paper works even better (the weirder and more personal the object, the greater the deterrent). Best of all is a dead mackerel dangling from the handle, though, in truth, the kids who ride in the stroller prefer the other methods.

Baby-Sitting   Child-care services are unavailable in the theme park, but Disneyland Paris Resort hotel guests can avail themselves of in-room baby-sitting.

Care for Infants and Toddlers   The Disneyland Paris theme park has special centralized facilities for the care of infants and toddlers. Everything necessary for changing diapers, preparing formulas, or warming bottles and food, is available in ample quantity. A broad selection of baby supplies is on hand for sale, and there are even rockers and special chairs for nursing mothers. Dads in charge of little ones are welcome at the Baby Care Center and can avail themselves of most services offered. In addition, babies can be changed without inconvenience in most of the larger rest rooms. The Baby Care Center is adjacent to the Plaza Gardens Restaurant at the central-hub end of Main Street. No baby-sitting services are offered.

Disney, Kids, and Scary Stuff

Disneyland Paris is a family theme park. Yet some of the Disney adventure rides can be intimidating to small children. On certain rides, such as the Big Thunder Mountain roller coaster and Star Tours (a spaceflight simulation ride), the ride itself may be frightening. On other rides such as the Phantom Manor and Blanche-Neige et les Sept Nains (Snow White and the Seven Dwarfs), it is the special effects. We recommend a little parent-child dialogue coupled with a "testing the water" approach. A child who is frightened by Les Voyages de Pinocchio should not have to sit through the Phantom Manor. Likewise, if Star Tours is too much, don't try Big Thunder Mountain.

Disney rides and shows are adventures. They focus on the substance and themes of all adventure, and indeed of life itself: good and evil, quest, death, beauty and the grotesque, fellowship and enmity. As you sample the variety of attractions at Disneyland Paris, you transcend the mundane spinning and bouncing of midway rides to a more thought-provoking and emotionally powerful entertainment experience. Though the endings are all happy, the impact of the adventures, with Disney's gift for special effects, is often intimidating and occasionally frightening to small children.

There are rides with menacing witches, rides with burning towns, and rides with ghouls popping out of their graves, all done tongue-in-cheek and with a sense of humor, provided you are old enough to understand the joke. And bones, lots of bones: human bones, cattle bones, dinosaur bones, and whole skeletons everywhere you look. There have got to be more bones at Disneyland Paris than at all the medical schools of Europe combined. There is a skull-shaped rock on Adventure Isle, a veritable platoon of skeletons sailing ghost ships in Pirates of the Caribbean, a haunting assemblage of skulls and skeletons in the Phantom Manor, with more skulls, skeletons, and bones punctuating Blanche-Neige et les Sept Nains (Snow White and the Seven Dwarfs), Peter Pan's Flight, and Big Thunder Mountain, to name a few.

One reader wrote us the following after taking his preschool children on Star Tours:

> *We took a four-year-old and a five-year-old, and they were scared to death at Star Tours. We did this first thing in the morning, and it took hours of [Peter Pan] and It's a Small World to get back to normal.*

> *Our kids were the youngest by far in Star Tours. I assume that either other adults had more sense or were not such avid readers of your book.*
> *Preschoolers should start with Dumbo and work up to Pinocchio in the late morning, after being revved up and before getting hungry, thirsty, or tired. Pirates of the Caribbean is out for preschoolers. You get the idea.*

The reaction of young children to the inevitable system overload of Disneyland Paris should be anticipated. Be sensitive, alert, and prepare for almost anything, even behavior that is out of character for your child at home. Most small children take Disney's variety of macabre trappings in stride, and others are quickly comforted by an arm around the shoulder or a little squeeze of the hand. For parents who have observed a tendency in their kids to become upset, we recommend taking it slow and easy by sampling more benign adventures like Peter Pan's Flight, gauging reactions, and discussing with children how they felt about the things they saw.

Sometimes small children will rise above their anxiety in an effort to please their parents or siblings. This behavior, however, does not necessarily indicate a mastery of fear, much less enjoyment. If children come off a ride in ostensibly good shape, we recommend asking if they would like to go on the ride again (not necessarily right now, but sometime). The response to this question will usually give you a clue as to how much they actually enjoyed the experience. There is a lot of difference between having a good time and mustering the courage to get through something.

Evaluating a child's capacity to handle the visual and tactile effects of Disneyland Paris requires patience, understanding, and experimentation. Each of us, after all, has our own demons. If a child balks at or is frightened by a ride, respond constructively. Let your children know that lots of people, adults as well as children, are scared by what they see and feel. Help them understand that it is okay with you if they get frightened and that their fear does not lessen your love or respect. Take pains not to compound the discomfort by making a child feel inadequate; try not to undermine self-esteem, impugn courage, or subject a child to ridicule. Most of all, do not induce guilt, as if your child's trepidation is ruining the family's fun. When older siblings are present, it is sometimes necessary to restrain their taunting and teasing.

A visit to Disneyland Paris is more than an outing or an adventure for a small child. It is a testing experience, a sort of controlled rite of passage. If you help your little one work through the challenges, the time can be immeasurably rewarding and a bonding experience for both of you.

The Fright Factor

Though each youngster is different, them are essentially six attraction elements which, alone or combined, can punch a child's buttons:

1. The name of the attraction Small children will naturally be apprehensive about something called the "Phantom Manor" or "La Tanière du Dragon" (The Dragon's Den).

2. The visual impact of the attraction from outside Big Thunder Mountain, for example, looks scary enough to give adults second thoughts; to many small children such rides are visually terrifying.

3. The visual impact of the indoor queuing area Pirates of the Caribbean with its dark caves and dungeons and the Phantom Manor with its "stretch rooms" are capable of frightening small children before they even board the ride.

4. The intensity of the attraction Some attractions are so intense as to be overwhelming; they inundate the senses with sights, sounds, movement, and even smell. *Honey, I Shrunk the Audience,* for instance, combines loud sounds, lasers, lights, and 3D cinematography to create a total sensory experience. For some preschoolers, this is two or three senses too many.

5. The visual impact of the attraction itself As previously discussed, the sights in various attractions range from falling boulders to lurking buzzards, from burning timbers to exploding kegs of dynamite. What one child absorbs calmly may scare the owl poop out of another child the same age.

6. The ride itself; the tactile experience Some Disney rides, such as Star Tours, are downright wild; wild enough to induce motion sickness, wrench backs, and generally discombobulate patrons of any age.

SMALL CHILD FRIGHT POTENTIAL CHART

As a quick reference, we have provided a "Fright Potential Chart" to warn you which attractions to be wary of, and why. Remember that the chart represents a generalization and that all kids are different. The chart relates specifically to kids 3–7 years of age. On average, as you would expect, children at the younger end of the age range are more likely to be frightened than children in their sixth or seventh year.

Main Street U.S.A.
Disneyland Railroad: Not frightening in any respect.
Horse-Drawn Streetcar: Not frightening in any respect.
Main Street Vehicles: Not frightening in any respect.
Discovery and Liberty Arcades: Not frightening in any respect.

Adventureland
La Cabane des Robinson: Not frightening in any respect.
Adventure Isle: Moderately intense; a good test attraction for little ones. Take care not to get separated; it's an easy place for children to get lost.
Pirates of the Caribbean: Slightly intimidating queuing area; an intense boat ride with gruesome (though humorously presented) sights and two short, unexpected slides down chutes.
Indiana Jones and the Temple of Peril: This thrill ride loops upside down and is certain to terrify most children under age nine.

Frontierland
Big Thunder Mountain: Visually intimidating from the ou side with moderately intense visual effects. The roller coaster is wild enough to frighten many adults, particularly senior citizens. Switching-off option provided (see page 114).
Phantom Manor: Name of attraction raises anxiety, as do sights and sounds of waiting area. An intense attraction with humorously presented macabre sights. The ride itself is gentle.

Frontierland (continued)

Indian Canoes: Not frightening in any respect.

River Rogue Keelboats: Not frightening in any respect.

Thunder Mesa Riverboat Landing: Not frightening in any respect.

Critter Corral: Not frightening for children who are at ease with live animals.

Rustler Roundup Shootin' Gallery: Not frightening in any respect.

Disneyland Railroad: Not frightening in any respect.

Fantasyland

Le Château de la Belle au Bois Dormant/La Tanière du Dragon: The dragon scares a majority of preschoolers; prepare young children before entering.

Mad Hatter's Tea Cups: Midway-type ride can induce motion sickness in all ages.

Blanche-Neige et les Sept Nains: Moderately intense spook-house genre attraction with some grim characters; not much of a threat to kids over age six.

Dumbo the Flying Elephant: A tame midway ride; a great favorite of most small children.

Le Carrousel de Lancelot: Not frightening in any respect.

It's a Small World: Not frightening in any respect.

Peter Pan's Flight: Not frightening in any respect.

Alice's Curious Labyrinth: Pretty benign, but frightens a small percentage of preschoolers.

Les Voyages de Pinocchio: Less frightening than Blanche-Neige et les Sept Nains but scares a few very young preschoolers. The sudden appearance of a whale frightens many small children.

Fantasy Festival Stage: Not frightening in any respect.

Disneyland Railroad: Not frightening in any respect.

Le Pays des Contes de Fées: Not frightening in any respect.

Casey Jr.—Le Petit Train du Cirque: Cagelike cars frighten some preschoolers.

Les Pirouettes du Vieux: A small Ferris wheel that occasionally frightens very young children.

Discoveryland

Star Tours: Extremely intense visually for all ages; the ride itself is one of the wildest in Disney's repertoire. Switching-off option provided (see page 114).

Orbitron-Machines Volantes: Waiting area is visually intimidating to preschoolers. The ride is actually tame.

Le Visionarium: Not frightening in any respect, but audience must stand.

Videopolis: Not frightening in any respect.

Honey, I Shrunk the Audience: Intense visual and tactile effects can frighten guests of any age. Not a good bet for children under age nine.

Space Mountain: An exceedingly wild roller coaster in the dark that frightens guests of all ages.

Les Mystères du Nautilus: A tame walk-through attraction that frightens some preschoolers.

Autopia: The noise in the waiting area slightly intimidates preschoolers; otherwise, not frightening.

ATTRACTIONS THAT EAT ADULTS

You may spend so much energy worrying about Junior's welfare that you forget to take care of yourself. If the ride component of the attraction (that is, the actual motion and movement of the conveyance itself) is potentially disturbing, persons of any age may be adversely affected. The attractions most likely to cause motion sickness or other problems for older children and adults are:

Adventureland	Indiana Jones and the Temple of Peril
Discoveryland	Star Tours
	Space Mountain
Fantasyland	Mad Hatter's Tea Cups
Frontierland	Big Thunder Mountain

Waiting Line Strategies for Adults with Small Children

Children hold up better through the day if you minimize the time they have to spend in lines. Arriving early and using the

Touring Plans in this guide will reduce waiting time immensely. Here are some additional measures you can employ to reduce stress on little ones.

1. Line Games It is a smart parent who anticipates how restless children get waiting in line and how a little structured activity can relieve the stress and boredom. In the morning kids handle the inactivity of waiting in line by discussing what they want to see and do during the course of the day. Later, however, as events wear on, they need a little help. Watching for and counting Disney characters is a good diversion. Simple guessing games like "20 Questions" also work well. Lines for rides move so continuously that games requiring pen and paper are cumbersome and impractical. Waiting in the holding area of a theater attraction though, is a different story. Here tic-tac-toe, hangman, drawing, and coloring can really make the time go by.

2. Last-Minute Entry If a ride or show can accommodate an unusually large number of people at one time, it is often unnecessary to stand in line. The Mark Twain Riverboat in Frontierland is a good example. The boat holds about 400 people, usually more than that are waiting in line to ride. Instead of standing uncomfortably in a crowd with dozens of other guests, grab a snack and sit in the shade until the boat arrives and loading is well under way. After the line has all but disappeared, go ahead and board.

At large-capacity theaters like *Le Visionarium* in Discoveryland, ask the entrance greeter how long it will be until guests are admitted to the theater for the next show. If the answer is 15 minutes or more, use the time for a rest room break or to get a snack; you can return to the attraction just a few minutes before the show starts. You will not be permitted to carry any food or drink into the attraction, so make sure you have time to finish your snack before entering. The following is a list of attractions that you can sometimes enter at the last minute:

Frontierland	Thunder Mesa Riverboat
Discoveryland	*Honey, I Shrunk the Audience*
	Le Visionarium
	Videopolis

3. The Hail-Mary Pass Certain waiting lines are configured in such a way that you and your smaller children can pass under the rail to join your partner just before boarding or entry. This technique allows the kids and one adult to rest, snack, cool off, or tinkle, while another adult or older sibling does the waiting. Other guests are understanding when it comes to using this strategy to keep small children content. You are likely to meet hostile opposition, however, if you try to pass older children or more than one adult under the rail. Attractions where it is usually possible to complete a Hail-Mary Pass include:

Fantasyland	Mad Hatter's Tea Cups
	Les Voyages de Pinocchio
	Dumbo the Flying Elephant
	Le Carrousel de Lancelot
	Peter Pan's Flight
Discoveryland	Orbitron

4. Switching Off (also known as The Baby Swap)   Several attractions have minimum height and/or age requirements, usually 102 centimeters (3'4") tall to ride with an adult, or seven years of age and 102 centimeters tall to ride alone. Some couples with children too small or too young forgo these attractions, while others split up and take turns riding separately. Missing out on some of Disney's best rides is an unnecessary sacrifice and waiting in line twice for the same ride is a tremendous waste of time.

A better way to approach the problem is to take advantage of an option known as "switching off" or "The Baby Swap." To switch off there must be at least two adults. Everybody waits in line together, both adults and children. When you reach a Disney attendant (known as a "greeter"), say you want to switch off. The greeter will allow everyone, including the small children, to enter the attraction. When you reach the loading area, one adult will ride while the other stays with the kids. The riding adult disembarks and takes responsibility for the children while the other adult rides. A third adult in the party can ride twice, once with each of the switching-off adults, so they do not have to experience the attraction alone.

Switching off is routinely practiced at Big Thunder Mountain in Frontierland, Star Tours and Space Mountain in Discoveryland, and at Indiana Jones and the Temple of Peril in Adventureland.

5. How to Ride Twice in a Row without Waiting   Many small children like to ride a favorite attraction two or more times in succession. Riding the second time often gives the child a feeling of mastering an accomplishment. Unfortunately, repeat rides can be time consuming, even in the early morning. If you ride Dumbo, for instance, as soon as Disneyland Paris opens, you will only have to wait a minute or two for your first ride, but when you come back for your second ride, your wait will be about 12 minutes. If you want to ride a third time, count on a 20-minute or longer wait.

The best way of getting your child on the ride twice (or more) without blowing your whole morning is by using the "Chuck Bubba Relay" (named in honor of a reader from Kentucky):

a. Mom and little Bubba enter the waiting line;

b. Dad lets a certain number of people go in front of him (34 in the case of Dumbo) and then gets in line;

c. As soon as the ride stops, Mom exits with little Bubba and passes him to Dad to ride the second time;

d. If everybody is really getting into this, Mom can hop in line again, no less than 34 people behind Dad.

The Chuck Bubba Relay will not work on every ride, because of differences in the way the waiting areas are configured (in other words, it is impossible in some cases to exit the ride and make the pass). For those rides where the Bubba Relay does work, however, here are the number of people to count off:

Mad Hatter's Tea Cups: 36 people

Dumbo the Flying Elephant: 34 people

Le Carrousel de Lancelot: 70 people

Peter Pan's Flight: 58 people

Orbitron: 26 people

Indian Canoe: 104 people, if 6 canoes are operating;
    64 people if 4 canoes are operating

If you are the second adult in line, you will reach a point in the waiting area that is obviously the easiest place to make the hand-off. Sometimes this point is where those exiting the ride pass closest to those waiting to board. In any event, you will know it when you see it. Once there, if the first parent has not arrived with little Bubba, just let those behind you slip past until they show up.

6. Last-Minute Cold Feet   If your small child gets cold feet at the last minute after waiting for a ride (where there is no age or height requirement), you can usually arrange with the loading attendant for a switch off. This situation arises frequently at Pirates of the Caribbean—small children lose their courage en route to the loading area.

There is no law that says you have to ride. If you get to the boarding area and someone is unhappy, just tell a Disney attendant you have changed your mind, and he or she will show you the way out.

7. Elevator Shoes for the Short and Brave   If you have a child who is crazy to go on the rides with height requirements, but who is just a little too short, slip heel lifts into his Nikes before he gets to the measuring point. Be sure to leave the heel lifts in, because he may get measured again at the boarding area.

8. Catch-22 at the Discoveryland Autopia   Though Autopia is a great treat for small children, they are required to be 132 cm (4'4") tall in order to drive. Since very few children six and under top this height, the ride is essentially withheld from the very age group that would most enjoy it. To resolve this Catch-22, go on the ride with your small child. The attendants will assume that you will drive. After getting into the car, however, shift your child over behind the steering wheel. From your position you will still be able to control the foot pedals, but your child will feel like he or she is driving. The car travels on a self-guiding track, incidentally, so there is no way your child can make a mistake while steering.

Lost Children

Lost children normally do not present much of a problem at Disneyland Paris. All Disneyland Paris employees are schooled in handling such situations. If you lose a child while touring, report the situation to a Disney employee, then check at Lost Children, in the Baby Care Center, as well as at City Hall, where lost children "logs" are maintained. There is no paging at Disneyland Paris, but in an emergency an "all points bulletin" can be issued throughout the park through internal communications.

Lost children under the age of seven are pretty easy to spot. More often than not, they will be standing right in the middle of a pedestrian thoroughfare sniffling or screaming. When detected by a Disney cast member, they are gently escorted to the Lost Children facility. Here, a multilingual attendant endeavors to ascertain their name, their parents' names, and other relevant information. This intelligence is communicated to City Hall where it is placed in a logbook. Children delivered to the Lost Children center are attended there until their parents come to claim them.

It is amazingly easy to lose a child (or two) at Disneyland Paris. We suggest that children under eight be color-coded by dressing them in purple T-shirts or equally distinctive attire. It is also a good idea to sew a label into each child's shirt that states his or her name, your name, and the name of your hotel. The same thing can be accomplished less elegantly by writing the information on a strip of masking tape. Hotel security professionals suggest that the information be printed in small letters, and that the tape be affixed to the outside of the child's shirt five inches or so below the armpit.

How Kids Get Lost

Children get separated from their parents every day at Disneyland Paris under circumstances that are remarkably similar (and predictable).

1. Preoccupied Solo Parent   In this scenario the only adult in the party is preoccupied with something like shopping, buying refreshments, loading the camera, or using the rest room. Junior is there one second and gone the next.

2. Hidden Exit   Sometimes parents wait on the sidelines while allowing two or more young children to experience a ride together. As it usually happens, the parents expect the kids to exit the attraction in one place, and, lo and behold, the young ones pop out somewhere else. The exits of some Disney attractions are considerably distant from the entrances. Make sure you know exactly where your children will emerge before letting them ride by themselves.

3. After the Show   At the completion of many shows and rides, a Disney staffer will announce, "Check for personal belongings, and take small children by the hand." When dozens, if not hundreds, of people leave an attraction at the same time, it is easy for parents to temporarily lose contact with their children unless they have them directly in tow.

4. Rest Room Problems   Mom tells six-year-old Tommy, "I'll be sitting on this bench when you come out of the rest room." Three situations: One, Tommy exits through a different door and becomes disoriented (Mom may not know there is another door). Two, Mom decides belatedly that she will also use the rest room, and Tommy emerges to find her absent. Three, Mom pokes around in a shop while keeping an eye on the bench, but misses Tommy when he comes out.

If you cannot be with your child in the rest room, make sure there is only one exit. Designate a meeting spot more distinctive than a bench, and be specific and thorough in your instructions: "I'll meet you by this flagpole. If you get out first, stay right here." Have your child repeat the directions to you.

5. Shopping Arcades   Almost all of the retail shops and restaurants have multiple entrances and exits. If you dawdle over a trinket too long and Johnny becomes bored, he may slip into an adjacent shop. Once separated, you have about a 30% chance in most stores of exiting through the same door as did the child. If you exit through a different door, of course, the problem is quickly compounded. Children small enough to be hidden from view by a counter or display do not even need to exit the shop to get lost. Either keep your children close while you shop or sit them down someplace (preferably with something to munch on) where you know they will stay put. Children do not have much patience with shopping, even at Disneyland Paris, so don't push your luck.

6. Parades   There are many special parades and shows at the theme park during which the audience stands. Children naturally tend to jockey around for a better view. By moving a little this way and a little that way, it is amazing how much distance kids can put between you and them before anyone notices.

7. Mass Movements   Another situation to guard against occurs when huge crowds disperse after fireworks, a parade, or at park closing. With 20,000–40,000 people suddenly moving at once, it is very easy to get separated from a small child or others in your party. Extra caution is recommended following the evening parades and fireworks. Families should develop specific plans for what to do and where to meet in the event they are separated.

8. Character Greetings   A fair amount of activity and confusion is commonplace when the Disney characters are on the scene. See the section on meeting the Disney characters (pages 120–121).

The Disney Characters

For many years the costumed, walking versions of Mickey, Minnie, Donald, Goofy, and others have been a colorful supporting cast at Disney developments. Known unpretentiously as the "Disney characters," these large and friendly figures help provide a link between Disney animated films and the Disney theme parks.

Audiences cry during the sad parts of Disney animated films and cheer when the villain is vanquished. To the emotionally invested, the characters in these features are as real as next-door neighbors, never mind that they are drawings on plastic. In recent years, the theme park personifications of Disney characters have likewise become real to us. For thousands of visitors, it is not just some person in a mouse costume they see, it is really Mickey. Similarly, running into Goofy or Snow White in Fantasyland is a memory to be treasured, an encounter with a real celebrity.

About 300 of the Disney animated film characters have been brought to life in costume. Of these, a relatively small number (about 45) are "greeters" (the Disney term for characters who mix with the patrons). The remaining characters are relegated exclusively to performing in shows or participating in parades. Some appear only once or twice a year, usually in Christmas parades or Disney anniversary celebrations.

Character Watching   Character watching has developed into a pastime. Where families were once content to stumble across a character occasionally, they now relentlessly pursue them, armed with autograph books and cameras. For those who pay attention, some characters are much more frequently encountered than others. Mickey, Minnie, and Goofy, for example, are seemingly everywhere, while Winnie the Pooh comes out only on rare occasions. Other characters can be seen regularly, but limit themselves to a specific location.

The fact that some characters are seldom seen has turned character watching into character collecting. Mickey Mouse may be the best known and most loved character, but from a collector's perspective he is also the most common. To get an autograph from Mickey is no big deal, but Daisy Duck's signature is a real coup. Commercially tapping into the character collecting movement, Disney sells autograph books throughout Disneyland Paris.

Preparing Your Children to Meet the Characters   Since most small children are not expecting Minnie Mouse to be the size of a forklift, it's best to discuss the characters with your kids before you go. Almost all of the characters are quite large, and several, like Brer

Bear, are huge! All of them can be extremely intimidating to a preschooler.

On first encounter, it is important not to thrust your child on the character. Allow the little one to come to terms with this big thing from whatever distance the child feels safe. If there are two adults present, one should stay close to the youngster while the other approaches the character and demonstrates that the character is safe and friendly. Some kids warm to the characters immediately, but some never do. Most take a little time and often need several different encounters.

The characters do not talk or make noises of any kind. Because the cast members could not possibly imitate the distinctive cinema voice of the character, the Disney folks have determined it is more effective to keep them silent. Lack of speech notwithstanding, the characters are extremely warm and responsive and communicate very effectively with gestures. As with the character's size, children need to be forewarned that the characters do not talk.

Parents need to understand that some of the character costumes are very cumbersome and that cast members often suffer from very poor visibility. You have to look close, but the eye holes are frequently in the mouth of the costume or even down on the neck. What this means in practical terms is that the characters are sort of clumsy and have a limited field of vision. Children who approach the character from the back or the side may not be noticed, even if the child is touching the character. It is perfectly possible in this situation for the character to accidentally step on the child or knock him down. The best way for a child to approach a character is from the front, and occasionally not even this works. For example, Donald, Daisy, and the various other duck characters have to peer around their bills. If it appears that the character is ignoring your child, pick your child up and hold her in front of the character until the character responds.

It is okay to touch, pat, or hug the character if your child is so inclined. Understanding the unpredictability of children, the characters will keep their feet still, particularly refraining from moving backward or to the side. Most of the characters will sign autographs or pose for pictures. Once again, be sure to approach from the front, so that the character will understand your intentions.

"Then Some Confusion Happened"   Be forewarned that character encounters give rise to a situation in which small children sometimes get lost. There is usually a lot of activity around a character, with both adults and children touching it or posing for pictures. In the most common scenario, the parents stay in the crowd while their child marches up to get acquainted. With the excitement of the encounter, all the milling people, and the character moving around, a child may get turned around and head off in the wrong direction. In the words of one mother: "Milo was shaking hands with Dopey one minute, then some confusion happened, and he [Milo] was gone." Families with several small children and parents who are busy fooling around with cameras can lose track of a youngster in a heartbeat. Our recommendation for parents of preschoolers is to stay with the kids when meeting the characters, stepping back only long enough to take a picture if necessary.

Meeting Characters   You can *see* the Disney characters in live shows and in parades. For times consult your daily entertainment schedule. If you have the time and money, you can share a meal with the characters (more about this later). But if you want to *meet* the characters, get autographs, and take photos, it's helpful to know where they hang out.

There will almost always be a character next to City Hall on Main Street and usually one or more in Town Square or around the railroad station. Characters make appearances in all the "lands" but are particularly thick in Fantasyland by the castle. Also look for characters around the central hub and at Videopolis in Discoveryland. The Disneyland Paris handout park map lists times and locations for meeting characters but does not specify which characters will be present.

Characters are featured in the afternoon and evening parades, shows at Le Théâtre du Château amphitheater (to the right front of the castle), and shows on the Fantasy Festival Stage near the Fantasyland train station. Characters sometimes also appear in productions on the Videopolis stage in Discoveryland. Performance times for all of the shows and parades are listed in the Disneyland Paris daily entertainment schedule (on the back of the park handout map). Characters will sometimes stick around to greet the audience after the shows.

Character Dining

Character dining is a phenomenon that began in the American Disney parks, where the food is so bad that guests had to be lured into the restaurants with other enticements. Following a bit of experimentation, some bright marketing person hit on the idea of the guests dining with the Disney characters. The characters, who of course do not really eat—or talk—mainly mix with the guests and pose for photographs.

Aside from being a strategy for charging a grand price for a *petit déjeuner,* the character meals provide a familiar, controlled setting in which small children can warm to the characters in a relaxed, unhurried way. Characters featured at the meals usually include some combination of Mickey, Minnie, Goofy, Pluto, and Chip 'n' Dale.

Character breakfasts are offered at Inventions Restaurant in the Disneyland Hotel, Manhattan Restaurant in Hotel New York, and Crockett's Tavern at Davy Crockett Ranch. These breakfasts are sold as extras on Disneyland Paris packages. They are hard to get into on the spur of the moment, but seats are sometimes available through the concierge at your Disney hotel. In the park, a character lunch is served from noon to 3:30 p.m., and a Tea Party is held from 4 to 5 p.m. at the Lucky Nugget Saloon. Make reservations before you arrive or at City Hall on the day you visit. Sometimes you can get a table by just walking in.

Character Dining: What to Expect   Character meals are bustling affairs, held in hotels' or the theme park's largest full-service restaurants. Character breakfasts offer a fixed menu served family style or a buffet. The typical family-style breakfast includes scrambled eggs; bacon, sausage, and ham; hash browns; waffles or French toast; biscuits, rolls, or pastries; and fruit. The meal is served in large skillets or platters at your table. If you run out of something, you can order seconds (or thirds) at no additional charge. Buffets offer much the same fare, but you have to fetch it yourself.

Character lunches and dinners range from a set menu served family or buffet style. At all meals, characters circulate around the room while you eat. During your meal, each of the three to five characters present will visit your table, arriving one at a time to cuddle the kids (and sometimes the adults), pose for photos, and sign autographs. Keep autograph books (with pens) and loaded cameras handy. For the best photos, adults should sit across the table from their children. Always seat the children where characters can reach them most easily. If a table is against a wall, for example, adults should sit with their backs to the wall and children on the aisle.

Part Four

Disneyland Paris in Detail

Arriving and Getting Oriented

If you arrive at Disneyland Paris by train, take the escalator up to ground level and follow signs to the theme park. If you arrive by bus, you will disembark next to the train station. Once again, follow the signs to the theme park.

If you drive, Disney parking attendants will direct you to an assigned parking space. Parking costs FF 45 ($6). Since the parking lot is about the size of Liechtenstein, it is a good idea to write down the number of the row in which you parked (having to canvas the parking lot looking for your car after an exhausting day in the theme park is absolutely maddening). Next, proceed to the canopied area in the center of the parking lot. Here you will find a "moving walkway" (a conveyor belt for pedestrians), which will

Not to Be Missed at Disneyland Paris	
Frontierland	Phantom Manor
	Big Thunder Mountain
Adventureland	Pirates of the Caribbean
Fantasyland	Peter Pan's Flight
Discoveryland	Star Tours
	Honey, I Shrunk the Audience
	Le Visionarium
	Space Mountain

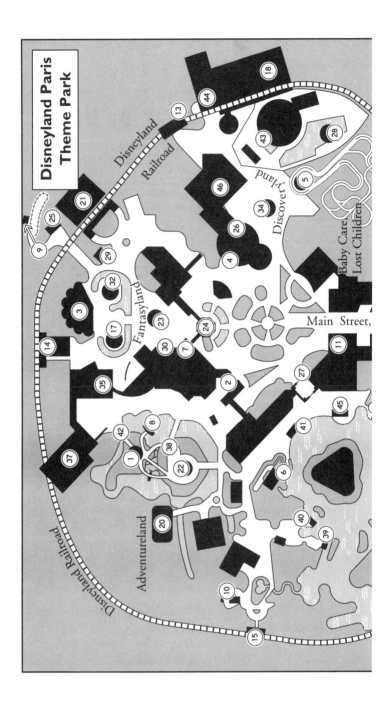

Disneyland Paris
Theme Park

Disneyland Railroad

Disneyland Railroad

Fantasyland

Discoveryland

Adventureland

Main Street,

Baby Care,
Lost Children

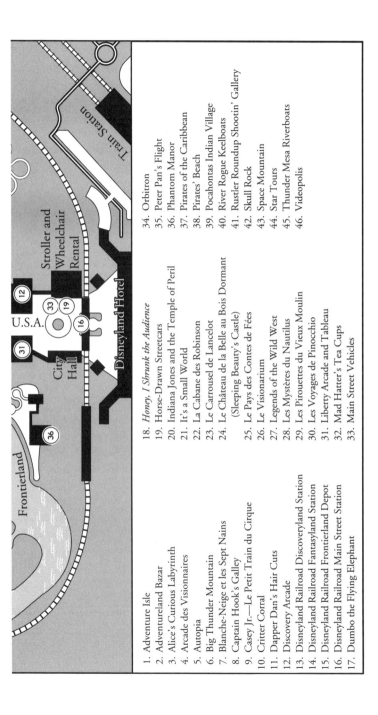

1. Adventure Isle
2. Adventureland Bazar
3. Alice's Curious Labyrinth
4. Arcade des Visionnaires
5. Autopia
6. Big Thunder Mountain
7. Blanche-Neige et les Sept Nains
8. Captain Hook's Galley
9. Casey Jr.—Le Petit Train du Cirque
10. Critter Corral
11. Dapper Dan's Hair Cuts
12. Discovery Arcade
13. Disneyland Railroad Discoveryland Station
14. Disneyland Railroad Fantasyland Station
15. Disneyland Railroad Frontierland Depot
16. Disneyland Railroad Main Street Station
17. Dumbo the Flying Elephant
18. *Honey, I Shrunk the Audience*
19. Horse-Drawn Streetcars
20. Indiana Jones and the Temple of Peril
21. It's a Small World
22. La Cabane des Robinson
23. Le Carrousel de Lancelot
24. Le Château de la Belle au Bois Dormant
    (Sleeping Beauty's Castle)
25. Le Pays des Contes de Fées
26. Le Visionarium
27. Legends of the Wild West
28. Les Mystères du Nautilus
29. Les Pirouettes du Vieux Moulin
30. Les Voyages de Pinocchio
31. Liberty Arcade and Tableau
32. Mad Hatter's Tea Cups
33. Main Street Vehicles
34. Orbitron
35. Peter Pan's Flight
36. Phantom Manor
37. Pirates of the Caribbean
38. Pirates' Beach
39. Pocahontas Indian Village
40. River Rogue Keelboats
41. Rustler Roundup Shootin' Gallery
42. Skull Rock
43. Space Mountain
44. Star Tours
45. Thunder Mesa Riverboats
46. Videopolis

transport you to stairs leading to the entrance plaza. From here follow signs to the theme park. Depending on where in the lot your assigned space is located, it will take 8–13 minutes to get to the theme park admission turnstiles.

Admission ticket booths are located on the ground level directly beneath the Disneyland Hotel. Currency exchange booths are also located here. On the very far right you will find the Guest Services and Group Sales offices.

After purchasing your admission, the entrance to the theme park is straight ahead. Having passed through the turnstiles, coin-operated storage lockers are available on the ground floor of the elevated train station. On the far side of the train station is Town Square. Wheelchair and stroller (push chair) rentals are to your right at Town Square Terrace. To your left are rest rooms and City Hall. City Hall serves as the primary guest information and services center for the theme park. Information specialists on duty are multilingual and assist guests with special needs from the routine to the extraordinary. Lost and found is also located at City Hall.

If you haven't already been given an official Disneyland Paris "Guest Guide," City Hall is the place to pick one up. The guide contains maps and the daily schedule for live entertainment; gives tips for good photos; lists all the attractions, shops, and eating places; and provides helpful information that covers first aid, baby care, and assistance for the disabled.

Notice on your map that Main Street ends at a central hub, from which four other sections of Disneyland Paris begin: (moving clockwise) Frontierland, Adventureland, Fantasyland, and Discoveryland. Le Château de la Belle au Bois Dormant (Sleeping Beauty's Castle) serves as the entrance to Fantasyland and is a focal point and the visual center of the park. The castle is a great place to meet if your group decides to split up for any reason during the day, and it can serve as an emergency meeting place if you are accidentally separated. If you use the castle as a meeting place, however, bear in mind that it is a pretty big place. Specify a particular spot at the castle, for example, the wishing well by the moat.

Starting the Tour

Everyone will soon find his or her own favorite and not-so-favorite attractions in Disneyland Paris. Be open-minded and adventuresome. Do not dismiss a particular ride or show as being not for you until *after* you have tried it. Our personal experience as well as our research indicates that visitors are different in terms of which Disney offerings they most enjoy. So do not miss seeing an attraction because a friend from home did not like it; that attraction could turn out to be your favorite.

We do recommend that you take advantage of what Disney does best: the fantasy adventures like Star Tours and Peter Pan's Flight and the audio-animatronic attractions (talking robots, so to speak), such as the Pirates of the Caribbean and *Le Visionarium*. Try to minimize the time you spend on carnival-type rides; you have probably got an amusement park, carnival, or local fair closer to your hometown. Do not, however, mistake rides like Big Thunder Mountain for amusement park rides. Although they are of the roller coaster genre, they represent pure Disney genius. Unless you have almost unlimited time, do not burn a lot of daylight browsing through the shops. Except for some special Disney souvenirs, you can find most of the same merchandise elsewhere. Similarly, do not devote a lot of time to waiting in line for meals. Eat a good early breakfast before you arrive, snack on vendor-sold foods during the touring day, or follow the suggestions for meals incorporated into the various touring plans presented.

Main Street, U.S.A.

This section of Disneyland Paris is where you will begin and end your visit. We have already mentioned that assistance and information are available at City Hall. The Disneyland Paris Railroad stops at the Main Street Station, and you can board here for a grand circle tour of the park, or you can get off the train in Frontierland or Fantasyland.

Main Street is a replication of a turn-of-the-century American small-town street. Many visitors are surprised to discover that all the buildings are real, not just elaborate props. Attention to detail here is exceptional: interiors, furnishings, and fixtures conform to the period. As with any real Main Street, the Disney version is essentially a collection of shops and eating places, with a City Hall and a Fire Station.

Attractions in Main Street, U.S.A., include the Statue of Liberty Tableau, a modest mixed-media exhibit that chronicles France's gift of the Statue of Liberty to the United States, and an antique car showroom. Finally, horse-drawn trolleys, fire engines, and horseless carriages offer rides along Main Street and transport visitors to the central hub (properly known as the Central Plaza).

Running parallel to Main Street are two enclosed, heated arcades: the Discovery Arcade on the right, and the Liberty Arcade on the left. Though the arcades contain exhibits on the many revolutionary inventions and developments of the late nineteenth and early twentieth centuries, their primary purpose is to provide sheltered access to the shops and restaurants of Main Street during cold or inclement weather.

Main Street Services

Most of the park's service facilities are centered in Main Street, including the following:

Wheelchair and Stroller Rental	To the right of the main entrance after passing under the railroad station
Banking Services	BNP automatic teller machines are located in each of the two arcades
Currency Exchange	At City Hall
Storage Lockers	On ground level of train station and at guest storage outside the park entrance
Lost & Found	At City Hall
Live Entertainment & Parade Information	At City Hall
Lost Persons	At City Hall
Disneyland Paris & Local Attraction Information	At City Hall
First Aid	At the central hub end of Main Street adjacent to the Plaza Gardens Restaurant (phone: 64-74-23-00)
Baby Care Center/ Baby Care Needs	At the central hub end of Main Street adjacent to the Plaza Gardens Restaurant

Main Street Attractions
Disneyland Railroad

Type of Attraction: Scenic railroad ride around the perimeter of Disneyland Paris; also transportation to Frontierland and Fantasyland

When to Go: After 4 p.m. or when you need transportation

Special Comments: The Frontierland station is usually the least congested boarding point

Overall Appeal by Age Group:

Pre-school	Grade School	Teens	Young Adults	Over 30	Senior Citizens
★★★★	★★★★	★★★	★★★	★★★★	★★★★

Author's Rating: ★★½ [Critical ratings are based on a scale of 0 to 5 stars; 5 stars is the best possible rating.]

Duration of Ride: About 22 minutes for a complete circuit

Average Wait in Line per 100 People Ahead of You: 8 minutes

Assumes: 3 trains operating

Loading Speed: Moderate

Description and Comments   This transportation ride blends a glimpse of all the lands and provides an energy-saving way of getting around the park. Passenger cars on the train are covered and partially enclosed to protect guests from inclement weather.

Touring Tips   In comparison with other Disneyland Paris attractions, the train is not a big deal. Almost everything that you can see from the train can also be seen while walking or while enjoying other attractions. In the American and Japanese parks, the train is regarded primarily as a transportation option rather than a bona fide attraction. In Disneyland Paris, however, the train is unbelievably popular. In fact, it is one of the attractions that is most difficult to experience without suffering a long wait. Our opinion is that a ride on the Disneyland Paris Railroad is not worth the sacrifice of much time or energy. If you love trains and are bound and determined to ride, however, try the Disneyland Paris Railroad late in the afternoon. Be sure to board at the less congested Frontierland station, located on the far side of Cottonwood Creek Ranch.

The Statue of Liberty Tableau

Type of Attraction: Nostalgic rendition of how France gave the United States the Statue of Liberty

When to Go: During the crowded period of the day

Overall Appeal by Age Group:

Pre-school	Grade School	Teens	Young Adults	Over 30	Senior Citizens
½	½	½	½	★	★½

Author's Rating: Dull; ★

Duration of Presentation: Operates continuously

Preshow Entertainment: None

Probable Waiting Time: Usually no wait

Description and Comments   A small walk-in exhibit that combines a diorama depicting the Statue of Liberty in New York Harbor with a narration detailing France's gift of the statue to the Americans. The continuously running, recorded narration and dramatic dialogue are primarily in French. The viewing area is able to hold only ten or so standing guests at a time, but it is rarely occupied, much less full.

Touring Tips   Liberty Court and the Statue of Liberty Tableau resemble an elaborate department store window display. Whenever we dropped in, the attraction was babbling away to an empty room. Check out the tableau while you are waiting for your companion(s) to come out of the nearby rest rooms.

Main Street Vehicles

Type of Attraction: Small exhibit of antique cars

When to Go: Whenever you want

Overall Appeal by Age Group:

Pre-school	Grade School	Teens	Young Adults	Over 30	Senior Citizens
★	★	★	★	★½	★★

Author's Rating: Adds a touch of realism to Main Street; ★

Duration of Presentation: Operates continuously

Preshow Entertainment: None

Probable Waiting Time: No waiting

Description and Comments   The walk-in exhibit consists of several well-preserved antique automobiles from the early twentieth century. By the way, the cars are actually for sale.

Touring Tips   A good place to get out of the sun or rain, or to kill time while others in your group shop on Main Street. It's fun, but not something you cannot afford to miss.

Transportation Rides

Description and Comments   Trolleys, buses, etc., which add color to Main Street.

Touring Tips   Will save you a walk to the central hub, but not worth a wait in line.

Main Street Eateries and Shops

Description and Comments   Snacks, food, and specialty/souvenir shopping in a nostalgic, happy setting. The Emporium on Main Street offers the park's largest selection of Disney trademark souvenirs.

Touring Tips   The shops are fun, but the merchandise can be had elsewhere (except for certain Disney trademark souvenirs). If seeing the park attractions is your objective, save the Main Street eateries and shops until the end of the day. If shopping is your objective, you will find the shops most crowded during the noon hour and near closing time. Remember, Main Street opens at least a half hour earlier, and closes a half hour to an hour later, than the rest of Disneyland Paris.

Frontierland

Frontierland is the first land to the left of Main Street and is reached via the central hub or an enclosed pedestrian walkway adjoining the Liberty Arcade. The theme in Frontierland is the American West of the late 1800s, with its cowboys, fur trappers, gold miners, Native American Indians, dance hall girls, and traders. The entrance to Frontierland is a log stockade, which opens to a Western trail town and a Southwestern adobe village, both spread along the "Rivers of the Far West" waterfront.

Big Thunder Mountain

Type of Attraction: Roller coaster with exciting special effects

When to Go: Before 9:30 a.m. and after 6:30 p.m.

Special Comments: Children must be 102 cm (3'4") tall and 3
   years old to ride (see "Switching Off" on page 114); those
   under 7 must ride with an adult

Overall Appeal by Age Group:

Pre-school	Grade School	Teens	Young Adults	Over 30	Senior Citizens
★★★	★★★★½	★★★★½	★★★★	★★★★	★★★

Author's Rating: Great effects though a relatively tame ride;
★★★★

Duration of Ride: 3½ minutes

Average Wait in Line per 100 People Ahead of You: 4 minutes

Assumes: 5 trains operating

Loading Speed: Moderate to fast

Description and Comments   A roller-coaster ride through and around a Disney "mountain." The time is gold rush days in the American West, and the idea is that you are on a runaway mine train. Along with the usual thrills of a roller-coaster ride (about a five on a "scary scale" of ten), the ride showcases some first-rate examples of Disney creativity: lifelike scenes depicting a mining town, falling rocks, an earthquake, and dynamite explosions, all animated humorously.

Touring Tips   A superb Disney experience, but not too wild a roller coaster; the emphasis here is much more on the sights than on the thrill of the ride itself. Regardless, it's a "not to be missed" attraction. For the time being, Big Thunder Mountain ranks with Star Tours (in Discoveryland) as the most popular attraction in the park. This popularity, coupled with the clockwise touring orientation of many guests, ensures that the attraction is virtually inundated with riders all day long. The only way to experience Big Thunder Mountain without a long wait is to ride in the first 30–45 minutes after the park opens—or after 6:30 p.m.

   As an example of how differently guests experience Disney attractions, consider this letter we received from an older lady:

> *Being in the senior citizens' category and having limited time, my friend and I confined our activities to those attractions rated as [good] for seniors.*
>
> *Because of your recommendation, and because you listed it as "not to be missed," we waited for one hour to board the Big Thunder Mountain [mine train], which you rated a "5" on a scary scale of "10." After living through 3½ minutes of pure terror, I will rate that attraction a "15" on a scary scale of "10." We were so busy holding on and scream-*

ing and even praying for our safety that we did not notice any falling rocks, a mining town, or an earthquake. In our opinion Big Thunder Mountain should not be recommended for seniors or preschool children.

Disneyland Railroad

Description and Comments   The Disneyland Paris Railroad stops in Frontierland on its circle tour around the park. See the description of the Disneyland Paris Railroad under Main Street for additional details regarding the sights en route.

Touring Tips   A pleasant and feet-saving way to commute to Fantasyland and/or Main Street. The Frontierland Station is located in the far corner of Frontierland, past Cottonwood Creek Ranch, so many guests overlook it. For this reason it is usually the least crowded of any of the train stations. On the negative side, fewer people on average disembark at Frontierland than at the other two stations. This means that there is less available space on board to accommodate new passengers.

Phantom Manor

Type of Attraction: Elaborate, high-tech Disney spookhouse
When to Go: Before 11:30 a.m. or after 6:30 p.m.
Special Comments: Frightens some very small children
Overall Appeal by Age Group:

Pre-school	Grade School	Teens	Young Adults	Over 30	Senior Citizens
Varies	★★★★	★★★★	★★★★	★★★★	★★★★

Author's Rating: Some of Disneyland Paris's best special effects;
★★★½
Duration of Ride: 5½-minute ride plus a 2-minute preshow
Average Wait in Line per 100 People Ahead of You: 3 minutes
Assumes: Both stretch rooms operating
Loading Speed: Fast

Description and Comments   A fun attraction more than a scary one, with some of the best special effects in the Disney repertoire. The ride begins in a preshow "stretch room," which delivers guests to the loading area of the actual ride. The main ride winds through the rooms and grounds of Phantom Manor. Though an excellent attraction, the Disneyland Paris rendition lacks the pace and intensity of sister attractions in the American parks. At Disneyland Paris the designers have attempted to incorporate a story line: something about a new bride who is forsaken by an evil husband. Whatever the story is supposed to be, it's muddled beyond comprehension and detracts markedly from the attraction's excellent holographic and audio-animatronic effects. A taped audio narration, partially in English but mostly in French, compounds the confusion.

Touring Tips   Even though Phantom Manor is a disappointment compared to its American predecessors, we nevertheless rate it as "not to be missed." Try to see Phantom Manor before 11:30 a.m. or after 6:30 p.m. If there is a long line when you arrive, do not despair. Phantom Manor is well designed when it comes to moving guests. Parents should be forewarned that some youngsters build a lot of anxiety concerning what they think they will see. The actual attraction scares almost nobody.

Indian Canoes

Type of Attraction: Scenic canoe ride

When to Go: Before 11 a.m.

Special Comments: Open seasonally

Overall Appeal by Age Group:

Pre-school	Grade School	Teens	Young Adults	Over 30	Senior Citizens
★★★★	★★★★	★★★★	★★★★	★★★★	★★★★

Author's Rating: Most fun way of seeing "Rivers of the Far West"; ★★★

Duration of Ride: 8–10 minutes depending on how fast you paddle

Average Wait in Line per 100 People Ahead of You: 12½ minutes

Assumes: 6 canoes operating

Loading Speed: Slow

Description and Comments   Paddle-powered (your paddle and power) ride around Big Thunder Mountain on the "Rivers of the Far West." The sights essentially are the same as on the riverboats or on the keelboats. The ride is a little different, however, in that the patrons actually paddle the canoe and in that the canoes are the only Disney ride that is not on some sort of track. We think the Indian Canoes are the most fun of any of the various river trips. Long lines beginning at about 11 a.m. reflect the popularity of this attraction. The Indian Canoes operate only on busier days and always close at dusk.

Touring Tips   The canoes represent one of three ways to see the same waterways. Since the canoes and keelboats are slower in loading and have a smaller passenger carrying capacity, we usually opt for the larger riverboats if we are on a tight schedule. If you are not up for a boat ride, a different view of most of the same sights can be had by hoofing from the graveyard at Phantom Manor around the waterfront to the canoe loading area. If you elect to canoe, try to ride before 11 a.m. or just before dusk.

Critter Corral and Cottonwood Creek Ranch

Type of Attraction: Walk-through American Western ranch and petting zoo
When to Go: Any time (closes at dusk)
Special Comments: Animals are real
Overall Appeal by Age Group:

Pre-school	Grade School	Teens	Young Adults	Over 30	Senior Citizens
★★★	★★½	★★	★★	★★	★★

Author's Rating: Something different for Disney; ★★
Touring Time: 5–10 minutes
Average Wait in Line per 100 People Ahead of You: Usually no waiting, though the petting zoo gets congested on busier days

Description and Comments   Cottonwood Creek Ranch is a replica of an Old Western homestead complete with a walk-through "Critter Corral" that serves as a petting zoo. Located on a path that winds from the Frontierland waterfront to the Frontierland train station, the ranch seems to be more of a space-filler than a true-blue Disney attraction. The petting zoo is small, with children usually outnumbering the animals by a wide margin. The animals and their enclosures, however, are clean and well maintained, and adults touring with children will find the ranch a pleasant rest stop.

Touring Tips   Visit whenever your schedule allows, but do not waste time here standing in line. If the ranch is too crowded for you to just walk in, skip it.

Chaparral Theater

Type of Attraction: Amphitheater
When to Go: Per the daily entertainment schedule
Author's Rating: Varies according to what's playing
Appeal by Age Group: Varies according to what's playing
Duration of Presentations: About 22 minutes

Description and Comments This open-air venue offers stage shows based on recent Disney movies and animated features, most having nothing to do with the Old West theme of Frontierland, where the theater is situated. Some productions are excellent, and some, like *The Tarzan Encounter* (which played during much of 2000), fall short.

Touring Tips The Chaparral Theater, tucked like a dimple next to the railroad track on the extreme left side of Frontierland, is somewhat hard to find. If you decide to catch a show there, give yourself extra time to find the theater. Though some productions are better than other, all shows are professionally done and generally worth seeing. The first and last scheduled performances of the day are usually the least crowded.

Rustler Roundup Shootin' Gallery

Type of Attraction: Electronic shooting gallery
When to Go: Whenever convenient
Special Comments: Not included in your admission price
Overall Appeal by Age Group:

Pre-school	Grade School	Teens	Young Adults	Over 30	Senior Citizens
★★★	★★★½	★★★	★★½	★★½	★★

Author's Rating: A very nifty shooting gallery; ★★½

Description and Comments A very elaborate shooting gallery which costs FF 10 ($1.35) to play, it's one of the few attractions in Disneyland Paris not included in the admission pass.

Touring Tips Good fun for those who enjoy shooting, but definitely not a place to blow time if you are on a tight schedule. Try it on your second day if time allows.

River Rogue Keelboats

Type of Attraction: Scenic boat ride

When to Go: Before 11 a.m.

Special Comments: Do not ride if lines are long; closes at dusk

Overall Appeal by Age Group:

Pre-school	Grade School	Teens	Young Adults	Over 30	Senior Citizens
★★★	★★★½	★★★	★★½	★★½	★★½

Author's Rating: ★★½

Duration of Ride: 7½ minutes

Average Wait in Line per 100 People Ahead of You: 18 minutes

Assumes: 3 boats operating

Loading Speed: Slow

Description and Comments Small river keelboats, which circle Big Thunder Mountain on the "Rivers of the Far West," taking the same route as the Indian Canoes and the larger riverboats. The top deck and the lower bow seats of the keelboat afford the best view but are exposed to the elements.

Touring Tips This trip covers the same circuit traveled by the canoes and riverboats. The canoes are the most fun, but the big riverboats are the most time efficient in terms of seeing the sights without a long wait. The other way to see much of the area covered by the respective boat tours is to walk the waterfront and then take a round-trip on the train starting at the Frontierland Station.

Thunder Mesa Riverboats

Type of Attraction: Scenic boat ride

When to Go: Between 11 a.m. and 5 p.m.

Overall Appeal by Age Group:

Pre-school	Grade School	Teens	Young Adults	Over 30	Senior Citizens
★★★	★★★	★★½	★★★	★★★	★★★

Author's Rating: Provides an excellent vantage point; ★★★

Duration of Ride: About 16 minutes

Average Wait to Board: 10 minutes

Assumes: Both boats operating

Loading Method: En masse

Description and Comments Large-capacity paddle wheel riverboats, which navigate the "Rivers of the Far West," circling Big Thunder Mountain and passing settler homesteads, dinosaur fossils, and spouting geysers among other things. Beautiful crafts, the riverboats provide a lofty perch from which to see Frontierland.

Touring Tips   One of three boat rides that survey the same real estate. Since the Indian Canoes and the River Rogue Keelboats accommodate considerably fewer guests, we think the riverboats make more efficient use of touring time. If you are not in the mood for a boat ride, many of the same sights can be seen by hiking around the waterfront and then taking the train for a circuit trip around the park. If you tour Disneyland Paris on a cold or rainy day, both riverboats have comfortably heated, albeit small, indoor cabins. Finally, the riverboats are the only Frontierland watercraft that operate after dusk.

Frontierland Eateries and Shops

Description and Comments   Frontierland offers two upscale, albeit informal, restaurants. The Lucky Nugget Saloon serves lunch and sometimes dinner buffets, usually with Disney characters in attendance. The Silver Spur Steakhouse features grilled meats.

Frontierland is so packed during the midday meal that it's difficult to obtain fast food without a long wait. The best bet for quick service midday or evening in Frontierland is the Cowboy Cookout Barbecue, all the way around the waterfront next to the petting zoo. In addition to serving decent barbecue, the Cowboy Cookout features live bluegrass music. Though crowded at mealtimes, Frontierland's Fuente del Oro Restaurante is the theme park's only Tex-Mex restaurant. An interesting vendor-cart snack in Frontierland is called the "Railroad Spike Potato," a potato that is baked from the inside out by hammering a red hot railroad spike into it.

Shops in Frontierland are stocked with cowboy hats, coonskin caps, toy rifles and pistols, American Western clothing (including blue jeans and cowboy boots), leather goods, cattle horns, American Indian pottery and jewelry, wood carvings, and Disney T-shirts.

Touring Tips   Do not waste time browsing in shops or standing in line for food, unless you have a very relaxed schedule or came specifically to shop.

Adventureland

Adventureland lies between Frontierland and Fantasyland. Approaching from the central hub, you enter a North African bazaar. Beyond the bazaar, Adventureland makes a transition to a Central African safari theme, and, moving toward Fantasyland, to a Caribbean theme. Mixed metaphors notwithstanding, the various architectural elements are nicely integrated and work well together. An interesting aside: The Disney landscapers have not quite figured how to keep bamboo, palm, and other tropical flora alive in the chilly French climate. In other words, if you visit Disneyland Paris during the winter, Adventureland vegetation might be a little sparse.

Adventure Isle

Type of Attraction: Walk-through exploration area

When to Go: Any time

Overall Appeal by Age Group:

Pre-school	Grade School	Teens	Young Adults	Over 30	Senior Citizens
★★★½	★★★½	★★★	★★½	★★½	★★½

Author's Rating: Exotic exercise; ★★½

Touring Time: About 12–20 minutes for most guests

Probable Waiting Time: None

Description and Comments   Adventure Isle is an exotic walk-through attraction featuring swinging bridges, caves, mountain lookouts, teetering rocks, lagoons, waterfalls, and a pirate ship. Thematically, it serves as a transition between La Cabane des Robinson (Swiss Family Treehouse) and Pirates of the Caribbean. Functionally, it provides an opportunity for kids to run, climb, explore, and generally let off steam. Visually stimulating to guests of all ages, and executed with exacting attention to detail, Adventure Isle can be explored in its entirety in less than a half hour.

Touring Tips   This is a good attraction to see during the crowded late morning and early afternoon, or, if you have two days, on your second day. Getting around Adventure Isle involves nothing more strenuous or risky than going up and down a lot of stairs. Children love Adventure Isle and can rummage around in its caverns for quite a while without getting bored. Most adults, however, get the general idea and call it quits in less than 15 minutes. All guests, but especially senior citizens, should be alert for slippery spots near the waterfalls and poorly lighted stairs in the cavern passageways. Parents should be warned that the caverns are labyrinthine and have multiple entrances and exits. Locating a child who has gotten loose in the caverns is no easy proposition.

La Cabane des Robinson (Swiss Family Treehouse)

Type of Attraction: Walk-through exhibit

When to Go: Before 11 a.m. and after 5 p.m.

Special Comments: Requires climbing a lot of stairs

Overall Appeal by Age Group:

Pre-school	Grade School	Teens	Young Adults	Over 30	Senior Citizens
★★★	★★★½	★★½	★★★	★★★	★★★

Author's Rating: A very creative exhibit; ★★★

Touring Time: 6–12 minutes

Average Wait in Line per 100 People Ahead of You: 7 minutes

Assumes: Normal staffing

Loading Speed: Does not apply

Description and Comments   This imposing replication of the shipwrecked family's tree-house home will fire the imagination of the inventive and the adventurous. Underneath the tree house, with entrances apart from the attraction per se, is a maze that winds among the root system of the huge artificial banyan tree.

Touring Tips   A self-guided walk-through tour that involves a lot of climbing up and down stairs but no ropes or ladders or anything fancy. People stopping during the tour to look extra long or to rest sometimes create bottlenecks. We recommend visiting this attraction in the late afternoon or early evening if you are on a one-day touring schedule. Stay close to your children in the root maze under the tree house, or you may become an unwilling participant in a lengthy game of hide and seek.

Pirates of the Caribbean

Type of Attraction: A Disney adventure boat ride

When to Go: Before 12:30 p.m. or after 4:30 p.m.

Special Comments: Frightens some small children

Overall Appeal by Age Group:

Pre-school	Grade School	Teens	Young Adults	Over 30	Senior Citizens
★★★	★★★★★	★★★★★	★★★★★	★★★★★	★★★★★

Author's Rating: Disney at its best; ★★★★★

Duration of Ride: Approximately 10 minutes

Average Wait in Line per 100 People Ahead of You: 3 minutes

Assumes: 40 boats operating

Loading Speed: Fast

Description and Comments   An adventure boat ride, this time indoors, through a series of amazingly detailed and realistic sets depicting a pirate raid on an island settlement, from the bombardment of the fortress to the debauchery that follows the victory—all in good, clean fun. Pirates of the Caribbean represents state-of-the-art Disney audio animatronics (robotics), exemplifying Disney attraction design at its wry best. Almost everyone is impressed by this attraction, and a large number of guests consider it to be the best attraction in the park. We rank Pirates of the Caribbean second only to Star Tours in Discoveryland.

Touring Tips   Another "not to be missed" attraction. Though engineered to move large crowds, this ride is sometimes overwhelmed briefly in the early afternoon. Even when the line appears long, however, the wait will usually not exceed 20 minutes.

Indiana Jones and the Temple of Peril (FASTPASS)

Type of Attraction: Small roller coaster

When to Go: Before 10 a.m. or use FASTPASS

Special Comments: Switching off available (see page 114)

Overall Appeal by Age Group:

Pre-school	Grade School	Teens	Young Adults	Over 30	Senior Citizens
★★	★★★½	★★★	★★½	★

Author's Rating: The queuing area is more interesting than the ride; ★★½

Duration of Ride: 1¼ minutes

Average Wait in Line per 100 People Ahead of You: 8 minutes without FASTPASS

Loading Speed: Slow

Description and Comments   Indiana Jones and the Temple of Peril is a thrill ride where you zip down a modest hill, loop upside down, and then ascend another small hill. Having stopped at the top of the second hill, you are allowed to roll backward to complete the same course in reverse. The attraction has next to nothing to do with Indiana Jones, though the queuing area is designed to resemble an archaeological dig site. The ride itself is exceedingly short and really does not offer any of Disney's trademark visuals or special effects. Loop forward, loop back: that's it. Added to attract more teens to the park at a time when Disneyland Paris finances were in disarray, Indiana Jones is a great example of an attraction developed on the cheap. It was, however, the wildest thing in the park until Space Mountain came on line. Curiously, and most likely because the park offer so few thrill rides, guests continue to endure long waits to ride.

Touring Tips   Indiana Jones is impossibly slow loading and not one-tenth as exciting as Space Mountain. If, however, you feel you can't miss it, use FASTPASS.

Adventureland Eateries and Shops

Description and Comments   The Adventureland restaurant, Colonel Hathi's Pizza Outpost, is usually the least crowded fast-food eatery in the park during midday, while the full-service Blue Lagoon Restaurant, with a romantic tropical moonlight theme, is the most evocative and visually stunning restaurant in the entire Disneyland Paris development. If you eat at the Blue Lagoon, avoid the red snapper. The Blue Lagoon requires reservations.

Shops in Adventureland sell such necessities as safari clothing, animal wood carvings, straw hats, pirate hats, African baubles and jewelry, rubber snakes, and, of course, Disney T-shirts. Most of the merchandise is overpriced and can be had for less in Paris and elsewhere.

Touring Tips   Skip the shops if you are on a tight schedule, or try them on your second day. Make reservations for any full-service restaurant at the door of the restaurant.

Fantasyland

Truly an enchanting place, spread gracefully like a miniature alpine village beneath the towers of Le Château de la Belle au Bois Dormant (Sleeping Beauty's Castle), Fantasyland is the heart of the park. Here Disney has created its own fanciful version of a quaint storybook village, steeped in the traditions of European folklore and children's fairy tales.

Before the park opened, many critics were skeptical that Disney could create in Fantasyland a castle and *petit village* that would captivate a European population accustomed to enjoying the real thing. Now that the park has been open a while, however, most Europeans concede that Fantasyland is much more a romantic fiction brought to life than an artificial reproduction of real castles or villages. History is history, and Fantasyland is fantasy. Period.

Disneyland Railroad

Description and Comments   The Disneyland Paris Railroad stops in Fantasyland on its circuit around the park. The station is located to the left of Alice's Curious Labyrinth and more or less on top of the Fantasy Festival Stage. From this usually uncrowded boarding point, transportation is available to Main Street and to Frontierland. A more extensive description of the Disneyland Paris Railroad can be found in the coverage of Main Street, U.S.A.

Le Château de la Belle au Bois Domant (Sleeping Beauty's Castle)

Type of Attraction: Walk-through exhibit

When to Go: Any time

Special Comments: Overlooked by many visitors

Overall Appeal by Age Group:

Pre- school	Grade School	Teens	Young Adults	Over 30	Senior Citizens
★★★	★★★	★★½	★★½	★★★	★★★½

Author's Rating: A fun surprise; ★★★

Description and Comments   Unnoticed by many visitors, small unobtrusive signs mark the entrances to each of the two attractions located in the *château* (castle). Stepping inside, the visitor can ascend a spiral staircase to a gallery where the story of Sleeping Beauty is told through ornate tapestries and stained glass. In a cave under the castle is La Tanière du Dragon (The Dragon's Den), inhabited by a huge, presumably life-size, audio-animatronic dragon. The dragon is awakened every few minutes by guests (who, more often than not, stumble into his lair by accident). On being roused, the beast flails his head and tail, roars, blows steam from his nostrils, and finally gets bored and goes back to sleep. While most visitors think the dragon is pretty slick, young children are frequently terrified.

Touring Tips   A pleasant change of pace for adults and a sort of adventure for kids, the dragon Audio Animatronics are some of Disney's best, and the stained glass is definitely worth the four minutes it takes to run upstairs and look around. See the gallery and the dragon at your convenience whenever you are in the neighborhood.

If the dragon is napping, stick around for a minute until he wakes up. There is no line for either of these small attractions.

It's a Small World

Type of Attraction: Scenic boat ride

When to Go: Any time except right after a parade

Overall Appeal by Age Group:

Pre-school	Grade School	Teens	Young Adults	Over 30	Senior Citizens
★★★	★★★	★★½	★★½	★★★	★★★½

Author's Rating: Relaxing; ★★★

Duration of Ride: 8 minutes

Average Wait in Line per 100 People Ahead of You: 1½ minutes

Assumes: Busy conditions with 30+ boats operating

Loading Speed: Fast

Description and Comments   A happy, upbeat attraction with a world brotherhood theme and a catchy tune that may require electroshock therapy to remove from your head. Small boats convey visitors on a tour around the world, with singing and dancing dolls showcasing the dress and culture of each nation. Almost everyone enjoys It's a Small World, but it stands as an attraction that some could take or leave, while others think it is one of the real masterpieces of Disneyland Paris. Try it, and form your own opinion.

Touring Tips   It's a Small World is a fast-loading ride that's usually a good bet during the busier times of the day. The boats are moved along by water pressure, with the pressure increased by added boats. Thus the more boats in service when you ride, the shorter the duration of the ride (and wait). The entire ride is indoors.

Peter Pan's Flight (FASTPASS)

Type of Attraction: A Disney fantasy adventure

When to Go: Before 10 a.m. and after 6 p.m. or use FASTPASS

Overall Appeal by Age Group:

Pre-school	Grade School	Teens	Young Adults	Over 30	Senior Citizens
★★★★	★★★★	★★★½	★★★★	★★★★	★★★★

Author's Rating: Happy, mellow, and "not to be missed"; ★★★★

Duration of Ride: 2½ minutes

Average Wait in Line per 100 People Ahead of You: 8 minutes without FASTPASS

Assumes: Normal operation

Loading Speed: Slow

Description and Comments   Though not considered one of the major attractions, Peter Pan's Flight is superbly designed and absolutely delightful, with a happy theme, a reunion with some unforgettable Disney characters, beautiful effects, and charming music. The ride consists of a journey in a small pirate ship over the sleeping city of London and then to Neverland.

Touring Tips   We classify it as "not to be missed." Try to ride before 10 a.m. or use FASTPASS. The entire ride is indoors.

Le Carrousel de Lancelot

Type of Attraction: Merry-go-round

When to Go: Before 11:30 a.m. or after 5 p.m.

Special Comments: Adults enjoy the beauty and nostalgia of this ride

Overall Appeal by Age Group:

Pre-school	Grade School	Teens	Young Adults	Over 30	Senior Citizens
★★★★	★★½	★	★★½	★★★	★★★

Author's Rating: A beautiful children's ride; ★★★

Duration of Ride: A little under 2 minutes

Average Wait in Line per 100 People Ahead of You: 8 minutes

Assumes: Normal staffing

Loading Speed: Slow

Description and Comments   A merry-go-round to be sure, but certainly one of the most elaborate and beautiful you will ever see, especially when lighted at night.

Touring Tips   Unless there are small children in your party, we suggest you appreciate this ride from the sidelines. If your children insist on riding, try to get them on before 11:30 a.m. or after 5 p.m. Though nice to look at, the carousel loads and unloads very slowly.

Blanche-Neige et les Sept Nains
(Snow White and the Seven Dwarfs)

Type of Attraction: Disney version of a spookhouse track ride

When to Go: Before 10 a.m. and after 6 p.m.

Special Comments: Not really very scary

Overall Appeal by Age Group:

Pre-school	Grade School	Teens	Young Adults	Over 30	Senior Citizens
★★★	★★★	★★½	★★½	★★½	★★½

Author's Rating: Worth seeing if the wait is not long; ★★★

Duration of Ride: About 2 minutes

Average Wait in Line per 100 People Ahead of You: 7 minutes

Assumes: Normal operation

Loading Speed: Slow

Description and Comments   Here you ride in a mining car through a spookhouse with a Perils-of-Pauline flavor, starring Snow White as she narrowly escapes harm at the hands of the wicked witch. The action and effects are a little better than those of Les Voyages de Pinocchio but not nearly as good as those of Peter Pan's Flight.

Touring Tips   This jerky ride is enjoyable but not particularly compelling. Experience it if the lines are not too long or on a second-day visit. Ride before 10 a.m. or after 6 p.m., if possible. Parents should be advised that the witch, who appears throughout the ride, badly frightens many young children. Writes one mother:

> *The outside looks cute and fluffy, but inside the evil witch just keeps coming at you. My five-year-old, who rode [the roller coaster] three times and took other scary rides right in stride, was near panic when our car stopped unexpectedly twice during Snow White. [After Snow White] my six-year-old niece spent a lot of time asking "if a witch will jump out at you" before other rides. So I suggest that you explain a little more what this ride is all about. It is tough on preschoolers who are expecting forest animals and dwarfs.*

Alice's Curious Labyrinth

Type of Attraction: Walk-through maze

When to Go: Before 11 a.m. and after 5 p.m.

Special Comments: Does not require much exertion

Overall Appeal by Age Group:

Pre-school	Grade School	Teens	Young Adults	Over 30	Senior Citizens
★★★	★★★½	★★½	★★½	★★½	★★★

Author's Rating: Aesthetically pleasing as well as imaginative; ★★★

Touring Time: 8–20 minutes

Average Wait in Line per 100 People Ahead of You: 9 minutes

Assumes: Normal staffing

Loading Speed: Does not apply

Description and Comments Alice's Curious Labyrinth is a Disney first, one of the few attractions created especially for Disneyland Paris. The theme is drawn from Disney's classic *Alice in Wonderland* in which the mean Queen of Hearts had an elaborate rose garden. The attraction is a nifty labyrinth consisting of a convoluted arrangement of beautifully manicured hedges about 1.75 meters (5'10") tall, embellished by fountains and audio-animatronic (robotic) characters from the story. Of particular interest are the "jumping fountains," a series of fountains in which spurts of water literally vault over the heads of guests going through the maze.

Touring Tips A self-guided walk-through attraction that involves some limited (but optional) step climbing. If you work through the entire labyrinth, you will come to a diminutive castle and tower with steps up and slides (for children only) back down. If you have had enough of hedges and such, you are given the opportunity to exit the maze before reaching the tiny castle. From a garden and landscaping perspective, Alice's Curious Labyrinth is a lovely piece of work. When seen from above (possible from the tower or from nearby Dumbo), the entire maze takes on the shape of a huge Cheshire cat. The labyrinth itself is rather straightforward, and not at all difficult to progress through, although people stopping to look extra long or to rest sometimes create bottlenecks that slow crowd flow. Disney attendants are posted around the maze to assist small children should they become disoriented or frustrated. Alice's Curious Labyrinth, very much an outdoor attraction, is obviously vulnerable to bad weather.

Les Voyages de Pinocchio

Type of Attraction: Disney dark (spookhouse-type) track ride

When to Go: Before 10:30 a.m. and after 5:30 p.m.

Overall Appeal by Age Group:

Pre-school	Grade School	Teens	Young Adults	Over 30	Senior Citizens
★★½	★★★	★★½	★★½	★★½	★★½

Author's Rating: Below average; ★★½

Duration of Ride: 2½ minutes

Average Wait in Line per 100 People Ahead of You: 6 minutes

Assumes: Normal operation

Loading Speed: Slow

Description and Comments   Another indoor track ride. This attraction, which falls a little short of Blanche-Neige and way short of Peter Pan, chronicles the adventures of Pinocchio, the wooden puppet who wants to be a real boy, as he tries to find his way home.

Touring Tips   Pinocchio does not quite live up to expectations. The action is difficult to follow and lacks continuity. The special effects are O.K.—just O.K. This attraction has been such a dud at Disneyland in California that we are surprised Disney elected to build a copy in France. The best time to ride Pinocchio is before 10:30 a.m. and after 5:30 p.m. Finally, a note to parents: Though Pinocchio is a pretty tame ride, there is one place where a whale jumps up unexpectedly, frightening many small children.

Dumbo the Flying Elephant

Type of Attraction: Disneyfied midway ride

When to Go: Before 9:30 a.m. and during parades

Special Comments: The favorite Disney ride of many small children

Overall Appeal by Age Group:

Pre-school	Grade School	Teens	Young Adults	Over 30	Senior Citizens
★★★★★	★★★½	★	★	★	★

Author's Rating: An attractive children's ride; ★★½

Duration of Ride: A little under 2 minutes

Average Wait in Line per 100 People Ahead of You: 15 minutes

Assumes: Normal staffing

Loading Speed: Slow

Description and Comments   A nice, tame, happy children's ride based on the lovable Disney flying-elephant character. It's an upgraded rendition of a ride that can be found at state fairs and amusement parks around the world. Shortcomings notwith-standing, Dumbo is the favorite Disneyland Paris attraction of most preschoolers.

Touring Tips   This is a slow-load ride that we recommend you bypass, unless you are on a very relaxed touring schedule. If your kids are excited about Dumbo, try to get them on the ride before 9:30 a.m. or try during parades or just before the park closes.

A lot of readers take us to task for lumping Dumbo in with carnival midway rides. These comments from a Canadian mother are representative:

> *I think you have acquired a jaded attitude. I know [Dumbo] is not for everybody, but when we took our oldest child (then just four), the sign at the end of the line said there would be a 90-minute wait. He knew and he didn't care, and he and I stood in the hot afternoon sun for 90 blissful minutes waiting for his 90-second flight. Anything that a four-year-old would wait for that long and that patiently must be pretty special.*

Mad Hatter's Tea Cups

Type of Attraction: Midway-type spinning ride

When to Go: Before 11 a.m. and after 5 p.m.

Special Comments: You can make the tea cups spin faster by turning the wheel in the center of the cup

Overall Appeal by Age Group:

Pre-school	Grade School	Teens	Young Adults	Over 30	Senior Citizens
★★★½	★★★★	★★★★½	★★★	★★	★★

Author's Rating: Fun but not worth much of a wait; ★★

Duration of Ride: A little under 2 minutes

Average Wait in Line per 100 People Ahead of You: 8 minutes

Assumes: Normal staffing

Loading Speed: Slow

Description and Comments   Well done in the Disney style, but still just an amusement park ride. *Alice in Wonderland's* Mad Hat-ter provides the theme for this attraction, where guests whirl around feverishly in big tea cups. A rendition of this ride, sans Dis-ney characters, can be found at almost every local carnival and fair.

Touring Tips   This ride, aside from not being particularly unique, is notoriously slow loading. Skip it on a busy schedule if the kids will let you. Ride in the morning of your second day if your schedule is more relaxed. A warning for parents who have not given this ride much thought: Teenagers love to lure an adult onto the Tea Cups and then turn the wheel in the middle (which makes the cup spin faster) until the adults are plastered against the side of the cup and are on the verge of throwing up. Unless you want to be a test subject in a human centrifuge, do not even consider getting on this ride with anyone younger than 21 years of age.

Les Pirouettes du Vieux Moulin (The Old Mill Ferris Wheel)

Type of Attraction: Tiny ferris wheel

When to Go: Before 10 a.m.

Special Comments: Offers a slightly elevated view of Alice's Curious Labyrinth

Overall Appeal by Age Group:

Pre-school	Grade School	Teens	Young Adults	Over 30	Senior Citizens
★★★½	★½	½	½	½	½

Author's Rating: Not worth a 10-minute wait for anyone over age 5; ½

Duration of Ride: 1½ minutes

Average Wait in Line per 100 People Ahead of You: 20 minutes

Loading Speed: Slow

Description and Comments   Les Pirouettes is a tiny ferris wheel tacked onto the back side of a fast-food kiosk. It's not a bad place to introduce preschoolers to Ferris wheels, but otherwise it's a waste of time.

Touring Tips   If you have a little one who wants to ride, get on before 10 a.m.

Casey Jr.—Le Petit Train du Cirque (The Little Circus Train)

Type of Attraction: Miniature train ride

When to Go: Before 11 a.m. or after 5 p.m.

Overall Appeal by Age Group:

Pre-school	Grade School	Teens	Young Adults	Over 30	Senior Citizens
★★★★	★★★½	★★	★★★	★★★	★★★½

Author's Rating: A quiet, scenic ride; ★★★
Duration of Ride: About 3 minutes
Average Wait in Line per 100 People Ahead of You: 12 minutes
Assumes: 2 trains operating
Loading Speed: Slow

Description and Comments   A pet project of Walt Disney, Casey Jr. circulates through a landscape of miniature towns, farms, and lakes. There are some stunning bonsai specimens visible from this ride, as well as some of the most manicured landscaping you are ever likely to see.

Touring Tips   This ride covers the same sights as Le Pays des Contes de Fées but does it faster and with less of a wait. Accommodations for adults, however, are less than optimal on this ride, with some passengers having to squeeze into diminutive caged cars (after all, it is a circus train). Also, some preschoolers are frightened by being enclosed. If you do not have children in your party, you can enjoy the same sights more comfortably by riding Le Pays des Contes de Fées.

Le Pays des Contes de Fées (Storybook Land)

Type of Attraction: Scenic boat ride
When to Go: Before 10:30 a.m. and after 5:30 p.m.
Overall Appeal by Age Group:

Pre-school	Grade School	Teens	Young Adults	Over 30	Senior Citizens
★★★★	★★★½	★★	★★★	★★★	★★★½

Author's Rating: Pretty, tranquil, and serene; ★★★
Duration of Ride: 7 minutes
Average Wait in Line per 100 People Ahead of You: 16 minutes
Assumes: 7 boats operating
Loading Speed: Slow

Description and Comments   Guide-operated boats wind along canals situated beneath the same miniature landscapes visible from the Casey Jr. Circus Train. This ride, offering stellar examples of bonsai cultivation, selective pruning, and miniaturization, is a must for landscape gardening enthusiasts

Touring Tips   The boats are much more comfortable than the train, the view of the miniatures is better, and the pace is more leisurely. On the down side, lines are long, and if not long, definitely slow-moving, and the ride itself takes a lot of time. Our recommendation is to ride Casey Jr. if you have children or are in a hurry. Take the boat if your party is all adults or your pace is more leisurely.

Le Théâtre du Château

Type of Attraction: Amphitheater
When to Go: As per the daily entertainment schedule
Special Comments: A good place to watch parades
Overall Appeal by Age Group:

Pre-school	Grade School	Teens	Young Adults	Over 30	Senior Citizens
★★★	★★★½	★★½	★★★	★★★	★★★

Author's Rating: ★★★
Duration of Presentation: About 30 minutes
Preshow Entertainment: None
Probable Waiting Time: None

Description and Comments   This amphitheater is actually situated outside Fantasyland across the moat from the front, right side of the castle (as you face it from the central hub). Various productions are staged at Le Théâtre du Château. Most shows feature Disney characters, and many performances involve audience participation. Dialogue and lyrics are mostly in French.

Touring Tips   Performance times for productions at Le Théâtre du Château are listed on the daily entertainment schedule in your park handout map. Seating is first come, first served; so if you want a seat in front, arrive at least 15–20 minutes early. Because both afternoon and evening parades pass right in front of Le Théâtre du Château, it has the distinction of being one of the few places where guests can enjoy a parade while seated. The theater is totally exposed to the weather, however, thus making it an uncomfortable place during the hot part of a summer day or any time of year when it is raining, snowing, or unusually cold.

Fantasy Festival Stage

Type of Attraction: Musical show featuring the Disney characters
When to Go: As per the daily entertainment schedule
Special Comments: The best place to see the Disney characters
Overall Appeal by Age Group:

Pre-school	Grade School	Teens	Young Adults	Over 30	Senior Citizens
★★★★½	★★★★½	★★★½	★★★½	★★★★	★★★★

Author's Rating: Funny, lively, and upbeat; ★★★★
Duration of Presentation: About 30 minutes
Preshow Entertainment: None
Probable Waiting Time: None

Description and Comments   The Fantasy Festival Stage is situated to the left of Alice's Curious Labyrinth. This covered (but not fully enclosed) theater is home to excellent productions featuring the Disney characters. In one presentation the characters (including Mickey, Minnie, Donald, Goofy, Chip 'n' Dale, Dopey, Brer Bear, Pinocchio, and Baloo) take the audience on a romping, musical tour of the various theme park lands. The quality of the rollicking, fast-paced show is evident in the cheering, clapping, and foot stomping of the appreciative crowds. Musical lyrics at the Fantasy Festival Stage are mostly in French and English. Spoken dialogue is primarily in French.

Touring Tips   Performance times for productions at the Fantasy Festival Stage are listed on the daily entertainment schedule available at City Hall. Arrive 20 minutes or so early to get a good seat. Though the theater entrance is roped off just before show time, late arrivals can view the presentation from the walkway leading to the Fantasyland train station (to the left of the theater). The audience at the Fantasy Festival Stage is protected from sun and precipitation, but not from wind. During the colder weather months, Fantasy Festival Stage productions are moved to the Videopolis stage in Discoveryland.

Fantasyland Eateries and Shops

Description and Comments   It's no big secret that we find the food in Disneyland Paris edible but incredibly expensive. Fantasyland food is no exception. Fantasyland's only full-service dining room, Auberge de Cendrillon, is also Disneyland Paris's only

French restaurant. Though the food at Auberge is good and the service attentive and friendly, it does not compare to the French cuisine available in Paris and some of the little villages surrounding Disneyland Paris. The most frequently overlooked fast-food restaurant in Fantasyland (at least before the afternoon parade) is Pizzeria Bella Notte, located out of the way on the walkway connecting It's a Small World with Discoveryland.

Touring Tips   Shopping in Fantasyland is ho-hum, with the possible exception of La Boutique du Château, which specializes in Christmas decor year-round. Do not waste time on the shops unless you have a relaxed schedule or unless shopping is a big priority. If you want to eat at the Auberge, make reservations in person at the door of the restaurant sometime before 11 a.m.

Discoveryland

Discoveryland is a mix of rides and experiences that relate to the technological development of humankind and our expectations (both now and retrospectively) of life in the future. Most of the architecture of Discoveryland is ageless, reflecting a nostalgic vision of the future as imagined by dreamers and scientists of Jules Verne's era. Discoveryland is both fun and educational, stimulating your intellect and curiosity while allowing you to jump in and try the future on for size.

Space Mountain (FASTPASS)

Type of Attraction: Roller coaster in the dark

When to Go: Immediately after the park opens or use FAST-PASS

Special Comments: Switching off available (see page 114)

Overall Appeal by Age Group:

Pre-school	Grade School	Teens	Young Adults	Over 30	Senior Citizens
N/A	★★★★	★★★★★	★★★★★	★★★★	★★½

Author's Rating: The wildest ride at Disneyland Paris; ★★★★

Duration of Ride: A little over 1 minute

Average Wait in Line per 100 People Ahead of You: 4 minutes without FASTPASS

Loading Speed: Moderate

Description and Comments The only thing that this Space Mountain shares with similarly named attractions in the United States is the name. Space Mountain at Disneyland Paris is the baddest coaster found in any Disney theme park and makes the other Space Mountains seem as tame as Peter Pan's Flight. For starters, you're launched like a jet off an aircraft carrier, hitting speeds of almost 50 miles per hour before you reach the first hill. From there it's inverted loops, corkscrews, and camelbacks all the way to the end. The ride is short, but plenty long enough for all but the most rabid coaster freaks.

Touring Tips Space Mountain is the most popular attraction in the park, so ride as soon as the park opens or use FASTPASS. Readers who are prone to motion sickness should stay away. Most children under age ten will find Space Mountain way too frightening. If you're undecided about whether your child should ride, test him on Big Thunder Mountain first. If he handles Big Thunder well and is willing to tackle a coaster about three times as wild, he'll be fine on Space Mountain. Minimum height requirement for children is 4'7".

Star Tours

Type of Attraction: Spaceflight-simulation ride

When to Go: Before 10 a.m. or just before park closes

Special Comments: Frightens many small children; expectant mothers also advised against riding

Overall Appeal by Age Group:

Pre-school	Grade School	Teens	Young Adults	Over 30	Senior Citizens
★★★★	★★★★★	★★★★★	★★★★★	★★★★★	★★★★

Author's Rating: A blast; not to be missed; ★★★★★

Duration of Ride: Approximately 5 minutes

Average Wait in Line per 100 People Ahead of You: 4 minutes

Assumes: 6 simulators operating

Loading Speed: Fast

Description and Comments This attraction is so amazing, so real, and so much fun that it just makes you grin and giggle. It is the only Disney ride anywhere for which we have voluntarily waited 45 minutes in line, not once, but three times in succession. The attraction consists of a ride in a flight simulator modeled after

those used in the training of pilots and astronauts. Guests, sup-
posedly on a little vacation outing in space, are piloted by a droid
(android, a.k.a. humanoid, a.k.a. robot) on his first flight with
real passengers. Mayhem ensues almost immediately as scenery
flashes by at supersonic speed and the simulator bucks and pitches.
You could swear you are moving at light speed. After several minutes of this, the droid somehow gets the spacecraft landed, and
you discover you are much happier than you were before you
boarded. Speaking strictly for the research team, we would like to
see a whole new generation of Disney rides on the order of Star
Tours. Star Tours and its waiting area are completely indoors.
Almost all of the dramatic dialogue is in French.

Touring Tips   This ride will be a Disneyland Paris headliner for
a long time to come and can be counted on to draw large crowds
throughout the day. Ride first thing in the morning or just before
the park closes. Note also that crowds at Star Tours ebb and flow.
This is because the other two featured attractions in Discoveryland—*Le Visionarium* and *Honey, I Shrunk the Audience*—are
large-capacity theater attractions. When these two attractions con-
clude a performance, they disgorge 800 and 700 people, respectively, many of whom hop right in line for Star Tours. Though
Star Tours is an efficient, fast-loading ride, it can be overwhelmed
by the arrival of the theater guests. If you arrive at Star Tours and
discover that it has suddenly become the third-largest city in
Europe, chalk it up to bad luck and try again later.

Autopia

Type of Attraction: Drive-'em-yourself miniature cars
When to Go: Before 10 a.m.
Special Comments: Must be 132 cm (4'4") tall to drive
Overall Appeal by Age Group:

Pre-school	Grade School	Teens	Young Adults	Over 30	Senior Citizens
★★★½	★★★	★	½	½	½

Author's Rating: Boring for adults (★); great for preschoolers
Duration of Ride: Approximately 3¼ minutes
Average Wait in Line per 100 People Ahead of You: 12 minutes
Assumes: At least 100 cars in operation

Loading Speed: Slow

Description and Comments   An elaborate miniature freeway with gasoline-powered cars that will travel at speeds of up to seven miles an hour. The raceway design, with its sleek cars, auto race noises, and highway signs, is quite alluring. The cars poke along on a track, however, leaving the driver with little to do—pretty ho-hum for most adults and teenagers. Of those children who would enjoy the ride, many are excluded by the requirement that drivers be 1.3 meters (4'4") tall.

Touring Tips   This ride is appealing to the eye, but it is definitely expendable on an adult tour. Preschoolers love it. If your preschooler is too short to drive, ride along and allow him or her to steer (the car runs on a guide rail) while you work the foot pedal.
   One mother we encountered had this to say:

> *I was truly amazed by the number of adults in line. Please emphasize to your readers that these cars travel on a guided path and are not a whole lot of fun. The only reason I could think of for adults to be in line was an insane desire to go on absolutely every ride. The other feature about the cars is that they tend to pile up at the end, so it takes almost as long to get off as it did to get on. Parents riding with their preschoolers should keep the car going as slow as it can without stalling. This prolongs the preschooler's joy and decreases the time you will have to wait at the end.*

   We clocked a man and his son on the Autopia. First they waited 42 minutes to board. Once in the car, they sat for 90 seconds waiting for cars ahead of them to move. They completed the circuit in 3 minutes, after which they sat in the car for 5 minutes just waiting to disembark. Clearly, this attraction can be a nightmare. We recommend avoiding it completely, unless you are touring the park on a low-attendance day or you ride before 10 a.m. Note that Autopia is totally exposed to the weather.

Orbitron
Type of Attraction: Very mild midway-type thrill ride
When to Go: Before 10 a.m. or during the hour before the park
   closes

Overall Appeal by Age Group:

Pre-school	Grade School	Teens	Young Adults	Over 30	Senior Citizens
★★★★	★★★½	★★★	★★	★	★

Author's Rating: Not worth the wait; ★½

Duration of Ride: About 1¾ minutes

Average Wait in Line per 100 People Ahead of You: 17 minutes

Assumes: Normal staffing

Loading Speed: Slow

Description and Comments A carnival-type ride involving small rockets, which rotate on arms around a central axis.

Touring Tips With an hourly capacity of less than 400 people, Orbitron is arguably the most inefficient ride in the park. We suggest you skip it entirely. If your children blackmail you into letting them ride, get them on board by 10 a.m. If you take a preschooler on this ride, place your child in the seat first and then seat you self.

Honey, I Shrunk the Audience

Type of Attraction: 3D film with special effects

When to Go: Before 10 a.m. or just before park closes.

Special Comments: Loud, intense show with tactile effects frightens some young children

Overall Appeal by Age Group:

Pre-school	Grade School	Teens	Young Adults	Over 30	Senior Citizens
★★★	★★★★½	★★★★½	★★★★½	★★★★½	★★★★

Author's Rating: An absolute hoot! Not to be missed; ★★★★½

Preshow Entertainment: 8 minutes

Probable Waiting Time: 12 minutes (at suggested times)

Description and Comments *Honey, I Shrunk the Audience* is a 3D offshoot of Disney's feature film *Honey, I Shrunk the Kids.* Played strictly for laughs, *Honey, I Shrunk the Audience* features an array of special effects, including simulated explosions, smoke, fiber optics, lights, water spray, and moving seats.

Touring Tips The sound level is earsplitting, frightening some young children. Many adults report that the loud soundtrack is distracting, even uncomfortable. While *Honey, I Shrunk the Audience* is a huge hit, it can be overwhelming for preschoolers, as this American mom reports:

> *Our three- and four-year-olds loved all the rides. They giggled through Thunder Mountain three times, thought Space Mountain was the coolest, and begged to ride Star Tours over and over. They even "fought ghosts" at [Phantom Manor]. But, Honey, I Shrunk the Audience, dissolved them into sobbing, sniveling, shaking, terrified preschoolers.*

Honey, I Shrunk the Audience has become one of the park's most popular attractions. Try to work it in before 11 a.m. Avoid seats in the first several rows: if you're too close to the screen, the 3D images don't focus properly.

Les Mystères du Nautilus (The Mysteries of the Nautilus)

Type of Attraction: Walk-through submarine

When to Go: Anytime

Overall Appeal by Age Group:

Pre-school	Grade School	Teens	Young Adults	Over 30	Senior Citizens
★★★½	★★★★	★★★	★★★	★★★½	★★★½

Author's Rating: Well done—exceeds expectations; ★★★½

Touring Time: About 10 minutes

Average Wait in Line Per 100 People Ahead of You: 7 minutes

Assumes: Normal staffing

Description and Comments Les Mystères du Nautilus offers a walk-through tour of the *Nautilus,* Captain Nemo's submarine from the Jules Verne novel (and Disney movie) *20,000 Leagues Under the Sea.* The self-guided tour takes you through the captain's cabin, the bridge (where a giant squid attacks periodically), the diving chamber, and the engine room, among others. Although most guests under age 40 never saw the movie or read the book, it doesn't take much imagination to get the idea.

Touring Tips Crowds ebb and flow, but the wait for the Nautilus is usually not long. Tour at your discretion whenever you're in Discoveryland. Unlike Robinson Crusoe's treehouse in Adventureland, touring the Nautilus does not require a lot of climbing up and down stairs. Obviously you must descend into the sub, but an elevator is provided for the disabled.

Le Visionarium

Type of Attraction: Time-travel movie adventure

When to Go: In the morning

Special Comments: Audience must stand throughout presentation

Overall Appeal by Age Group:

Pre-school	Grade School	Teens	Young Adults	Over 30	Senior Citizens
★★	★★★	★★★★	★★★★	★★★★	★★★★

Author's Rating: Outstanding; ★★★★

Duration of Presentation: About 20 minutes

Preshow entertainment: Robots, lasers, and movies

Probable Waiting Time: 15–25 minutes

Description and Comments   *Le Visionarium* was designed specifically for Disneyland Paris. Visitors first view a preshow introducing Timekeeper (a humanoid) and 9-Eye (a time-traveling robot so named because she has nine cameras to serve as eyes). Following the preshow, the audience is ushered into the main theater, where the audio-animatronic (robotic) Timekeeper places 9-Eye into a time machine and dispatches her on a crazed journey into the past and then into the future. What 9-Eye sees on her odyssey (through her nine camera eyes) is projected onto huge screens that completely surround the audience, providing a 360-degree perspective of all the action. The robot's travel takes her back to prehistoric Europe and then forward to meet French author and visionary Jules Verne, who hitches a ride with 9-Eye into the future. Circle-Vision film technology, Disney audio animatronics, and high-tech special effects combine to establish *Le Visionarium* as one of Disneyland Paris's premier attractions. We rate it as "not to be missed." Though the dialogue is in French, there is a phone at each guest-viewing position which allows the guest (by turning a knob) to tune in a choice of an English, German, or Spanish translation.

Touring Tips   *Le Visionarium* is extremely popular and draws large crowds from midmorning on. The theater is huge, however, accommodating 800 guests per showing. If you try *Le Visionarium* before noon, your wait should be in the 10–20-minute range. During the crowded middle of the day, expect a 15–30-minute wait.

Videopolis

Type of Attraction: Rock and roll dance and concert hall

When to Go: As per the daily entertainment schedule

Special Comments: The best place for rock and roll at Disneyland Paris

Overall Appeal by Age Group:

Pre-school	Grade School	Teens	Young Adults	Over 30	Senior Citizens
★★★½	★★★★½	★★★★½	★★★★½	★★★★	★★★½

Author's Rating: Loud, wild, and well done; ★★★★

Duration of Presentation: About 20 minutes

Preshow Entertainment: Rock music

Probable Waiting Time: None

Description and Comments Videopolis is a huge indoor theater and disco complex with fast-food counter service on the side. The exterior of the building is styled as an aircraft hangar with a Jules Verne airship suspended over the entrance. Inside multiple tiers of seats and dining tables rise in a semicircle around a large stage. Between the stage and the seating area is a good-sized hardwood dance floor. Three to six times a day (depending on park operating hours), a stage show is presented. High powered, imaginatively choreographed, and frenetically energetic, the productions feature a large cast of talented dancers augmented by a daunting array of special effects. Everything in these shows from set design to the musical score is first rate. The Videopolis stage also hosts special concerts and limited-engagement shows starring top musical and dance talent from all over the world. Though the music is loud, guests of all ages enjoy the Videopolis productions. Teens (not unexpectedly), many school-age children, and a goodly number of adults rate the Videopolis productions as the best of Disneyland Paris's live entertainment offerings.

Touring Tips It is still unclear whether Videopolis is a fast-food restaurant with a stage show on the side—or the other way around. Either way the place is huge and teeming with people from about 10 a.m. on. The restaurant, Café Hyperion, offers expensive but edible pizza, sandwiches, and burgers. Videopolis is so gargantuan that you can almost always find a place to sit. If the complex is especially crowded, and you cannot find a place to roost, squeeze in with any guests who are occupying a table that exceeds their group size. If you are not eating anything, there is row seating (no tables) down front. You do not have to buy anything to watch the show.

Discoveryland Eateries and Shops

Description and Comments Discoveryland in the only "land" that does not offer full-service dining. If you want to eat in Discoveryland, you are relegated to eating what Disney considers to be the "food of the future": American fast food. Café Hyperion in the mammoth Videopolis complex serves hamburgers, sandwiches, salads, and sausages and is usually pretty crowded. For an out-of-the-way restaurant, try Buzz Lightyear's Pizza Planet (and playground) to the right of *Honey, I Shrunk the Audience*.

Discoveryland shops sell Disney trademark toys, souvenirs, and clothing, as well as games and gift items.

Touring Tips The creativity in Discoveryland was apparently exhausted before the planners got around to shopping and menus. In any event, there is not much to stimulate the appetite or the shopping reflex. Lunch at the Café Hyperion can, however, be a time saver if you eat about noon and combine lunch with an early show on the Videopolis stage (consult your daily entertainment schedule for show times).

Live Entertainment at Disneyland Paris

Live entertainment in the form of bands, Disney character appearances, parades, singing and dancing, and ceremonies further enliven and add color to Disneyland Paris on a daily basis. For specific information about what's going on the day you visit, stop by City Hall as you enter the park. Be forewarned, however, that if you are on a tight schedule, it is impossible to see both the park's featured attractions *and* take in the numerous and varied live performances offered. In our One-Day Touring Plans we exclude the live performances in favor of seeing as much of the park as time permits. This is a considered tactical decision based on the fact that some of the parades and other performances siphon crowds away from the more popular rides, thus shortening waiting lines.

But the color and pageantry of live happenings around the park are an integral part of the Disneyland Paris entertainment mix and a persuasive argument for second-day touring. The following is an incomplete list of those performances and events that are scheduled with some regularity and require no reservations.

Disneyland Paris Band	Disneyland's all-purpose band entertains around the park
Casey's Corner Pianist	Ragtime piano favorites at Casey's Corner at the central-hub end of Main Street
Barbershop Quartet	A barbershop quartet sings nostalgic tunes in Town Square and along Main Street
Sax Quintet	A versatile quintet of saxes plays on Main Street
Barn Dance	Bluegrass and country music at the Cowboy Cookout Barbecue in Frontierland
Frontierland Stuntmen	Wild West brawl and shoot-out in Frontierland in front of the Lucky Nugget Saloon
Mariachi Band	A strolling mariachi band plays in the courtyard of Fuente del Oro Restaurante in Frontierland
Steel Drums	Caribbean steel drums in Adventureland on the patio of the Explorers Club
Disney Rock Groups	High-energy Disney rock groups perform in Discoveryland and elsewhere according to the daily entertainment schedule
Stage Shows	Live productions are performed several times each day on the Videopolis stage in Discoveryland, at the Chaparral Theater in Frontierland, on the Fantasy Festival Stage in Fantasyland, and outside at Le Théâtre du Château amphitheater to the right of

the castle. Descriptions of these productions are included in the coverage of attractions in the respective lands. Consult the daily entertainment schedule (available at City Hall) for show times.

Fireworks | A thunderous and spectacular fireworks display marks the conclusion of each Disneyland Paris day when the park is open late. Consult the daily entertainment schedule for show time.

Disney Characters | On most days a character is on duty next to City Hall for photo posing. Disney character shows are performed according to the daily entertainment schedule on the Fantasy Festival Stage in Fantasyland. Disney characters are also featured in productions at Le Théâtre du Château amphitheater on the outside right of the castle. Finally, characters roam the park throughout the day but can almost always be found in Fantasyland.

PARADES

Parades are a big deal at Disneyland Paris, with dozens of Disney characters, enormous floats, and some amazing special effects. Demonstrating Disney's singular talent for showmanship and pageantry, the Disneyland Paris parades are eye-popping celebrations, larger, more colorful, and more elaborate than any Disney street productions to date. We rate both the afternoon and evening parades as not to be missed.

In addition to providing great entertainment, the parades also serve to lure guests away from the attractions. If getting on rides is more appealing than watching a parade, you will find the wait for all attractions substantially diminished just before and during parades. Because the parade route does not pass through Frontierland, Adventureland, or Discoveryland, attractions in these lands are particularly good bets.

Afternoon Parade

Usually staged at 3 p.m., the afternoon parade is a full-fledged spectacular with elaborate floats, music, Disney characters, and dancers. Many afternoon parades originated at other Disney parks where they were immensely well received. Holiday parades are substituted at Christmas and other seasonal celebrations.

Evening Parade(s)

There is a parade each night the park is open after 8 p.m. The Main Street Electrical Parade, one of Disney's most beautiful and beloved parades, is featured. Like all Disney parades, it showcases music and the Disney characters. What distinguishes the Electrical Parade, however, is that each float is composed of thousands of tiny light bulbs, with almost three-quarters of a million twinkling lights in the parade overall. To augment the stunning effect of this sparkling galaxy, park lighting is dimmed all along the parade route. The Main Street Electrical Parade is a delightful, happy event. We rate it as "not to be missed." Consult the daily entertainment schedule for parade time(s).

Parade Route and Vantage Points

The parade route begins near It's a Small World in Fantasyland and proceeds past Pizzeria Bella Notte and then under the Fantasyland arch into the plaza between Discoveryland and the castle moat. Here parades turn to pass in front of Le Théâtre du Château amphitheater, and then go on to the central hub. Having circled the central hub, the route continues down Main Street, around Town Square, and exits through a gate by the Buttons & Bows Hat Shop. Sometimes the parades run the reverse route, starting on Main Street and terminating in Fantasyland.

Many guests view parades from the central hub or from the curb on Main Street. The upper platform of the Disneyland Paris Railroad station at the Town Square end of Main Street offers one of the best vantage points and is certainly one of the most popular (that is, contested). This is also a particularly good place for watching the evening fireworks show. Unfortunately, though, you literally have to stake out your position on the train platform 30 to 45 minutes before the parade begins.

Since the majority of spectators pack Main Street and the central hub, we recommend watching parades from Fantasyland or from where parades pass in front of Le Théâtre du Château. In fact, there are several good vantage points that are frequently overlooked:

1. The entrance concourse of It's a Small World. Simply ascend the entrance ramp of It's a Small World in Fantasyland as if you were going to board the ride. Stop midway up and position yourself on the elevated ramp overlooking the parade route.

2. The wall in front of Pizzeria Bella Notte. There is a waist-high wall on which you can stand in front of this pizza restaurant in Fantasyland. Claim your position 10–12 minutes before parade time.

3. The elevated walkway from the castle to the wishing well. From the inner courtyard of the castle (facing toward the castle drawbridge and Main Street beyond), you can reach a walled walkway, which zigzags down the outside of the castle to a bridge crossing the moat by a wishing well. Standing along this walkway provides a good, elevated vantage point for watching parades.

4. The wishing well. Alongside the castle moat is a wishing well. If you take up a position along the wooden rail by the wishing well, you will have a good view of passing parades.

5. Le Théâtre du Château. As mentioned above, parades pass right in front of Le Théâtre du Château amphitheater. Not only does the amphitheater afford an excellent view, but it is also one of the few places where you can watch the parade while comfortably seated. Claim your seat at least 20–30 minutes before parade time.

6. Le Théâtre du Château production balcony. There is an elevated, railed area used by sound technicians and other production staff for performances at Le Théâtre du Château. When no show is in progress at Le Théâtre (as is the case during parades), this elevated vantage point offers guests a good view of the parade but no place to sit.

7. Town Square Balcony. A tiny balcony to the immediate left of the Town Square entrance to the Liberty Arcade is elevated about a meter and can hold approximately six or seven people. Next to the upper platform of the train station, it provides the best vantage point for seeing the parade over the heads of the crowd. Small and inconspicuous, the balcony often remains unoccupied during parades.

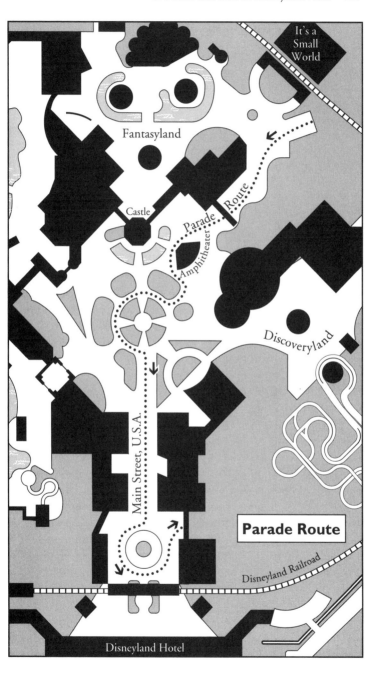

Shopping in Disneyland Paris

Shops in Disneyland Paris add realism and atmosphere to the various theme settings and make available an extensive inventory of souvenirs, clothing , novelties, decorator items, and more. Much of the merchandise displayed (with the exception of Disney trademark souvenir items) is available back home and elsewhere. In our opinion, shopping is not one of the main reasons for visiting Disneyland Paris. We recommend bypassing the shops on a one-day visit. If you have two or more days to spend in Disneyland Paris, browse the shops during the early afternoon when many of the attractions are crowded. Remember that Main Street—with its multitude of shops—opens earlier and closes later than the rest of the park. Lockers in Main Street allow you to stash your purchases safely.

Our recommendations notwithstanding, we realize that for many guests Disney souvenirs and memorabilia are irresistible. If you have decided that you would look good in a Goofy hat with shoulder-length floppy ears, you are in the right place. What's more, you have plenty of company. One of our readers writes:

> *I've discovered that people have a compelling need to buy Disney stuff when they are at [Disneyland Paris]. When you get home you wonder why you ever got a cashmere sweater with Mickey Mouse embroidered on the breast, or a tie with tiny Goofys all over it. Maybe it is something they put in the food.*

Part Five

Dining

Eating in Disneyland Paris

Over the years dining at Disneyland Paris has evolved. There are fewer full-service restaurants in the park, and at Disney Village, American chain restaurants like McDonald's, Planet Hollywood, and the Rainforest Cafe are slowly but certainly replacing Disney eateries. Prices have held steady in regard to the dollar and the pound but have escalated markedly in regard to the French franc. In terms of quality, the food on average is not as good as when the park opened in 1992, but generally better than that served at other Disney parks and resorts.

Theme has always been an integral part of any Disney dining experience—until now, that is. At Disneyland Paris you can no longer make an assumption about a restaurant's cuisine based on the name and theme of the establishment. You'll find Chinese stir-fries in a cowboy restaurant, Italian dishes in a New England seafood joint, Indian curry at a steakhouse, and pizza almost everywhere. As recently as four years ago, the Disneyland Paris restaurants were highly differentiated. Today, with a couple of exceptions, the bills of fare are pretty much the same. The guest need only choose the setting in which he prefers to eat his steak, pizza, or pasta.

I will tell you forthrightly that you can expect good, albeit expensive, food at the Disneyland Paris theme park, at Disney Village, and at the resort hotels. Will it knock you out? Probably not. Is it as good as the food served at comparable prices in Paris? Surely not. But consider as you climb down from Dumbo that you are not *in* Paris. For the moment you are captive on the alien planet of Disneyland Paris, and you can either eat what is available or go without.

The predominant cuisine at Disneyland Paris is American, with almost all American regional specialties represented. Steak is featured in many restaurants, as is barbecue. You will also be able to find New England, Florida, and Pacific Northwestern seafood. Hamburgers abound, and Southwestern/Mexican specialties can be found both in and out of the park. Then, of course, there is that most pretentious manifestation of American culinary art, California nouveau cuisine. The essence of this school of cooking is to turn basic American dishes (catfish, hamburger, pork chops, and such) into exotic creations by arranging the food in miniscule quantities on the plate and garnishing it with endive, watercress, and avocado.

California nouveau cuisine notwithstanding, portions at all the park and resort restaurants are large: too large, in fact, for many Europeans. All meals (breakfast, lunch, and dinner) are available, as well as limited late-night dining. Both bulk-loading American breakfasts and the traditional French *petit déjeuner* can be had in the resort hotel and theme park restaurants. Dress is casual for all meals. Even restaurants that specify that a jacket and tie are required for gentlemen will admit guests dressed in jeans and T-shirts.

Children are welcome at all Disney restaurants. Wait staff and managers understand how itchy children get when they have to sit for an extended period. Your server will keep the small one supplied with bread and butter and will get your meal on the table faster than in comparable restaurants elsewhere. Comments from patrons suggest that being served too quickly is a much more frequent occurrence than having to wait a long time. Finally, most Disneyland Paris restaurants have special children's menus, and all have booster seats and high chairs.

To help you make the most of the meals you eat at Disneyland Paris, we provide summarized versions of the menus of each of the full-service restaurants in the theme park, at Disney Village, and at the resort hotels. We also provide tips for eating in the park, which will help you avoid crowds and save money.

ALTERNATIVES AND SUGGESTIONS FOR EATING IN THE DISNEYLAND PARIS THEME PARK

In the theme park, there are 4 table-service restaurants; 16 counter service, full-menu restaurants; 10 limited-menu sandwich, dessert, and beverage shops; and a number of vendor carts selling snacks. The table-service restaurants generally require reservations, made either at the door of the restaurant or through the concierge/information desk at your Disneyland Paris Resort hotel or campground. All other park restaurants and food concessions operate on a walk-up, first-come first-served basis.

Where and what you eat will be determined primarily by your touring objectives and budget. If you have only one day to spend at the park, you will not have much time for long, leisurely meals in the full-service restaurants. If you are touring on a restricted budget, you will need to locate affordable food (not an easy proposition at Disneyland Paris). In both cases you will want to avoid crowded conditions and long waits at the restaurants. To assist you in conserving time and money, we suggest the following:

1. Eat a good breakfast before arriving at Disneyland Paris. You do not want to waste early-morning touring time eating breakfast in the theme park. If the cost of breakfast is a consideration, buy a supply of croissants, fruit, or whatever at a local market before you check into your hotel or campground.

2. Having eaten a good breakfast, keep your stomach happy as you tour by purchasing snacks from the many vendors stationed throughout the park. This is especially important if you are on a tight schedule; you cannot afford to spend a lot of time waiting in line for food.

3. Most Disneyland Paris guests prefer to eat a late lunch and a late dinner. If you are willing to eat your midday meal before 12:30 p.m. and your evening meal before 7 p.m., you will avoid most of the rush. You also will have eaten in time to enjoy the afternoon and/or evening parade(s).

4. There are several counter-service, full-menu restaurants, which are typically overlooked by the crowds. They are:

Main Street	Victoria's (pot pies and salads)
Frontierland	Cowboy Cookout Barbecue (barbecue and hamburgers)
Adventureland	Colonel Hathi's Pizza Outpost
Fantasyland	Pizzeria Bella Notte (before 12:20 p.m.)
Discoveryland	Buzz Lightyear's Pizza Planet

All of the above serve decent food, though Victoria's is a cut below the other four. Pizzeria Bella Notte should be avoided immediately following parades and productions at Le Théâtre du Château. Colonel Hathi's is the best counter-service restaurant in the park (at both lunch and dinner) for avoiding the crowds.

5. If you are on a tight schedule and the park closes early, stay until closing time and eat dinner outside of the theme park and Disneyland Paris Resort. If you are lodging in Paris, wait until you return to the city to dine. If you are lodging at Disneyland Paris, try one of the excellent and affordable restaurants in the villages around Disneyland Paris. L'Auberge de la Brie, in Couilly–Pont-aux-Dames is one of our personal favorites. What you save on the price of food will more than pay for your cab fare.

6. Exit the park (be sure to get your hand stamped for same-day re-entry) and try one of the restaurants in the Disneyland Hotel or at Disney Village. At the Disneyland Hotel, the Inventions lunch and dinner buffets are outstanding, and the California Grill is arguably the best restaurant in the resort. Walking time to the Disneyland Hotel is less than four minutes, and to Disney Village about five or six minutes.

7. Many of the theme park counter-service restaurants serve a cold sandwich or salad. Buy your cold lunch before the restaurants get crowded, and carry your food (or store it in a locker) until you are ready to eat. Come prepared with some plastic freezer bags to wrap the food. Drinks can be purchased at an appropriate time from any convenient Disney street vendor.

8. Most fast-food eateries in the theme park have more than one service window. Regardless of the time of day, check out the lines at all of the windows before waiting. Sometimes a staffed but out-of-the-way window will have a much shorter line or no line at all.

9. Many of the full-service restaurants that accept reservations for lunch and/or dinner fill their respective seatings quickly. To obtain reservations, hot-foot it over to the restaurant(s) of your choice before 10:30 a.m. Better yet, if you are a guest at a Disneyland Paris Resort hotel, have your concierge/

information desk make your reservations for you. If you do it at the door of the restaurant, you will be given a hand-written card as confirmation and documentation. Later, when you return to eat, present this card to the maître d' hotel.

10. For your general information, the Disney people have a park rule against bringing in your own food and drink. Operational procedures may change, but during the periods when we were researching this guide, theme park entrance attendants actually searched guests' diaper bags, large purses, shopping bags, daypacks, fanny packs, and other pieces of personal luggage.

The Cost of Fast Food in the Theme Park

Fast food can be purchased at counter-service restaurants with relatively varied menus and from vendor carts with limited selections. As you can see from the prices quoted below, at Disneyland Paris "fast" food is not synonymous with "cheap" food.

Tea or cola (large)	FF 18 ($2.40)
Tea or cola (small)	FF 12 ($1.60)
Coffee or hot chocolate	FF 8–10 ($1–1.40)
Beer	FF 16 ($2)
Bottled water	FF 12 ($1.60)
Vendor snacks (popcorn, ice cream, and such)	FF 10–20 ($1.40–2.70)
Sandwiches (hot dogs, hamburgers, tacos, and such)	FF 10–38 ($1.40–5)
Soups	FF 24–32 ($3.20–4.30)
Salads	FF 15–36 ($2–4.80)
Pizza	FF 44–50 ($5.90–6.70)

DISNEYLAND PARIS RESTAURANTS RATED AND RANKED

Listed below are the table-service restaurants (and two upscale buffets) of Disneyland Paris ranked according to the quality of food served. Beside the name of the restaurant is its location. If the restaurant is in the theme park, the land where it is located is specified. If it is in a hotel, the name of the hotel is given. Finally, several restaurants are located in Disney Village, a dining, shopping, and entertainment complex next to the train station.

Each restaurant is assigned an overall star rating, which encompasses the entire dining experience, including style, service, and ambience, in addition to the taste, presentation, and quality of the food. Five stars is the highest rating possible and connotes the best of everything. Four-star restaurants are exceptional, and three-star restaurants are well above average. Two-star restaurants are good. A one-star is an average restaurant that demonstrates an unusual capability in some area of specialization, for instance, an otherwise unmemorable place that serves great barbecued chicken. After the star rating, there is a numerical food-quality score, based on a scale of 100, with 100 representing the best possible quality.

In our evaluation we make no attempt to compare Disney restaurants to restaurants in Paris or to restaurants in the surrounding villages of Marne-la-Vallée. Since Disney restaurants serve American food, we rate them according to how they would stack up against similar restaurants in the United States. It's all a matter of taste, of course, but France strikes us as a strange place to go for American food. See the section titled "Dining outside Disneyland Paris" for a word about good restaurants in nearby small villages.

Next to the quality score is a value rating, defined as follows:

A   Exceptional value, a real bargain
B   Good value
C   Fair value; you get exactly what you pay for
D   Somewhat overpriced
F   Significantly overpriced

Disneyland Paris Restaurants Rated and Ranked				
Restaurant	Location	Star Rating	Quality Rating	Value Rating
California Grill	Disneyland Hotel	★★★★	90	D
Inventions (buffet)	Disneyland Hotel	★★★★	88	B
Hunter's Grill	Sequoia Lodge	★★★½	86	C
Club Manhattan	Hotel New York	★★★½	84	F

Disneyland Paris Restaurants (continued)				
Blue Lagoon	Adventureland	★★★½	84	C
Yacht Club	Newport Bay	★★★	79	D
Auberge de Cendrillon	Fantasyland	★★★	77	C
The Steak House	Disney Village	★★★	76	F
Planet Hollywood	Disney Village	★★★	76	C
Park Side Diner	Hotel New York	★★★	73	D
Cape Cod (buffet)	Newport Bay	★★★	72	C
L.A. Bar & Grill	Disney Village	★★★	72	D
Beaver Creek Tavern	Sequoia Lodge	★★★	72	C
Rainforest Cafe	Disney Village	★★★	71	C
Walt's	Main Street	★★★	70	D
Annette's Diner	Disney Village	★★★	70	D
Silver Spur	Frontierland	★★½	69	F
Billy Bob's	Disney Village	★★½	69	C
Lucky Nugget	Frontierland	★★½	66	D
Crockett's Tavern	Davy Crockett Ranch	★★½	65	D
Chuck Wagon Cafe	Hotel Cheyenne	★★	64	D
La Cantina	Hotel Santa Fe	★★	60	D

DISNEYLAND PARIS DINING DURING COLD WEATHER MONTHS

From October through mid-April, when crowds are normally light, Disneyland Paris changes and scales down its food-service operations. Most theme park restaurants are open only for the midday meal, except during winter holidays. Many theme park counter-service restaurants are closed on weekdays. Conversely, at Disney Village during off-season, restaurants are closed at midday and open only in the evening.

DISNEYLAND PARIS MENUS

When it comes to flowery prose and whimsical description, menu writers are in a class by themselves. No novelist, poet, or even publicist can pilot a truckload of adjectives with the consummate finesse of the menu writer. A menu, for example, might list the following dish:

Fresh, young, free-range chicken trimmed from the bone and slowly simmered in its own natural juices with tender carrots and scallions   FF 110 ($15)

The *Unofficial* translation of this mouth-watering delicacy is: Chicken stew   FF 110 ($15)

Alas, whereas we are able to achieve some measure of success in distilling the menus' descriptive prose, we were singularly unable to do anything about the inflated prices.

Children's Menus

All theme park and resort table-service restaurants offer children's menus. In general, the children's menus offer pasta, fish, chicken, and hamburgers, with presentation and side dishes varying from restaurant to restaurant.

Prices

In the following restaurant profiles, price ranges are for main courses only and do not include starters, salads, desserts, or drinks. We use the following price designations.

Moderate	FF 60–120 ($8–16)
Expensive	FF 120–180 ($16–24)
Very Expensive	FF 180 and over ($24 and over)

DISNEYLAND PARIS FULL-SERVICE RESTAURANTS AND BUFFETS

ANNETTE'S DINER			QUALITY 70
American fast food	Moderate	★★★	VALUE D

Disney Village

Comments: Annette's Diner is a good replica of a 1950s American drive-in hamburger joint. Hostesses wear full skirts and oldies rock music plays continuously. The hamburgers are excellent—better than any hamburgers we have eaten in the States for years. The milkshakes and soda fountain concoctions are also very good. Expect to pay dearly, however, for your serving of vintage American food and nostalgia.

AUBERGE DE CENDRILLON			QUALITY 77
French	Expensive	★★★	VALUE C

Fantasyland

Comments: The only French restaurant in Disneyland Paris, Auberge is luxurious and formal in appearance, relaxed and friendly in style. Stained glass, tapestries, and vaulted ceilings help create an atmosphere in keeping with the adjacent Fantasyland castle.

BEAR CREEK TAVERN			QUALITY 72
American	Moderate	★★★	VALUE C

Sequoia Lodge

Comments: The Beaver Creek Tavern, located on the lower level of the Sequoia Lodge, is an informal restaurant specializing in burgers and salads with a few classier main courses available. A tavern it ain't.

BILLY BOB'S			QUALITY 69
Tex-Mex buffet	Moderate	★★½	VALUE C

Disney Village

Comments: Billy Bob's is more a U.S. country-western nightclub than a restaurant. It does, however, offer a Tex-Mex buffet each night between 7 and 11 p.m. The food is palatable, if not exactly authentic, and the atmosphere is upbeat (sometimes raucous). Billy Bob's is definitely not the place to go for a quiet meal.

BLUE LAGOON RESTAURANT			QUALITY 84
Caribbean seafood	Expensive	★★★½	VALUE C

Adventureland

Comments: Blue Lagoon, a Caribbean seafood restaurant, is one of the treasures of the park. At the Blue Lagoon, the moon is always rising and the stars constantly shining. Diners relax on verandas under thatched roofs and watch boats drift past on the river below (actually the beginning of the Pirates of the Caribbean ride). Though the food is decent, the main attraction is the romantic island ambience. On a cold French winter's day, a couple of hours at Blue Lagoon is worth the cost of Disneyland Paris admission.

CALIFORNIA GRILL			QUALITY 90
American	Very Expensive	★★★★	VALUE D

Disneyland Hotel

Comments: California Grill is the best restaurant anywhere at Disneyland Paris. Luxurious without being pretentious, the California Grill offers fine dining in a comfortable, clublike setting. Located on the second floor of the Disneyland Hotel, the restaurant overlooks the Disneyland Railroad station and theme park beyond. An easy four-minute walk from the park entrance, California Grill offers guests the opportunity to enjoy cocktails and wine with dinner without straying far from the theme park.

CAPE COD			QUALITY 72
Italian buffet	Moderate	★★★	VALUE C

Newport Bay Club

Comments: Cape Cod, like many Disneyland Paris restaurants, basically ignores its New England seafood theme, serving instead a buffet featuring Mediterranean seafood, pasta, and pizza. While not nearly as exotic or varied as the Inventions buffet at the Disneyland Hotel, the Cape Cod buffet selection is perhaps a better choice for picky eaters and families with children. In addition to the evening buffet, Cape Cod offers a character breakfast in the morning and a menu-selection lunch.

CHUCK WAGON CAFE			QUALITY
			64
American barbecue Moderate		★★	VALUE
			D

Hotel Cheyenne

Comments: Chuck Wagon Cafe is similar to La Cantina food court at the Santa Fe, except the Chuck Wagon's house specialty is barbecued chicken, ribs, and pork. Here you can also find stews, grilled meats, and, of course, that old cowboy favorite, Chinese stir-fried dishes. A number of serving stations or self-service food tables are arranged around a barn-size kitchen. Diners essentially wander from one serving area to another accumulating whatever items they desire. Cashiers tally the bill and collect payment before guests are seated. With each item charged à la carte, the tab can add up quickly. Expect to pay FF 95–255 ($13–34) per adult for dinner. With its beamed ceilings, wagon wheel chandeliers, and old-fashioned Western saloon bar, Chuck Wagon is a restaurant where families will feel at home.

CLUB MANHATTAN			QUALITY
			84
International	Very Expensive	★★★½	VALUE
			F

Hotel New York

Comments: Club Manhattan is one of Disneyland Paris's flagship restaurants. Chic, contemporary, and elegant, the restaurant offers some of the resort's better food, but at exorbitant prices. Sophisticated, and at the same time romantic in a formal New York way, Club Manhattan also offers ballroom dancing to aid diners in digesting their meals. Jackets are required for gentlemen.

CROCKETT'S TAVERN			QUALITY
			65
American	Moderate	★★½	VALUE
			D

Davy Crockett Ranch

Comments: Crockett's Tavern is a large, bustling, rustic place that would be very much at home in Frontierland. Decorated with various trapper paraphernalia, the Tavern specializes in salads and grilled items. Service is cafeteria style, i.e., self-serve, with a cashier waiting eagerly at the end to total it all up. Crockett's Tavern is fine if you're staying at Davy Crockett Ranch; otherwise, don't go out of your way to try it.

HUNTER'S GRILL			QUALITY 86
Spit-roasted meats	Expensive	★★★½	VALUE C

Sequoia Lodge

Comments: Hunter's Grill offers a fixed-price dinner, which includes servings of several meats. As you might expect, the decor is reminiscent of a hunting or ski lodge. Fresh cuts of meat are on display behind glass. Located on the lower level of Sequoia Lodge, Hunter's Grill is a 13–18-minute walk from the theme park (or a 5-minute bus ride from the train and bus transportation station).

INVENTIONS			QUALITY 88
Spit-roasted meats	Expensive	★★★★	VALUE B

Disneyland Hotel

Comments: Located, like the California Grill, on the second floor of the Disneyland Hotel, Inventions serves Disneyland Paris's most elaborate and well-prepared buffet. The ample table offers a wide selection that includes cold smoked meats, French and Scandinavian cheeses, Mexican guacamole, and Italian pasta and pepper salad. Hot dishes feature pastry-wrapped fish fillets, prime rib, and even sliced breast of duck. For visitors who enjoy ethnic variety and are big eaters, Inventions lunch and dinner buffets are highly recommended. Though not inexpensive, the buffets represent a good value for the money—less than five minutes from the park entrance.

LA CANTINA			QUALITY
			60
Mexican	Moderate	★★	VALUE
			D

Hotel Santa Fe

Comments: La Cantina is a food court—a number of small serving stations specializing in different main courses, as well as salads, vegetables, breads, and desserts. Hot offerings include grilled meats and poultry, soups, fajitas, and various Mexican and Southwestern American dishes. Guests can select items from about a dozen serving stations; each item is priced à la carte as at a cafeteria. La Cantina is less expensive than Disneyland Paris table-service restaurants, but not much. By the time you pay individually for everything on your plate, it is easy to run up a tab of FF 128–255 ($17–$34) without much effort. The La Cantina dining room is festive, with colorful American Southwestern decor. The restaurant has a bustling school cafeteria atmosphere: informal but certainly not romantic or intimate.

LOS ANGELES BAR AND GRILL			QUALITY
			72
Californian	Moderate	★★★	VALUE
			D

Disney Village

Comments: Los Angeles Bar and Grill is a busy, trendy California-style eatery specializing in pizza, fajitas, pasta, and salads. Contemporary in design with a decidedly youthful atmosphere, the restaurant exudes the feel and energy of a suburban American neighborhood hangout. About seven minutes by foot from the theme park entrance.

LUCKY NUGGET			QUALITY
			66
American buffet	Expensive	★★½	VALUE
			D

Disney Village

Comments: Lucky Nugget offers a Tex-Mex buffet that barely pays lip service to either cuisine. The setting, of course, is that of an American Wild West saloon. Most meals are character meals. During busier times of year reservations are a good idea.

PARK SIDE DINER			QUALITY 73
American	Moderate	★★★	VALUE D

Hotel New York

Comments: Park Side Diner is an upscale, Art Deco American hotel coffee shop: comfortable, informal, and bustling. Sandwiches, pasta, and salads are the specialties of the house.

PLANET HOLLYWOOD			QUALITY 76
American	Moderate	★★★	VALUE C

Disney Village

Comments: Planet Hollywood is one of a chain of American movie-theme restaurants owned by actors Bruce Willis and Demi Moore, among others. Loud and cavernous, with movie memorabilia covering the walls, Planet Hollywood specializes in sandwiches, burgers, dinner salads, pizza, and pasta.

RAINFOREST CAFE			QUALITY 71
American	Moderate	★★★	VALUE C

Disney Village

Comments: Rainforest Cafe, like Planet Hollywood, is an American chain theme restaurant. This time the theme is a rainforest jungle, complete with audio-animatronic animals. During busier times of year, the cafe makes a real (and time-consuming) production of getting a table. Menu offerings are extensive, but quality is not as consistent as Planet Hollywood.

SILVER SPUR			QUALITY 69
American steak house	Expensive	★★½	VALUE F

Frontierland

Comments: What you see is what you get at Silver Spur: a frontier saloon atmosphere augmented by art depicting the American Wild West.

THE STEAK HOUSE		QUALITY
		76
American steak house Expensive ★★★		VALUE
		F

Disney Village

Comments: The Steak House is a good imitation of an upscale Denver or Kansas City downtown club. Though informal, it captures the masculine feel of exclusive restaurants frequented by wealthy cattlemen. It's an 8–12-minute walk from the theme park.

WALT'S		QUALITY
		70
American Expensive ★★★★		VALUE
		D

Main Street, U.S.A.

Comments: Walt's is an elegantly appointed American restaurant offering decor and atmosphere consistent with its Main Street, U.S.A., turn-of-the-century setting.

YACHT CLUB RESTAURANT		QUALITY
		79
American Expensive ★★★		VALUE
		D

Newport Bay Club

Comments: The Yacht Club is an attractive and intimate restaurant with low ceilings and nautical decor. A huge display of fresh seafood gets you in the mood as you enter the door, on the ground floor of the Newport Bay Club. You can walk to the Newport Bay Club from the theme park in 15–20 minutes, or catch a bus (no charge) next to the train station.

Dining outside Disneyland Paris

Having a meal—a rather expensive meal—at the Steak House in Disney Village or at Club Manhattan in the Hotel New York is undoubtedly a pleasant experience. The surroundings are fairly elegant, the portions are large, and the service is friendly. Of course, the fare is basically just steak and chops, standard American "continental" cuisine found just about anywhere in the world.

You are in France, though, and you may wish to broaden your culinary experiences by dining outside the park. In fact, we strongly recommend this option. Consider what you could get for significantly less money in Paris, 40–50 minutes away. You could eat, for example, at Auberge des Deux Signes, just downstream from a floodlit Notre Dame. Perhaps you would order the preserved goose with wild mushrooms or the lentils steamed with a hint of lard. Or coquille St. Jacques (scallops) with safron. You would be eating authentic French cuisine in a French restaurant in France— and be seated in an exquisite table in a former medieval chapel!

The advantages are obvious. However, the downside is the inconvenience of leaving the park and taking time away from Disney adventures. There is a middle ground, however. It should be emphatically stated that you do not have to go all the way to Paris for an excellent and affordable French meal. There are a number of highly respectable, very French, and not particularly expensive restaurants just minutes away in the surrounding villages of the Seine-et-Marne departement. Visitors often ignore the fact that Disneyland Paris is located near the scenic Marne River, and many eateries have set their tables along the verdant banks of the river that French impressionist Auguste Renoir loved so much and captured in his passionate oils. And if you have your own car, finding nearby restaurants is a snap. Instead of ersatz American food at prices far higher than Americans would pay for it at home, you could explore the immediate region and eat in luxury while not venturing too far off the track. The villages of Lagny-sur-Marne, Condé–Ste. Libiaire, and others, although not very rural, offer both delightful cuisine and charming decor. L'Auberge de la Brie, in nearby Couilly–Pont-aux-Dames, offers an extremely reasonable five-course fixed-price menu, for example, that would bring you everything from an asparagus flan to a magnificent cheese cart to sinful desserts. Not to mention the elaborate wine list!

When you begin to crave meals that let you know you really are in France, remember culinary nirvana lies just beyond the park's gates. Even if you do not have a car, you are only a short taxi ride away from memorable five-course meals. Though there are buses to neighboring villages, the schedules are erratic and confusing— and fares are not that much cheaper than taxis. And the restaurants will call taxis for you for your return trip back to the park. Even including the taxi fare, you will pay less for dinner than you would at any Disneyland Paris table-service restaurant.

Main courses (called *plats* or *assiettes,* not *entrees,* which actually means appetizers or starters) at the restaurants we feature here run FF 75–125 ($10–17) at most of the restaurants listed. Many offer a prix fixe menu, however, which is almost always advantageous. A four- or five-course meal (appetizer, fish course, meat, cheese or salad, and dessert) can easily be less than FF 165 ($22).

Inexpensive below refers to a full meal without wine for under FF 125 ($17) per person; moderate, FF 125–250 ($17–34); expensive, over FF 250 ($34 and up). If you decide to go to one of the small villages for lunch or dinner, be aware the meal could last a couple of hours, and plan your day accordingly. And note that French restaurants are not open all day long. We have included only restaurants in the park's immediate vicinity, so you can get back to Mickey quickly. In fact, none are more than 20 minutes away by car or taxi. Remember to have your hand stamped when you leave the park if you want to return the same day. The stamp is in invisible ultraviolet ink, so you won't look foolish at an elegant French meal with a red Daffy beaming up at the waiter. Although lunch is a perfectly viable option, in most cases you'll feel more relaxed and less rushed taking your time in the evening.

Listed below by town are some personal restaurant recommendations:

Village	Restaurant
Condé–Ste. Libiaire (5 kilometers from the park)	Vallée de la Marne 2 Quai de la Marne tel. 01-60-04-31-01 Specialty: Seasonal, foie gras, game, and scallops Price: Moderate
Couilly–Pont-aux-Dames (10 minutes from the park)	L'Auberge de la Brie 14 ave Boulingre tel. 01-64-63-51-80 Specialty: Lobster with stewed tomatoes, scallops with foie gras de canard Price: Expensive Closes at 2:30 p.m.; reopens at 7:30 p.m.

Village	Restaurant
Lagny-sur-Marne (15 kilometers from the park)	Le Gourmandin 117 rue Claye tel. 01-64-30-22-94 Specialty: Fish Price: Moderate
	Auberge Le Tournesoleil 7 rue Marne tel. 01-60-43-49-30 Specialty: Fish and meat, Provençal decor Price: Moderate
L'Ermitage (4 kilometers from the park)	Ecluse de Chalifert On the riverfront tel. 01-60-43-41-43 Specialty: Traditional French "guinguette" dance hall with din ner, accordion music, and retro dancing Price: Moderate to Expensive Friday and Saturday at 8:30 p.m.
Montévrain (2 kilometers from the park)	La Bonne Auberge 37 route N 34 tel. 01-64-30-25-09 Specialty: Fish and meat, local Brie cheese, and famous local mustard Price: Inexpensive Closes at 2 p.m.; reopens at 7 p.m. Owners Brenda and Maurice speak English!
Villeneuve-le-Comte (10 minutes from the park)	La Bonne Marmite 15 rue Général de Gaulle (behind Davy Crockett Ranch) tel. 01-60-43-00-10 Specialty: Fresh game and fish Price: Expensive

Some General Advice

Closings Almost all these restaurants are closed Mondays, and some are closed other days as well. Some open on Sundays for lunch but close for dinner. Call ahead.

Reservations Always call to reserve. Nonsmokers should request a table away from the smoke. Usually restaurants will try to accommodate you as best as they can.

Dress Cut-off jeans may be fine at even the best of the park restaurants, but they are not acceptable attire beyond the gates, particularly in a small village. That does not mean tie and jacket are required, but you will feel more at ease and be more welcome in respectable dress: try to avoid T-shirts or shorts for men and women (unless they are dress shorts).

Part Six

Touring Plans

Touring Plans: What They Are and How They Work

When we interviewed Disneyland Paris visitors who toured the park on a slow day—say, in early October—they invariably waxed eloquent about the sheer delight of their experience. However, when we questioned visitors who toured on a moderate or busy day, they spent most of the interview telling us about the jostling crowds and how much time they stood in line. What a shame, they said, that you should devote so much time and energy to fighting the crowds in a place as special as Disneyland Paris.

Given this complaint, we descended on Disneyland Paris with a team of researchers to determine whether a touring plan could be devised that would move the visitor counter to the flow of the traffic and allow him or her to see virtually the whole park in one day with only minimal waits in line. On some of the busiest days of the year, our team monitored traffic flow into and through the park, noting how the park filled and how the patrons were distributed among the various lands. Likewise, we observed which rides and attractions were most popular and where bottlenecks were most likely to form.

After many long days of collecting data, we devised a number of preliminary touring plans, which we tested during one of the busiest weeks of the entire year. Each day individual members of our research team would tour the park according to one of the preliminary plans, noting how long it took to walk from place to place and how long the wait in line was for each ride or show.

Combining the knowledge gained through these trial runs, we devised a master plan, which we retested and fine-tuned. This plan, with very little variance from day to day, allowed us to experience all of the major rides and attractions (and most of the lesser ones) in one day; our average in-line wait at each ride/show was less than ten minutes.

From this master plan we developed a number of alternative plans that take into account the varying tastes and personal requirements of different Disneyland Paris patrons. We devised a plan, for instance, for adults touring without small children that takes advantage of their ability to move around the park quickly. Another plan was designed for parents touring with children under age eight. Each plan operates with the same efficiency as the master plan but addresses special needs and preferences.

Finally, after all the touring plans were tested by our staff, we selected everyday Disneyland Paris patrons to test the plans. We used convenience sampling; the only prerequisite for being in the test group was that the guest must be visiting a Disney theme park for the first time. A second group of ordinary Disneyland Paris patrons was chosen for a "control group": first-time visitors who would tour the park according to their own plans but who would make notes of what they did and how much time they spent in lines.

When the two groups were compared, the results were impressive. On days when the park's attendance exceeded 40,000 visitors, patrons touring on their own (without our plan) *averaged* two hours more waiting in line per day than those touring according to our plan—and they experienced only two-thirds as many attractions.

Will the Plans Continue to Work Once the Secret Is Out?

Yes! First, all of the plans require that a patron be on hand when Disneyland Paris opens. Many people on holiday simply refuse to make this early-rising sacrifice, even though you can see more in the one hour just after the park opens than in several hours once the park begins to fill. Second, it is anticipated that less than 1% of any given day's attendance will have been exposed to the plans, not enough to bias the results. Last, most groups will alter the plans somewhat, skipping certain rides or shows as a matter of personal taste.

Variables that Will Affect the Success of the Touring Plans

How quickly you move from one ride to another; when and how many refreshment and rest room breaks you take; when, where, and how you eat meals; and your ability (or lack thereof) to find your way around will all have an impact on the success of the plans. We recommend continuous, expeditious touring until around 11:30 a.m. After that, breaks and so on will not affect the plan significantly. If you are touring on a short-hours day (9 a.m.–6 p.m.) and attendance is large, you may wish to avail yourself of one of the time-saving lunch options listed in Part Five: Dining.

General Overview of the Touring Plans

The Disneyland Paris Touring Plans are step-by-step plans for seeing as much as possible with a minimum of time wasted standing in line. They are designed to assist you in avoiding bottlenecks on days of moderate to heavy attendance. On days of lighter attendance (see Selecting the Time of Year for Your Visit), the plans will still save you time but will not be as critical to successful touring.

Choosing the Right Touring Plan

Five different touring plans are presented:

- One-Day Touring Plan for Adults
- One-Day Touring Plan for Seniors
- One-Day Touring Plan for Adults with Small Children
- Two-Day Touring Plan A for Daytime Touring or for When the Park Closes Early (before 8 p.m.)
- Two-Day Touring Plan B for Morning and Evening Touring or for When the Park Is Open Late (after 8 p.m.)

If you have two days to spend at Disneyland Paris, the two-day touring plans are by far the most relaxed and efficient. Two-Day Touring Plan A takes advantage of early-morning touring opportunities when lines are short and the park has not yet filled with guests. This plan works well year-round and is particularly recommended for days when Disneyland Paris closes before 8 p.m. On the other hand, Two-Day Touring Plan B combines the efficiency of early-morning touring on the first day with the splendor of Disneyland Paris at night on the second day. This plan is perfect for guests who wish to sample both the attractions and the special magic of Disneyland Paris after dark, including parades and fireworks.

If you have only one day but wish to see as much as possible, use the One-Day Touring Plan for Adults. This plan will pack as much into a single day as is humanly possible but obviously does not permit long, leisurely meals or a lot of browsing in shops. The plan features what we consider the best Disneyland Paris has to offer, omitting midway rides and other less impressive attractions.

If you have small children, you may want to use the One-Day Touring Plan for Adults with Small Children. This plan includes many of the children's rides in Fantasyland and omits roller coaster rides and other attractions not suitable for small children (either because of Disney's age and height requirements or because the rides and shows are frightening). Since this plan calls for adult guests to sacrifice many of the better Disney attractions, it is not recommended unless you are touring Disneyland Paris primarily for the benefit of the children. An alternative would be to use the One-Day Touring Plan for Adults and take advantage of "switching off," a technique whereby children accompany adults to the loading area of rides with age and height requirements but do not actually ride (see page 114). Switching off allows adults to enjoy the wilder rides while keeping the whole group together.

Finally, for older persons (or others) who desire to minimize walking, we have created the One-Day Touring Plan for Seniors. Though it is impossible in a park the size of Disneyland Paris to avoid a fair amount of walking, we have eliminated in the Seniors itinerary much of the backtracking found in the other touring plans. The Seniors touring plan also omits such thrill rides as Big Thunder Mountain, Space Mountain, and Indiana Jones, even though many seniors enjoy these rides.

Preliminary Instructions for All Touring Plans

BEFORE YOU GO

1. Buy your admission in advance. One-, two-, or three-day passports can be obtained in advance by writing the Disneyland Paris Ticket Service as described on page 22. If you are lodging at a Disneyland Paris Resort hotel, you can purchase your passes at the hotel the night before you visit the park.

2. Call 64-74-30-00 the day before you go for the official opening time.

3. Read over the touring plan of your choice so that you will have a basic understanding of what you are likely to encounter.

4. Many of the touring plans make use of FASTPASS. Read the section about FASTPASS on pages 86–90 to make sure you understand the system.

AT DISNEYLAND PARIS

On days of moderate to heavy attendance, follow the touring plans exactly, deviating only when you do not wish to experience a listed attraction. For instance, the touring plan may direct you to Big Thunder Mountain, a roller coaster ride. If you do not like roller coasters, simply skip that step and proceed to the next.

1. For morning touring, if you have already bought your admission passes, arrive at the park about 40 minutes before official opening time. If you are touring on a summer weekend or during a holiday period, arrive 60 minutes before official opening time. If you have not yet purchased your admission, add another 15 minutes.

2. Admission pass in hand, wait at the entrance turnstile to be admitted. If your gate is not attended, don't worry; sometimes the gate operators are not posted until just a minute before opening.

3. Understand that certain attractions close early. Closing times for these attractions can be found in your handout park map.

4. Move expeditiously until about 11 or 11:30 a.m. After 11:30 feel free to slow your pace and work parades and stage shows into your itinerary. If you elect to see a stage show, try to arrive at the theater about 30 minutes before show time.

5. When you are admitted to the park, move as fast as you can, directed by your chosen touring plan, to the far end of Main Street. Disneyland Paris utilizes two basic opening procedures, so you will probably encounter one of the following:

    a. The entire park will be open. If this is the case, proceed as quickly as possible to the first attraction listed on your touring plan.

    b. Only Main Street will be open. In this case, station yourself by the rope barrier (at the place directed by your touring plan) and be ready to hustle to the first ride listed when the remainder of the park is opened.

One-Day Touring Plan for Adults

For: Adults without small children.

Assumes: Willingness to experience all major rides (including roller coasters) and shows.

Be forewarned that this plan requires a lot of walking and some backtracking; this is necessary to avoid long waits in line. A little extra walking coupled with some hustle in the morning will save you two to three hours of standing in line. Note also that you might not complete the tour. How far you get will depend on the size of your group, how quickly you move from ride to ride, how many times you pause for rest or food, how quickly the park fills, and what time the park closes. With a little zip and some luck, it is possible to complete the touring plan even on a busy day when the park closes early.

1. Arrive before official opening time (specifically as directed in the preliminary instructions to the touring plans) and purchase your admission if necessary.

2. Line up in front of an entrance turnstile and wait to be admitted to the park. Choose a turnstile as far to the right as possible. If you have not been given a park handout map, try to get one from the gate attendant as you pass through the turnstile. If you cannot obtain a map at the gate, pick one up at City Hall, on the left side of Town Square, once you have passed through the turnstile.

3. When you are admitted to the park, move posthaste to the far end of Main Street. When you reach the far end of Main Street, turn right toward Discoveryland. If there is no rope barrier, continue quickly and without stopping to Discoveryland and Space Mountain. If a rope barrier is in place, station yourself at the rope and wait to be admitted to Discoveryland. Position is everything at this point in the day. You will later be rewarded in great time savings for your early morning discipline. *Note:* The first ride on the touring plan is a roller coaster. If you do not like roller coasters, go directly to Step 5.

4. Ride Space Mountain.

5. On exiting Space Mountain bear right to Star Tours. Ride.

6. Backtrack to the entrance of Discoveryland and cross the central hub to Frontierland. Passing through the log stockade

without stopping, head directly to Big Thunder Mountain and ride. Big Thunder Mountain is also a roller coaster, so if you don't like roller coasters, proceed directly to Adventureland via the central hub and head for Pirates of the Caribbean in the upper left corner of the park. After riding Pirates, pick up the touring plan at Step 9.

7. After experiencing Big Thunder, turn left along the waterfront. Turn right after passing the Fuente del Oro Restaurante and enter Adventureland. Continue straight until you come to a bridge. Turn left *before* crossing the bridge and head for Indiana Jones and the Temple of Peril. This modest roller coaster loops you upside down. If you're not in the mood to be stood on your head, skip to Step 9.

Note: Indiana Jones is a FASTPASS attraction. If you want to ride and the posted wait time is less than 30 minutes, join the regular queue. If the posted wait exceeds 30 minutes, obtain FASTPASSes for your party and plan to return later.

8. After riding (or not riding) Indiana Jones, cross the bridge to the Swiss Family Treehouse (La Cabane des Robinson). Bypassing the tree house for the moment, bear left on the far side of the bridge and cross a second bridge leading to Adventure Isle. Continue, keeping the stream on your left until your reach a stone and concrete bridge. Turn left here and proceed to Pirates of the Caribbean. Ride.

9. Bear left after Pirates of the Caribbean and depart Adventureland for Fantasyland. In Fantasyland turn right toward the castle and check the posted wait time for Peter Pan's Flight. If the wait is 25 minutes or less, go ahead and ride. If the wait exceeds 25 minutes, skip Peter Pan for the moment. If the wait is prohibitive and you did not obtain a FASTPASS for Indiana Jones, get a FASTPASS for Peter Pan now.

10. Continue toward the castle; ride Les Voyages de Pinocchio.

11. Exit Pinocchio to the right and ride Blanche-Neige et les Sept Nains.

12. After Snow White (Blanche-Neige), cross between the Carousel and Dumbo to the Mad Hatter's Tea Cups. If you are prone to motion sickness, skip to Step 14. Otherwise, ride the tea cups.

13. Moving away from the castle, pass under the railroad tracks and ride Le Pays de Contes de Fées (Storyland Boats).

14. If you have an Indiana Jones FASTPASS, it should be about time to return and ride. If you are within your return period for your Indiana Jones FASTPASS, you will now be able to additionally pick up Peter Pan FASTPASSes on the way. Do so. If your return period has not begun, continue experiencing other attractions (or taking a break or having lunch) until the return period rolls around. At that time return to Indiana Jones, stopping en route at Peter Pan for FASTPASSes.

After using your Indiana Jones FASTPASS you will have most of the potential bottlenecks behind you. Feel free to relax your pace, grab something to eat, or interrupt the touring plan to enjoy some live entertainment (see the parades and shows schedule in your park handout map).

15. The next attraction on the touring plan is *Le Visionarium* in Discoveryland. *Le Visionarium* is located to the right just inside the main entrance to Discoveryland.

16. After *Le Visionarium,* cross the plaza toward Space Mountain. To the right of Space Mountain is the walk-through attraction, Les Mystères du Nautilus. Enjoy.

17. After Nautilus, walk to the far side of Space Mountain to *Honey, I Shrunk the Audience.* Enjoy the show.

18. Next go to the adjacent railroad station and take the Disneyland Railroad to the Fantasyland Station.

19. By the time you arrive at Fantasyland it should be time to use your FASTPASSes for Peter Pan's Flight. If not, skip ahead until time to return to Peter Pan.

20. On the far side of Fantasyland ride It's a Small World.

21. Exiting Small World to the right, cross Fantasyland and return to Adventureland. Take a left after passing through the entrance and continue to La Cabane des Robinson. Explore the tree house.

22. Return to Frontierland via the central plaza and ride the Thunder Mesa Riverboat.

23. Turn right after exiting the riverboat. Keeping the waterfront on your right, proceed to Phantom Manor. If the

queue looks intimidating, don't worry. Phantom Manor is a fast-loading attraction, so your wait will be tolerable.

24. This concludes the touring plan. If you still have time and energy, explore Adventure Isle and Skull Rock (both in Adventureland) and tour the castle. Be sure to check out the dragon in the cellar. Alternatively, check your daily entertainment schedule for parades, shows, and fireworks. Main Street stays open later than the other lands, so you might want to save your shopping. Be aware, however, that stores get very congested in the hour or so prior to park closing.

One-Day Touring Plan for Seniors

For: Older adults who wish to minimize walking.
Assumes: Willingness to experience all major rides (except thrill rides and roller coasters) and shows.

Because of the size of Disneyland Paris, there is no way to tour the entire park without walking a great deal. Although you will be doing some backtracking, the extra walking will save you as much as two hours of standing in line. Seniors would be best served seeing the park over two days with plenty of time for rest in between. But if your schedule limits you to a single day, the following touring plan will allow you to see the best the park has to offer, excluding the thrill rides: Big Thunder Mountain, Space Mountain, Indiana Jones and the Temple of Peril, and Star Tours.

If the park is open past 9 p.m. and you are lodging at the Disneyland Paris Resort, discontinue the plan at about 1 p.m. and go to your hotel for lunch and some rest. Return refreshed in the late afternoon or early evening to complete your tour. Note also that you might not complete the touring plan. How far you get will depend on the size of your group, how quickly you move from attraction to attraction, how many times you pause for rest or food, how quickly the park fills, and what time the park closes. If you do not spin your wheels, especially in the morning, it is possible to complete the touring plan even on a busy day when the park closes early.

1. Arrive before official opening time (specifically as directed in the preliminary instructions to the touring plans) and purchase your admission if necessary. If you wish to eat lunch in a table-service restaurant, we recommend the Blue Lagoon in Adventureland.

2. Line up in front of an entrance turnstile and wait to be admitted to the park. If you have not been given a park handout map, try to get one from the gate attendant as you pass through the turnstile. If you cannot obtain a map at the gate, pick one up at City Hall, on the left side of Town Square, once you have passed through the turnstile.

3. When you are admitted to the park, move posthaste to the far end of Main Street via the Discovery Arcade. The Discovery Arcade is an enclosed walkway that runs parallel to Main Street on the right. Its entrance is on the far right side of Town Square before you start down Main Street. When you reach the far end of the Discovery Arcade, move directly across the central hub and pass through the main entrance of the castle into Fantasyland. If a rope barrier is in place at the central hub, station yourself at the rope and wait to be admitted to the remainder of the park. Position is critical early in the morning. The time you spend now literally will save hours of waiting later in the day.

4. In Fantasyland (on your left after passing through the castle), ride Blanche-Neige et les Sept Nains (Snow White and the Seven Dwarfs).

5. On exiting Blanche-Neige, go next door to the left and ride Les Voyages de Pinocchio. After exiting Pinocchio, turn left and walk around the corner (keeping Au Chalet de la Marionnette restaurant on your left). Across the plaza (on your right), you will see Peter Pan's Flight. Ride.

6. After Peter Pan strike out across Fantasyland, passing Dumbo on your right. On your left across from the Tea Cups, explore Alice's Curious Labyrinth. This attraction and the next one on the touring plan are a must-see for garden and landscaping buffs.

7. Exit the labyrinth to the left and take a second left under the railroad tracks. Ride Le Pays des Contes de Fées (Storyland Boats). Don't be put off by the seemingly childish theme. This is one of the highest-ranking attractions in the park for seniors.

8. Pass back under the track, turn left to It's a Small World. Ride.

9. After Small World, return to the central hub via the walkway that runs to the left of the castle (as you face it from Small World). Enter Discoveryland.

10. On your left, not far past the entrance to Discoveryland, is *Le Visionarium*. Once again, the line will appear huge, but it will be largely absorbed when the show in progress concludes. See the show.

11. On exiting *Le Visionarium,* turn left and walk to the far end of Discoveryland. If you're feeling plucky, take a spin on Star Tours (a bumpy ride but totally wonderful attraction).

12. To the immediate right of Star Tours is *Honey, I Shrunk the Audience.* The line here also may look intimidating, but, as at *Le Visionarium,* it will disappear when the new audience is admitted. Seniors give this show high ratings and particularly enjoy the remarkable 3D special effects.

Note: This is about as far as you can go on a busy day before the crowds catch up with you, but you will have experienced many of the more popular rides and shows, and you will have cleared most of Disneyland Paris's major traffic bottlenecks. Remember, during the morning (through Step 12) keep moving. In the afternoon, adjust the pace to your liking.

Consult your live entertainment schedule. Note performance times for the afternoon parade and for stage shows around the park. Simply interrupt the touring plan as convenient to see the parade(s) and stage shows, resuming the touring plan afterward. For tips on finding a good vantage point for watching the parade(s), see pages 165–166. Likewise, from this point on, feel free to discontinue the touring plan for lunch and/or dinner. Advice on where and when to eat can be found under Alternatives and Suggestions for Eating in the Theme Park on pages 170–173.

13. Backtrack past Star Tours to the Discoveryland Railroad Station. Take the Disneyland Railroad to the Fantasyland Station.

14. After disembarking, head toward the castle, then take your first right into Adventureland.

15. In Adventureland continue to bear right to Pirates of the Caribbean. Do not worry if the line seems long: Pirates is an efficient, fast-loading ride, and you will not have a long wait. Ride.

16. Exit Pirates of the Caribbean and turn right. Pass through Adventure Isle. If you are feeling energetic, there are caverns and paths to explore (which require a lot of step climbing).

If you think you are getting enough exercise as it is, you can get a good look at Adventure Isle just by passing through.

17. From Adventure Isle make your way to La Cabane des Robinson (Swiss Family Treehouse). Touring the tree house involves climbing stairs but nothing challenging or tricky. Once again, you can appreciate much of this imposing structure by viewing it from the ground.

18. Exit Adventureland and enter Frontierland. Keep the waterfront on your right, past the entrance to Big Thunder Mountain and past the shooting gallery, until you reach the landing for the big riverboats. Take the riverboat for a ride on "Rivers of the Far West."

19. Exiting the riverboat, continue around the waterfront all the way to Phantom Manor. See Phantom Manor. Though the line may appear long, it will move quickly.

20. After exiting Phantom Manor, backtrack to the main log stockade entrance of Frontierland. Check out Legends of the Wild West.

21. After exiting the log fort on the central hub side, take the first path to the left and continue to the central hub entrance of Adventureland. Enter Adventureland and visit the bazaar.

22. Exit Adventureland toward the central hub and make an immediate left on the path leading to the lower part of the castle. On its lower left side, you will see a small, dark passage marked "La Tanière du Dragon" (The Dragon's Den). Stop and say *bonjour* to the dragon. Afterward take the steps up into the castle to its second floor. Check out the story of *Sleeping Beauty* as told in stained glass and tapestries.

23. If you have some time left before the park closes, backtrack to pick up attractions you may have missed or bypassed because the lines were too long. Check out any parades, fireworks, or live performances that interest you. Grab a bite to eat. Save Main Street until last, as it remains open after the rest of the park closes.

24. Continue to tour until everything except Main Street closes or you are ready to go. Finish your day by browsing along Main Street. If you are shopping for a Disney souvenir and the Main Street shops are packed, you can find almost the same selection at less-crowded Disney Village on the far side of the train station.

One-Day Touring Plan for Adults with Small Children

For: Parents who feel compelled to devote every waking moment to the pleasure and entertainment of their small children, and for rich people who are paying someone else to take their children to the theme park.

Assumes: Periodic stops for rest, rest rooms, and refreshment.

This touring plan represents a concession to the observed tastes of younger children. Included are many midway-type rides that your children may have the opportunity to experience (although in less exotic surroundings) at local fairs and amusement parks. These rides at Disneyland Paris often require long waits in line, consuming valuable touring time that could be better spent experiencing the many rides and shows found only at a Disney theme park and that best demonstrate the Disney genius.

To a large extent, adults supervising this plan stand around, wipe noses, pay for stuff, and generally watch the children enjoy themselves. Regardless of whether you are loving, guilty, masochistic, truly selfless, insane, or saintly, this touring plan will provide a small child with about as perfect a day as is possible at Disneyland Paris.

If you want to balance the touring plan a bit, try working out a compromise with your kids to forgo some of the carnival-type rides (Dumbo, The Mad Hatter's Tea Cups, Le Carrousel de Lancelot, Orbitron) or boring attractions (for adults), such as the Autopia.

Another alternative is to use the One-Day Touring Plan for Adults and take advantage of "switching off." This technique allows small children to be admitted to rides such as Big Thunder Mountain and Space Mountain. The children wait in the loading area as their parents ride one at a time; the nonriding parent waits with the children.

1. Arrive before official opening time (specifically as directed in the preliminary instructions to the touring plans) and purchase your admission if necessary.

2. Line up in front of an entrance turnstile and wait to be admitted to the park. If you have not been given a park handout map, try to get one from the gate attendant as you pass through the turnstile. If you cannot obtain a map at the gate, pick one up at City Hall (on the left side of Town Square) once you have passed through the turnstile.

3. When you are admitted to the park, move posthaste to the far end of Main Street. On reaching the far end of Main Street, proceed directly across the central hub and head for the main entrance to the castle and Fantasyland. If a rope barrier is in place across the end of Main Street, position yourself at the rope and wait to be admitted to the remainder of the park. Time you invest in staking out your position now will save you hours of standing in line later.

4. Pass directly through the castle without stopping and past the carousel to Dumbo. Ride Dumbo.

5. After riding Dumbo, head up the left side of Fantasyland to Peter Pan's Flight. Ride.

6. After Peter Pan, head across the plaza to experience the Mad Hatter's Tea Cups.

7. In Fantasyland ride Le Carrousel de Lancelot. Since the ride can accommodate almost 100 riders at a time, your wait should be short.

8. After the carrousel, ride Les Voyages de Pinocchio. *Note:* The whale in this attraction frightens some small children.

9. Turn right when you exit Pinocchio and go next door to Blanche-Neige et les Sept Nains (Snow White and the Seven Dwarfs). *Note:* The witch in this attraction frightens many children.

10. Next explore Alice's Curious Labyrinth, on the other side of the Mad Hatter's Tea Cups.

11. Exit the labyrinth to the left and pass under the railroad tracks. Two attractions, one a boat ride and the other a train, take you for a ride through Storyland. Ride either or both. Be aware that some preschoolers become alarmed by the confinement of the train. In addition the train is not particularly comfortable for adults.

12. Pass back under the railroad track and stay left until you reach It's a Small World. Ride.

13. After Small World, return to the central hub on the walkway that passes to the left of the castle (as you face it from Small World). Enter Discoveryland.

14. In Discoveryland ride Orbitron, situated in the center of the plaza.

15. Next door to Orbitron, ride Autopia. If your child is too small to drive, allow him or her to steer (the car is on a track); you work the accelerator and brake.

    Autopia and Orbitron are exceedingly slow-loading rides so you will be in for long waits at both. We recommend skipping Orbitron, which is like Dumbo, only a little higher and faster. When you see the wait at Autopia, you may want to skip it as well and try back later during a parade.

16. Next door to Autopia, tour the submarine *Nautilus.*

17. Proceed to the far side of Space Mountain to the Discoveryland station of the Disneyland Railroad. Take the railroad to the Fantasyland station.

Note: If you are staying at Disneyland Paris and would like to return to your hotel for lunch and a nap, take the train all the way around the park plus one stop, disembarking at the Main Street station the second time the train stops there. When you return to the park, catch the train to Fantasyland and resume the touring plan.

18. Bear to your right departing the Fantasyland station and pass Peter Pan's Flight. Enter Adventureland and turn right to Pirates of the Caribbean. Ride. *Note:* Pirates has macabre sights that frighten some small children. Do not worry if the line seems long; Pirates is an efficient, fast-loading ride, and you will not have a long wait.

19. After exiting Pirates of the Caribbean, turn right. Explore Adventure Isle. *Note:* It is very easy to lose a child in the labyrinthine tunnels and paths of Adventure Isle. Either stay close to your children or designate a very specific place to regroup in the event you get separated.

20. From Adventure Isle make your way to La Cabane des Robinson (Swiss Family Treehouse). You will not have any difficulty staying together as you explore the tree house. Underneath it, however, is a maze that meanders through the root system of the giant tree. It is very easy to lose a child here.

21. Depart Adventureland and enter Frontierland. Turn to your right and proceed to Critter Corral petting zoo.

22. Bear left on exiting the Critter Corral and keep the waterfront on your right. Take the riverboat cruise at Thunder Mesa Landing.

23. Exit right along the waterfront to Phantom Manor. Ride. *Note:* This attraction frightens some small children, but if your little one tolerated the witch in Blanche-Neige, there should be no problem with Phantom Manor.

24. Exit Frontierland through its main entrance, stopping to check out the log fort on the way.

25. Turn left after exiting Frontierland and follow the path past the entrance to Adventureland until you see a path leading to the lower part of the castle. On its lower left side, you will see a small, dark passage marked "La Tanière du Dragon" (The Dragon's Den). Stop and say *bonjour* to the dragon. *Note:* The lifelike dragon frightens many children. Be sure to inform your little ones (before you go in!) that the dragon is not real.

26. From the Dragon's Den go up the steps into the castle and explore the more light-hearted upper stories.

27. In Discoveryland there are three attractions, *Le Visionarium,* Star Tours, and *Honey, I Shrunk the Audience*, that are toss-ups for children under age eight. Star Tours and *Honey, I Shrunk the Audience* frighten younger children, whereas the audience at *Le Visionarium* must stand, making it hard for children to find a place where they can see. Of the three, expect the longest wait at Star Tours.

28. If you have some time left before the park closes, backtrack to pick up attractions you may have missed or bypassed because the lines were too long. Check out any parades, fireworks, or live performances of interest to you. Grab a bite to eat. Save Main Street until last, as it remains open after the rest of the park closes.

29. Continue to tour until everything except Main Street closes or you are ready to go. Finish your day by browsing along Main Street. If you are shopping for a Disney souvenir and the Main Street shops are jammed, you can find almost the same selection at the Disney Village on the far side of the train station.

Two-Day Touring Plan A for Daytime Touring or for When the Park Closes Early

For: Patrons wishing to spread their Disneyland Paris visit over two days and for those preferring to tour in the morning.

Assumes: Willingness to experience all major rides (including roller coasters) and shows.

Timing: The following Two-Day Touring Plan takes advantage of early-morning touring and is the most efficient of all the touring plans for comprehensive touring with the least waiting in line. On each day you should complete the structured part of the plan by 3 p.m. or so. If you are visiting Disneyland Paris during a period of the year when the park is open late (after 8 p.m.), you might prefer our alternate two-day touring plan, which offers morning touring on one day and late-afternoon and evening touring on the other day. Another highly recommended option is to return to your hotel by mid-afternoon for a nap and an early dinner and come back to the park by 7:30 or 8 p.m. for the Main Street Electrical Parade, fireworks, and live entertainment.

DAY ONE

1. Arrive before official opening time (specifically as directed in the preliminary instructions to the touring plans) and purchase your admission if necessary. Your touring plan today will take you primarily to Frontierland and Adventureland. If you want to eat lunch at a table-service restaurant, we recommend the Blue Lagoon in Adventureland. Simply make reservations at the door of the restaurant while you are touring Adventureland.

2. Line up in front of an entrance turnstile and wait to be admitted to the park. Choose a turnstile as far to the left as possible. If you have not been given a park handout map, try to get one from the gate attendant as you pass through the turnstile. If you cannot obtain a map at the gate, pick one up at City Hall, on the left side of Town Square, once you have passed through the turnstile.

3. When you are admitted to the park, move quickly to the far end of Main Street via the Liberty Arcade. The Liberty

Arcade is an enclosed walkway that runs parallel to Main Street on the left. Its entrance is on the far left side of Town Square before you start down Main Street. When you reach the far end of the Liberty Arcade, turn left and follow the rustic covered walkway. If there is no rope barrier, continue quickly and without stopping to Frontierland and Big Thunder Mountain. If a rope barrier is in place at the rustic walkway, position yourself at the rope and wait to be admitted to the remainder of the park. Resist the urge to troop around Main Street. To stay ahead of the crowds it is important to follow the touring plan precisely in the morning. *Note:* The first ride on the touring plan is a roller coaster. If you do not like roller coasters, go directly to Step 6.

4. The rustic covered walkway leads right to Frontierland, bypassing the central hub. At the end of the covered walkway, as you enter Frontierland, keep the waterfront on your left and proceed directly to Big Thunder Mountain. Though the ride appears to be on an island, the loading area is down the waterfront past the shooting gallery. Ride.

5. After riding Big Thunder Mountain, turn left on exiting and continue along with the waterfront on your left. Turn right after passing Fuente del Oro Restaurante (on your right) and enter Adventureland. Continue straight until you come to a bridge. Turn left *before* crossing the bridge and head for Indiana Jones and the Temple of Peril. This a modest roller coaster that loops you upside down. If two roller coasters back-to-back is one too many, cross the bridge and skip ahead to Step 6.

6. After riding (or not riding) Indiana Jones cross the bridge leading to the Swiss Family Treehouse (La Cabane des Robinson). Bypassing the tree house for the moment, bear left on the far side of the bridge, ultimately crossing a second bridge leading to Adventure Isle. Continue to keep the stream on your left until your reach a stone and concrete bridge. Turn left here. Once over the bridge, bear to the right and enter Fantasyland.

7. In Fantasyland turn right toward the castle and check the posted wait time for Peter Pan's Flight. Peter Pan is a FAST-PASS attraction. If you want to ride and the posted wait time is less than 25 minutes, join the regular queue. If the

posted wait exceeds 25 minutes, obtain FASTPASSes for your party and plan to return later.

8. Continue toward the castle, ride Les Voyages de Pinocchio.

9. Exit Pinocchio to the right and ride Blanche-Neige et les Sept Nains.

10. After Snow White (Blanche-Neige), cross between the Carrousel and Dumbo to the Mad Hatter's Tea Cups. Ride. If you are prone to motion sickness, skip to Step 11.

11. Backtrack to Adventureland. Experience Pirates of the Caribbean.

12. After Pirates of the Caribbean head back toward the entrance of Fantasyland but turn right just before the Fantasyland entrance. Continue with Skull Rock and Captain Hook's Ship on your right until you reach La Cabane des Robinson. Cross the bridge and explore the tree house.

13. If, after checking out the tree house, you'd like to tour Adventure Isle, the pirate ship, and Skull Rock more comprehensively, now's the time to do it. Otherwise skip ahead to Step 14.

14. Return to Frontierland. This is also a good time to check your daily entertainment schedule for performances at the Chaparral Theater. Near the theater is the Cowboy Cookout Barbecue, one of our favorite counter-service restaurants.

15. In Frontierland, continue along the waterfront to the Thunder Mesa Riverboat Landing. Take a cruise on "Rivers of the Far West."

16. Turn right on exiting the cruise and proceed to Phantom Manor. The lines will appear long, but because the Manor is a fast-loading attraction, your wait should be tolerable.

17. Keeping the waterfront on your left, backtrack to the main entrance of Frontierland. Take a look at Legends of the Wild West, a walk-through exhibit.

18. Exit Frontierland toward the central hub and bear left to the Adventureland main entrance. Explore the Bazaar.

19. Exit Adventureland toward the central hub and make an immediate left on the path leading to the lower part of the castle. On its lower left side, you will see a small, dark passage

marked "La Tanière du Dragon" (The Dragon's Den). Stop and say *bonjour* to the dragon. Afterward ascend the steps into the castle to its second floor. Check out the story of *Sleeping Beauty* as told in stained glass and tapestries.

20. This concludes the touring plan for day one. Consult your live entertainment schedule. Note performance times for the afternoon parade and for productions at the various stages in the park. For tips on finding a good vantage point for watching the parade(s), see pages 165–166. Likewise, from this point on, feel free to discontinue the touring plan for lunch and/or dinner. Advice on where and when to eat can be found under Alternatives and Suggestions for Eating in the Theme Park on pages 170–173. Cruise the shops on Main Street on your way to the park exit.

DAY TWO

1. Arrive before official opening time (specifically as directed in the preliminary instructions to the touring plans) and purchase your admission if necessary. Your touring plan today will take you primarily to Discoveryland and Fantasyland. If you wish to eat lunch in a table-service restaurant, we recommend Auberge de Cendrillon in Fantasyland. Another option is to enjoy a fast-food lunch while taking in a show on the Videopolis stage (consult the live entertainment schedule for show times).

2. Line up in front of an entrance turnstile and wait to be admitted to the park. If you have not been given a park handout map, try to get one from the gate attendant as you pass through the turnstile. If you cannot obtain a map at the gate, pick one up at City Hall, on the left side of Town Square, once you have passed through the turnstile.

3. When you are admitted to the park, move rapidly to the far end of Main Street via the Discovery Arcade, the enclosed walkway that runs parallel to Main Street on the right. The Discovery Arcade entrance is on the far right side of Town Square before you start down Main Street. When you reach the far end of the arcade, proceed to the entrance to Discoveryland. If Discoveryland is open, move as fast as your feet will carry you to Space Mountain. If a rope barrier is

in place at the central hub, station yourself at the rope and wait to be admitted. As soon as the barrier is removed zip directly to Space Mountain and ride.

4. Space Mountain is the favorite attraction of many guests. If you are a Space Mountain fan, obtain a FASTPASS (after riding) for a second ride later in the day. If you don't want to ride Space Mountain again, skip to Step 5.

5. Head toward the rear of Discoveryland, keeping the Videopolis on your left. Ride Star Tours.
There are two slow-loading rides in Discoveryland, Orbitron and Autopia. Both have great eye appeal but are not very interesting or exciting for most adults. We recommend bypassing them, but if you really want to ride, now's the time.

6. After Star Tours bear left to *Honey, I Shrunk the Audience.*

7. Exit *Honey, I Shrunk the Audience* and backtrack past Star Tours to the Discoveryland station of the Disneyland Railroad. Take the train to the Fantasyland station.

8. Turn left on exiting the Fantasyland station and explore Alice's Curious Labyrinth.

9. Exit the labyrinth to the left and turn left again, crossing under the railroad tracks. Ride Le Pays des Contes de Fées (Storyland Boats).

10. Return to the other side of the tracks and turn left to try It's a Small World.

11. Exit It's a Small World to the left and return to the central hub via the walkway that passes to the left of the castle (as you face it from Small World). From the central hub enter Discoveryland.

12. Keep left after entering Discoveryland. Check your daily entertainment schedule (in the park map) for shows on the Videopolis Stage. Interrupt the touring plan to take in a performance.

13. In Discoveryland, experience *Le Visionarium,* located on the left just inside the Discoveryland entrance.

14. In Discoveryland, take a walking tour of Captain Nemo's submarine at Les Mystères du Nautilus.

15. This concludes the touring plan for today. Revisit your favorite attractions or try attractions you may have missed

or bypassed because the lines were too long. Check out any parades or live performances that interest you. Browse the shops, saving Main Street until last. If your hotel is close by and the park is open past 9 p.m., you might consider going back to your room for some rest and then returning refreshed in the evening to enjoy Disneyland Paris at night.

Two-Day Touring Plan B for Morning and Evening Touring or for When the Park Is Open Late

For: Visitors who want to enjoy Disneyland Paris at different times of day, including evenings and early mornings.

Assumes: Willingness to experience all major rides (including roller coasters) and shows.

Timing: This Two-Day Touring Plan is for people visiting Disneyland Paris on days when the park is open late (after 8 p.m.). The plan offers morning touring on one day and late afternoon and evening touring on the other day. If the park closes early, or if you prefer to do all of your touring during the morning and early afternoon, use the Two-Day Touring Plan A.

DAY ONE

1. Arrive before official opening time (specifically as directed in the preliminary instructions to the touring plans) and purchase your admission if necessary. If you want to eat lunch at a table-service restaurant, we recommend the Blue Lagoon in Adventureland. Make reservations at City Hall or at the door of the restaurant.

2. Line up in front of an entrance turnstile and wait to be admitted to the park. Choose a turnstile as far to the right as possible. If you have not been given a park handout map, try to get one from the gate attendant as you pass through the turnstile. If you cannot obtain a map at the gate, pick one up at City Hall, on the left side of Town Square, once you have passed through the turnstile.

3. When you are admitted to the park, move posthaste to the far end of Main Street. When you reach the far end of Main Street, turn right toward Discoveryland. If there is no rope

barrier, continue quickly and without stopping to Discoveryland and Space Mountain. If a rope barrier is in place, station yourself at the rope and wait to be admitted to Discoveryland. Position is everything at this point in the day. You will later be rewarded in great time savings for your early-morning discipline. *Note:* The first ride on the touring plan is a roller coaster. If you do not like roller coasters, go directly to Step 5.

4. Ride Space Mountain.

5. Exit Space Mountain and bear right to Star Tours. Ride.

6. Return to the entrance of Discoveryland and cross the central hub to Frontierland. Pasings through the log stockade without stopping, head directly to Big Thunder Mountain and ride. Big Thunder Mountain is also a roller coaster, so if you don't like roller coasters, go to Fantasyland instead of Frontierland and pick up the touring plan at Peter Pan's Flight, Step 9.

7. After riding Big Thunder Mountain, turn left on exiting and continue along with the waterfront on your left. Turn right after passing Fuente del Oro Restaurante (on your right) and enter Adventureland. Continue straight until you come to a bridge. Turn left *before* crossing the bridge and head for Indiana Jones and the Temple of Peril. This modest roller coaster loops you upside down. If two roller coasters back-to-back is one too many, cross the bridge and skip ahead to Step 8.

8. After riding (or not riding) Indiana Jones cross the bridge leading to the Swiss Family Treehouse (La Cabane des Robinson). Bypassing the tree house for the moment, bear left on the far side of the bridge, ultimately crossing a second bridge leading to Adventure Isle. Continue to keep the stream on your left until your reach a stone and concrete bridge. Turn left here. Once over the bridge, bear to the right and enter Fantasyland.

9. In Fantasyland turn right toward the castle and check the posted wait time for Peter Pan's Flight. Peter Pan is a FASTPASS attraction. If you want to ride and the posted wait time is less than 25 minutes, join the regular queue. If the posted wait exceeds 25 minutes, obtain FASTPASSes for your party and plan to return later.

10. Continue toward the castle, ride Les Voyages de Pinocchio.

11. Exiting Pinocchio to the right, ride Blanche-Neige et les Sept Nains.

12. After Blanche-Neige, cross between the Carrousel and Dumbo to the Mad Hatter's Tea Cups. Ride the Tea Cups. If you are prone to motion sickness, skip to Step 13.

13. Moving away from the castle, pass under the railroad tracks and ride Le Pays des Contes de Fées (Storyland Boats).

14. Pass back under the tracks and turn left to It's a Small World. Ride.

15. Backtrack to Adventureland. Experience Pirates of the Caribbean.

16. After Pirates of the Caribbean head back toward the entrance of Fantasyland, but turn right just before the Fantasyland entrance. Continue with Skull Rock and Captain Hook's Ship on your right until you reach La Cabane des Robinson. Cross the bridge and explore the tree house.

17. Return to Frontierland. This is also a good time to check your daily entertainment schedule for performances at the Chaparral Theater. Near the theater is the Cowboy Cookout Barbecue, one of our favorite counter-service restaurants.

18. In Frontierland bear left along the waterfront to the Thunder Mesa Riverboat Landing. Take a cruise on "Rivers of the Far West."

19. Turn right on exiting the cruise and proceed to Phantom Manor. The lines will appear long, but because the Manor is a fast-loading attraction, your wait should be tolerable.

20. This concludes the touring plan for day one. Consult your live entertainment schedule. Note performance times for the afternoon parade and for shows at the Videopolis stage and at the Fantasy Festival Stage. All three live productions are excellent. For tips on finding a good vantage point for watching the parade(s), see page 165–166. From this point on, also feel free to discontinue the touring plan for lunch. Advice on where and when to eat can be found under Alternatives and Suggestions for Eating in the Theme Park on page 170–173.

DAY TWO

1. Plan to arrive at the park by 3:30 p.m.

2. Pick up a live entertainment schedule (in the park handout map) and note performance times for the evening parade(s) and fireworks. If you intend to eat at a table-service restaurant, make sure that your reservations give you sufficient time to finish dinner before the parade begins. Make the reservations first thing after arriving at the park at the door of your chosen restaurant. If you are a guest at a Disneyland Paris hotel or campground, make dining reservations through the concierge/information desk of your hotel before leaving for the park.

3. Check the daily entertainment schedule for performance times at the various stages in the park. Feel free to interrupt the touring plan to take in a show.

4. Go to Discoveryland via the central hub. Experience *Le Visionarium,* located to the left just inside the entrance.

5. Also in Discoveryland, explore the submarine from *20,000 Leagues Under the Sea* at Les Mystères du Nautilus.

6. Exiting the sub, proceed to the far side of Space Mountain to *Honey, I Shrunk the Audience,* located by the railroad tracks. If you are a Space Mountain fan, stop and pick up a Space Mountain FASTPASS for a ride later in the day en route to *Honey, I Shrunk the Audience.*

7. After *Honey, I Shrunk the Audience,* backtrack past Star Tours to the Discoveryland station of the Disneyland Railroad. Take the train to the Fantasyland station.

8. Head back through Fantasyland to the castle. Take the steps up into the castle to its second floor. Check out the story of *Sleeping Beauty* as told in stained glass and tapestries. Next descend into the dungeon named "La Tanière du Dragon" (The Dragon's Den). Stop and pay your respects to the dragon. Exit the dungeon at the opposite end from where you entered.

9. Go to Adventureland via its main entrance (off the central hub) and survey the Bazaar.

10. Depart Adventureland toward the central hub, making an immediate right just outside the entrance. Head to Frontierland and see Legends of the West, a walk-through exhibit in the fort at the Frontierland main entrance.

11. Eat dinner and enjoy the parades and fireworks. If you have time, backtrack to catch attractions you may have missed or bypassed because the lines were too long. Save Main Street until last, as it remains open after the rest of the park closes.

12. Continue to tour until everything except Main Street closes or until you are ready to go. Finish your day by browsing along Main Street. If you are shopping for a Disney souvenir and the Main Street shops are packed, you can find almost the same selection at less-crowded Disney Village on the far side of the train station.

Part Seven

Disneyland Paris at Night

The Disney folks contrive so cleverly to exhaust you during the day that the mere thought of night activity sends most visitors into anaphylactic shock. For the hearty and the nocturnal, however, there is lot to do in the evenings at Disneyland Paris.

In the Theme Park

The Disneyland Paris theme park is very different in the evening. As shadows lengthen and the lights come on, the park is transformed. The energetic festivity of the day gives way to the romantic rhythms of the night. In the evening the park is more than the sum of its attractions. Absent is the frenetic activity of daytime touring. At night, somehow, it is enough just to be there, to walk, to relax, to drink it all in. If you have a choice in the matter, do not miss an opportunity to experience the theme park at night.

When the theme park is open past 8 p.m., the major evening event is the Main Street Electrical Parade, followed by fireworks. In addition to the parade and the fireworks, there are shows at the Chaparral Theater, the Videopolis stage, the Fantasy Festival Stage, and at Le Théâtre du Château amphitheater. Between shows on the Videopolis stage, there is dancing. The music is contemporary rock, blasted through a sound system powerful enough to pulverize gallstones. For show times consult the daily live entertainment schedule. Besides scheduled events, there are impromptu appearances throughout the park by the Disney characters and by various musical groups.

In the Resort Hotels

The bars, lounges, and restaurants at the resort hotels become a refuge for Disneyland Paris guests, spent from a day at the theme park.

While you cannot exactly characterize the hotel bars as "happening" places, they do provide a change of pace and an opportunity to detox from one too many rides on It's a Small World. The Rio Grande Bar at the Hotel Santa Fe and the Red Garter Saloon at the Hotel Cheyenne are the most boisterous and upbeat of the hotel lounges. The Sequoia Lodge's Redwood Bar & Lounge, with its cozy fireside warmth, is the most romantic. Finally, Hotel New York features the New York City Bar. If you are really in a party mood, however, the nightspots at Disney Village are your best bet.

At Davy Crockett Ranch

Weather permitting, a campfire program is conducted each night at Camp Davy Crockett. Open only to campground guests, the event includes singing, stories, and, in the summer, character appearances and Disney feature films.

At Disney Village

Disney Village is a shopping, eating, and entertainment complex located between the theme park and the Disneyland Paris Resort hotels. Consisting of a broad promenade running between parallel rows of shops and restaurants, Disney Village serves as a sort of downtown for the Disneyland Paris Resort. Columns of polished metal, supporting a mesh umbrella of twinkling lights, stand sentrylike along the promenade. By day the mesh admits sunlight; at night it illuminates Disney Village with an electric galaxy of tiny stars.

There are seven restaurants at Disney Village (including a McDonald's), six shops, *Buffalo Bill's Wild West* (dinner) *Show,* three nightclubs, a French tourist office, a post office, and an eight-screen Gaumont cinema complex. The restaurants and shops are open both days and evenings. *Buffalo Bill's,* the circus, and the three clubs operate only at night. Disney Village is within easy walking distance of the resort hotels, the theme park, and the bus and train stations. Guests at the resort hotels have the option of catching a bus to the Disney Village. There is no admission charge to the Disney Village, or to any of its clubs or restaurants (except for the stage shows).

DISNEY VILLAGE NIGHTSPOTS

There are three dance clubs at Disney Village. Hurricane's features dancing to contemporary rock music (usually taped, but occasionally live) in a Florida beach shack setting. Billy Bob's, nearby, offers live American country music and dancing in a rustic, multifloored building. Finally, Rock 'n Roll America showcases live rock from the 1950s to the 1970s. There is usually no cover charge or minimum drink requirement in any of the establishments.

DISNEY VILLAGE RESTAURANTS

There are five table-service restaurants: Los Angeles Bar and Grill, Annette's Diner, The Steak House, Rainforest Cafe, and Planet Hollywood. All are described in Part Five: Dining. In addition to the table-service establishments, there are three fast-food eateries. New York Style Sandwiches specializes in (what else?) New York–style deli sandwiches, and the adjacent Sports Bar offers assorted appetizers and munchies along with a wide selection of beer. New York Style Sandwiches and the Sports Bar are populated most evenings by unwinding Disney employees. Last, there's McDonald's.

DISNEY VILLAGE SHOPPING

Shops at Disney Village include a Disney merchandise store, a toy store, a Disney art gallery, a Western goods (that is, cowboy-theme) emporium, a sporting goods shop, and a themed retail operation selling Hollywood movie memorabilia and posters and souvenirs from various U.S. cities. The shops and the restaurants are open both days and evenings.

BUFFALO BILL'S WILD WEST SHOW

The featured attraction of Disney Village is *Buffalo Bill's Wild West Show.* Staged in its own spacious indoor stadium, the show is a scaled-down rendition of the original *Wild West Show* that toured Europe in the late 1800s and was a great hit in Paris. The presentation brings back to life some of the most colorful characters of the American Wild West, including Buffalo Bill (William F.) Cody, sharpshooter Annie Oakley, and Sioux Indian Chief Sitting Bull.

The *Wild West Show's* arena is about the size of an ice hockey rink. Guests sit at counters, which ring the arena in concentric tiers. There is not much elbow room, and the seats (which are fixed in place) are too far away from the table for most young children. On the positive side, there is an unobstructed view from every seat in the house, and the acoustics are excellent. Unlike many dinner shows, there is no wasted time at *Buffalo Bill's*. Guests have something to nibble on virtually from the moment they sit down, and events in the arena commence as soon as the entire audience is in place.

Starring real American cowboys and Native American Indians, the current version of the *Wild West Show* does a creditable job of depicting the life and work of the American cowboy. A cattle drive, complete with real longhorn steers, is reenacted. The trail hands are seen working the cattle, roping and cutting, and then, when the day is done, relaxing around a campfire before bedding down. Later, America Indians dance in preparation for a buffalo hunt. The reenactment of the hunt, which features about ten live buffalo, is the high point of the show. A third sequence depicts an Indian attack on a stagecoach, and the subsequent rescue of the passengers by the cavalry.

When the *Wild West Show* operates in a historical context, revisiting the life and events of the old American West, the production is both moving and compelling. When it switches gears, however, becoming essentially a circus on horseback, the production falls flat. A supposed contest between hands from competing ranches (with each ranch representing a part of the audience) seems hopelessly contrived. Dinner waiters, in the unlikely role of cheerleaders, struggle mightily to get the audience to identify with the competitors from "their" ranch. More ridiculous yet is the trick-shooting display by the show's resurrected Annie Oakley. Patently fake, and without any semblance of realism, rigged targets drop like wounded ducks as Miss Oakley waves her six-shooter in the general direction of her mark. Conspicuous by its absence is the most exciting of all cowboy pastimes, the rodeo. How can you have a show about the American West without some bronco riding or steer wrestling?

On balance, *Buffalo Bill's Wild West Show* is a solid production, with its assets outweighing its liabilities. The sets are stunning, the horsemanship outstanding, and the pageantry colorful and impressive. When Buffalo Bill and Sitting Bull lead the whole entourage into the arena for the grand finale, you could swear you had stepped back 100 years in time.

The dinner served at the *Wild West Show* consists of chili, barbecued roast chicken, smoked ribs, corn on the cob, roasted potatoes, and apple cobbler with vanilla ice cream. (Vegetarians should register as such when they reserve seats.) The barbecue is quite good, but it is different from any we have ever had in the United States (Could there be a French cowboy running the chuck wagon?). The portions are large enough to make a buffalo founder. Draft beer, Coca-Cola, and coffee or tea, all served from pitchers, accompany the meal. Other drinks are available but cost extra. Waiters do a good job keeping your glass or cup filled.

Buffalo Bill's Wild West Show usually plays twice nightly at 6:30 and 9:30 p.m. The early show tends to be the more popular because it affords guests the opportunity to return to the theme park in time for a parade and fireworks (on nights when the park is open until 9 p.m. or later). The cost of the *Wild West Show* and dinner is FF 325 ($43) for adults and FF 195 ($26) for children 3 to 11 years old. The price of admission, which, incidentally, is higher than a one-day pass to the theme park, includes a souvenir cowboy hat.

Index

Unofficial Guide Reader Survey

If you would like to express your opinion about Disneyland Paris or this guidebook, complete the following survey and mail it to:

> *Unofficial Guide* Reader Survey
> P.O. Box 43673
> Birmingham, AL 35243

Inclusive dates of your visit _____

Members of your party:	Person 1	Person 2	Person 3	Person 4	Person 5
Gender (M or F)	_____	_____	_____	_____	_____
Age	_____	_____	_____	_____	_____

How many times have you been to Disneyland Paris? _____

On your most recent trip, where did you stay? _____

Concerning accommodations, on a scale with 100 best and 0 worst, how would you rate:

The quality of your room? _____ The value for the money? _____
The quietness of your room? _____ Check-in/checkout efficiency? _____
Shuttle service to the parks? _____ Swimming pool facilities? _____

Did you rent a car? _____ From whom? _____

Concerning your rental car, on a scale with 100 best and 0 worst, how would you rate:

Pickup processing efficiency? _____ Return processing efficiency? _____
Condition of the car? _____ Cleanliness of the car? _____
Airport shuttle efficiency? _____

Concerning your touring:

Who in your party was most responsible for planning the itinerary? _____
What time did you normally get started in the morning? _____
Did you usually arrive at the theme parks prior to opening? _____
Did you return to your hotel for rest during the day? _____
What time did you normally go to bed at night? _____
If a Disney Resort guest, did you participate in early entry? _____

On a scale with 100 best and 0 worst, rate how the touring plans worked:

Name of Plan	Rating
_____	_____
_____	_____
_____	_____
_____	_____

Concerning your dining experiences:

How many restaurant meals (including fast food) did you average per day? _____

How much (approximately) did your party spend on meals per day? _____

Favorite restaurant outside of Disneyland Paris? _____

Did you buy this guide: Before leaving? _____ While on your trip? _____

How did you hear about this guide?

Loaned or recommended by a friend _____   Radio or TV _____

Newspaper or magazine _____   Bookstore salesperson _____

Just picked it out on my own _____   Library _____

Internet _____

What other guidebooks did you use on this trip? _____
_____

On the 100 best and 0 worst scale, how would you rate them? _____
_____

Using the same scale, how would you rate the *Unofficial Guide?* _____

Are *Unofficial Guides* readily available in bookstores in your area? _____

Have you used other *Unofficial Guides?* _____ Which one(s)? _____

Comments about your Disneyland Paris vacation or about the *Unofficial Guide:* _____
_____
_____
_____
_____
_____
_____
_____
_____
_____
_____
_____
_____
_____
_____
_____
_____